STRENGTH IN
CHA S

STRENGTH IN
CHA☀S

THE ULTIMATE LEADERSHIP BLUEPRINT FOR MASTERING THE UNCONTROLLABLE

KEVIN BLACK

BLACK DINGO PRESS
SCOTTSDALE, ARIZONA

For permission requests, contact Kevin at:
Kevin@kevinblack.co

First Edition
Hardcover ISBN: 979-8-9929313-1-0
Paperback ISBN: 979-8-9929313-0-3
Ebook ISBN: 979-8-9929313-2-7
Library of Congress Control Number: 2025905487

This is a work of nonfiction. Some names and identifying details may have been changed to protect privacy.

This book is for informational purposes only and does not constitute legal, medical, or psychological advice.

Readers should consult appropriate professionals where necessary.

Printed in the United States of America

For my mother

"He robs present ills of their power who has perceived their coming beforehand."
— Seneca, *Letters to Lucilius,* Letter 78

Contents

PART III: LEADERSHIP, CHAOS, AND CONTROL

PART IV: CONSTRUCTIVE CHAOS

Illustrations

Images

1. Scipio Africanus Meets Hannibal Before the Battle of Zama, by Hermann Vogel, 19th century. Source: thecollector.com.

2. Map. *Italy and Vicinity, The Second Punic War: 218 BC – 212 BC.* Map courtesy of the United States Military Academy Department of History.

3. *The Battle Between Scipio and Hannibal at Zama*, print by Cornelis Cort, after Giulio Romano. (MET 59.570.439)

4. *The Continence of Scipio*, by Sebastiano Ricci (1659–1734), oil on canvas, c. 1706. (Image ID: 2HNAFF4)

5. Vintage map showing the march of the Anabasis of the Ten Thousand Greeks under Cyrus the Younger, 401 BC, from Sardis to Cunaxa and back (Catabasis). (Image ID: 2P9205A)

6. *The Battle of Cunaxa*, by Adrien Guignet. (Image ID: 2X18KGN)

7. *The Anabasis of Xenophon*, by Charles Anthon, LL.D. (Image ID: 2ANFNXG)

8. *The Sea! The Sea!*, engraving illustration from *Great Men and Famous Women* (1894). (Image ID: KB046C)

9. Andrew S. Grove (1936–2016), former Chairman and CEO of Intel Corporation. (Image ID: BAJ9R3)

10. Map. *Battle of the Nile (Battle of Aboukir Bay), Egypt*, 1–3 August 1798. Naval engagement between British (led by Nelson) and French forces. (Image ID: 2RGB7CY)

11. Horatio Nelson, 1st Viscount Nelson (1758–1805), British officer in the Royal Navy. (Image ID: M9DJ0R)

12. *Captain Horatio Nelson*, painted by John Francis Rigaud in 1781, with Fort San Juan in the background. (Image ID: M9DJ0R)

Acknowledgements

To my parents, for all the support in every way imaginable. Especially to Patty, whose uncanny ability to read natural behavior helped shape my earliest understanding of how people truly operate. That gift runs deep.

To Jennifer. This book would not exist without you. Your encouragement, your help, and above all, your tolerance of this nine-year odyssey made it possible. You didn't just live alongside this dream; you carried part of its weight.

To T.S. Ransdell, aka Travis the Author. Your unwavering support, interest in this subject, and belief in me never faded. You reminded me this work mattered and that it needed to be published.

To my friend Mike Clute, for your marketing insight, emotional support, and genuine excitement about this project. Your energy showed up when mine didn't.

To the Galvanize team, Miranda and Katelyn. Thank you for making my environment fun and entertaining. And most of all, to Katie Hurst, who gave me critical support at a critical moment, enabling me to keep working out of the best office space I've ever known. Without that, I may not have finished this.

To Chris Healy, who introduced me to the brilliant and wickedly accurate term *Malicious Compliance*, a concept that stuck with me ever since.

To Alex Petkas, for your unmatched knowledge of Xenophon and the Ten Thousand, and for keeping the ancient Greeks alive in modern minds. Your work sharpened mine.

To Donald Vandergriff and Jörg Muth, whose expertise in Mission Command and leadership selection was invaluable. Your insights helped shape an entire chapter.

To Melissa Davis, Director of Library and Archives at the George C. Marshall Foundation in Lexington, Virginia. Your knowledge, generosity, and respect for George Marshall—the man, the soldier, the statesman—made my work stronger and more honest.

To Andrew Jackson O'Shaughnessy, author of *The Men Who Lost America*. Thank you for your clarity and depth on the British perspective of the American Revolution, especially your insights on Lord Germain. Your scholarship brought historical fog into focus.

To Michael Vlahos, for your passion, your mind, and your enthusiasm as we discussed Cortés, the Conquistadors, and the Aztec world they collided with.

To Roger Hill. Thank you not just for your story in *Dog Company*, but for allowing me to tell it again. Your courage, personal example, and willingness to assist meant the world to me.

To Colonel (Ret.) Douglas Macgregor. Your response to my *USA Today* article on chaos never left me. Knowing that someone of your strategic insight, intellectual rigor, and real-world experience saw value in the work became a quiet directive: this book wasn't optional—it *had* to be completed.

And to all my friends who kept showing up with enthusiasm, curiosity, and encouragement. You may not know how much it mattered, but I do.

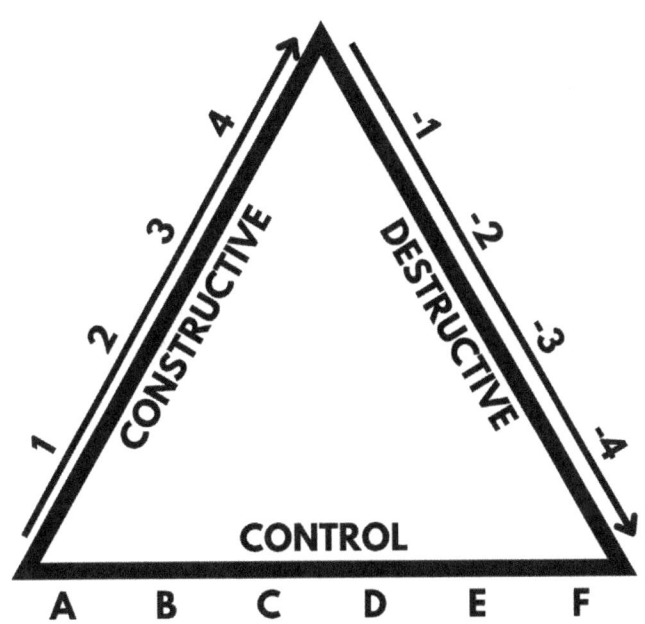

PART I

PROBLEM

&

SOLUTION

Chapter 1
Strength in Chaos

You are not a strong leader.

The good news is that it has nothing to do with your character or courage. The reason is simple: you are not prepared for chaos. Most leaders aren't.

This revelation should be shocking, given the enormous wealth of leadership resources available. Equally puzzling is the astronomical amount of money poured into leader development and team building every year. Yet, amid all this, one truth is apparent: chaos isn't going anywhere, and whether you're ready or not, you will have to face it.

Let's be clear: chaos isn't some rare condition. We all know it—too well, in fact. How often do we say in our daily lives, "This is chaos," or "We live in chaos," or "It's absolute chaos in there!" Yet, few of us can define it with the same precision as with a crisis or an emergency.

What are the consequences of our unpreparedness? In business, chaos leads to high turnover, missed deadlines, low employee engagement, and, of course, financial losses. In the military, it results in disciplinary problems, poor cultural climates, and unreliable equipment—all of which can lead to disaster or even death. On a personal level, chaos can tarnish reputations, grind down ambitions, and, frankly, drain away the drive to achieve something truly meaningful in life.

Without serious attention to chaos, we remain at its mercy—ensnared in its unpredictable grip. But what if, instead of being its victim, we could learn to master it?

A New Take on an Old Subject

I know chaos. I've experienced it in both the military and the private sector.

My first major encounter with it came as a cadet at the Virginia Military Institute. The U.S. Supreme Court ordered the school—the oldest state military college in the nation—to accept women into our ranks. Overnight, I found myself at the center of a whirlwind of change. Even the smallest misstep in our deep-seated traditions and language, the wrong word or a mistaken glance, could ignite a media firestorm and provoke the ire of the Department of Justice. From that point on, unpredictability loomed over us like a specter, forcing us hotblooded 20-year-old young men to tread carefully with every word, glance, or action—knowing that a single misstep could jeopardize not just our time at VMI but our futures.

Chaos followed me into the Army. As a rifle platoon leader, I served in the first unit to test the Medium Brigade—a new concept integrating Strykers, light armored vehicles, into infantry ranks. We were "trigger pullers," gritty and physically tough troops used to marching on foot with rucksacks stuffed with ammo and tobacco. Now, we were expected to manage million-dollar vehicles brimming with complex electronics. Beyond bullets, water, and food, we suddenly had to account for oil, fuel, parts, and relentless maintenance—an unwelcome burden for soldiers trained to thrive on simplicity.

Although we gained new, deadly capabilities, some leaders resisted the change. New ways of operating—and indeed, thinking—threatened their reputations and chances for promotion. The resulting chaos was palpable. It became exhausting and stressful to work under leaders who refused to fully embrace the potential of their new tools. Worse, those same leaders were responsible for reviewing and rating subordinates who were willing to challenge orthodoxy. This created an awkward dynamic: risk-taking subordinates sometimes outshone their more rigid superiors, deepening tensions and fueling professional jealousies.

In 2003, I deliberately invited chaos into my life. I volunteered for the coming war in Iraq, and, to my surprise, the Army sent me. But I wasn't on the frontlines as I had hoped; instead, I was assigned to military intelligence. Imagine an intense sales leader suddenly immersed in an Information Technology (IT) team. I found myself in a foreign land, in a strange world. I had to learn a technical language and collaborate with people whose skills and experiences were completely different from mine. The real challenge wasn't adapting to the complexity—it was bridging the competency gap in real-time, knowing that lives were on the line during actual combat operations.

After ten years in uniform (six active duty and four at VMI), I had a life-changing epiphany: I never liked taking orders. (Yes, I am a slow learner.) So, in 2005, I left the Army and swore I'd never work for "the Man" again. Instead, I stepped into a new and much more stressful realm of chaos: entrepreneurship. I would take my knowledge of leadership and strategy to the private sector.

Since then, I have worked with businesses ranging from $20 million to $5 billion in revenue, across a variety of industries, from medical device manufacturing to identity theft protection. Specifically, I help clients develop flexible strategies for their companies while building leaders and teams capable of executing them.

The work is incredibly rewarding and, most of all, fun. I use behavioral profiling and computer wargaming to engage clients in active learning. Rather than passively listening to lectures, they are fully immersed, learning critical lessons in leadership and teamwork through trial and error. Success requires them to support one another, adapt quickly, and solve complex challenges, all while their competitors are doing the same. In essence, they experience chaos—but in a controlled, professionally safe setting, free from judgment.

This approach gave me a profound new perspective on chaos. When harnessed correctly, chaos becomes a catalyst for growth and focus, driving teams to innovate and adapt under pressure. But the moment that focus wavers, the balance between order and disorder tips, and what was once a productive experience quickly spirals into catastrophe.

A Shocking Observation

Over the years, I began to notice something troubling: most leaders weren't prepared for chaos. The managerial and communication challenges that plagued a chief executive in a $200 million business were strikingly similar to those faced by a two-star general in a peacetime Army. The key difference? The general's Army couldn't just up and leave to join the competition.

Even pedigree didn't make a difference in chaos. Those with elite educations and impressive experiences were just as susceptible. The most common effect was tunnel vision. Senior executives, responsible for strategic goals, often became consumed by immediate, tactical problems. They lost sight of the bigger picture—and ultimately, their overall return on investment (ROI) to the company. In a sense, these corporate generals became over-paid captains and colonels.

What frustrated me most was how quickly executives aban-doned all the hard work we had completed together. Chaos be-came an excuse to forget or ignore prior commitments, shifting focus solely to the immediate crisis. Unsurprisingly, executing our agreed-upon strategies became difficult, which strained re-lationships. The collective focus shifted from driving success to simply holding everything together to avoid falling apart at the seams.

Strangely, though, chaos didn't defeat everyone. There were exceptions—truly impressive ones, in fact. These leaders and teams faced the same stresses as their peers, yet they not only endured but emerged successfully despite the challenges. One company client, for example, reached the pinnacle of corporate success by going public. This incredible feat was made more im-pressive considering they did so despite intense internal con-flicts, fierce competition, and intrusive government oversight.

Still, these people were rare. What stood out about them wasn't necessarily their tactical brilliance or strategic genius, but rather their resilience and adaptability. They knew how to navi-gate the struggles that tripped up others.

Why was this, I wondered? Was there a resource that could explain why some thrived in chaos and others did not? A blue-print, perhaps, to help the rest of us? Unfortunately, no. While memoirs and industry books mention chaos, I never found any-thing that objectively examined it in a practical, useful way for leaders and teams. So, I decided to create one myself.

Your Essential Resource to Chaos

One of the greatest leadership fallacies is the illusion of complete control—the belief that success depends on mastering every variable. It's like trying to direct your team as if they were chess pieces on a board: predictable, mechanical, and fully under your command. But real teams aren't chess pieces, and real leadership isn't a game of perfect control. Even the most accomplished leaders know this is impossible.

Why? Because some aspects of leadership are inherently uncontrollable—a harsh reality often overlooked in today's leadership development. Specifically, there are four:

- Chaos is inevitable

- Individuals respond to chaos differently

- People are largely uncontrollable

- Environments are constantly shifting

Fighting these forces doesn't just hinder success—it often intensifies the very chaos leaders fear most.

Here's the critical insight: **strength in chaos comes from mastering the uncontrollable**. It's not about ruling these forces but rather learning to harness them to your advantage. Chaos isn't the enemy—it's the arena where strong leaders are made. Those who master its forces gain a competitive edge that others can't match.

This is where *Strength in Chaos* comes in. This is the first book to measure chaos at both the leader and team levels. It gives you a practical blueprint to transform unpredictability into your greatest advantage. Whether you lead in the private sector or the armed forces, these tools will elevate your leadership to meet the demands of our hyper-paced, volatile world.

I've condensed the book into four key takeaways:

- **Chaos is inevitable**. Your team is already experiencing it, whether you realize it or not. If you're not preparing for chaos now, you're falling behind in today's hyper-paced world. The ability to embrace and adapt to chaos isn't just a necessity—it's your new competitive advantage.

- **Control is the source of chaos**. Chaos arises from how control is perceived, applied, or withheld at the individual level. Understanding how people react to control helps leaders mitigate the effects of chaos rather than escalate it.

- **Natural behaviors are the driver of chaos**. This scientifically measurable element of personality reveals how individuals respond to control and why. By understanding natural behaviors, you can anticipate specific reactions and thus be better prepared to manage team dynamics.

- **Chaos is measured using The Chaos Model**. This tool assists you in:

  o *Pinpointing* your team's position on the chaos and control scales.

  o *Predicting* upcoming challenges given your current trajectory.

  o *Preparing* your team to exceed expectations, no matter the odds.

A New Type of Leadership book

This isn't just another business or management book. It introduces something entirely new: Chaos Studies in Leadership. Grounded in my experiences as a veteran Army officer and management consultant—and enriched by insights from military history, philosophy, and behavioral science—this approach cuts through the noise to reveal what chaos really is and how to leverage it to your advantage. You'll learn to measure its impact and transform that knowledge into a competitive edge. Frankly, this is the book I wish I'd had as a junior officer in the army.

Chaos is universal, transcending time, culture, and geography. To prove it, I've drawn from over two millennia of examples spanning military, business, and political contexts. From a trapped Ancient Greek army fighting 1,500 miles to return home, to Spanish conquistadors clashing amidst hostile natives, to 18th-century British commanders turning a local conflict into a world war, to the former head of Intel struggling to save their business at its peak—you'll see how leaders across history faced chaos. Some triumphed spectacularly, while others, despite their advantages, failed just as dramatically.

The business examples come from my two decades in the private sector. They include a diverse set of leaders, managers, teams, and companies. While individual identities have been changed for privacy, the lessons remain authentic.

All the examples in this book are designed to sharpen your understanding of chaos and how to turn it into an advantage. They challenge conventional ideas of leadership, pushing you to think differently about it. As you reflect on these lessons and connect them to your own journey, remember: every challenge in chaos is a chance to grow stronger. The path to mastering chaos begins here—and you've already taken the first step.

Let's Establish Expectations....

This book is about how to think about chaos. It's not a tactical playbook—that comes later.

Before you can effectively address chaos, you need to understand its essence: what drives it, how control influences it, and why people respond to it in different ways.

Understanding chaos also requires an exploration into the field of natural behaviors. This incredibly valuable—but largely untapped—resource provides critical insight into how and why people react to both chaos and control.[1] As you read through the book, you'll no doubt feel the temptation to profile yourself or others. I strongly recommend against it. Without expert guidance and a reliable tool (both of which, in my experience, are rare), you risk setting false expectations about yourself and others. Worse, you could damage relationships and undermine your authority. Instead, approach this field with curiosity and respect for its complexity, recognizing the critical role it plays in leadership development.

Understanding must come before action, and that's why this book focuses on building your foundation first. The second book in this series will provide the tactics, techniques, and procedures to develop the specific leadership competencies required to grow strong in chaos. For now, focus on gaining a deeper understanding of chaos itself.

This is Your Opportunity

Chaos isn't going away—and neither is the pressure to lead through it. But those who understand it first, win first. This is your chance to gain that edge.

If you work in Corporate America or large institutions:

- **Become an invaluable asset** to your boss, by helping them achieve their ROI without getting mired in tactics of day-to-day business.

- **Anticipate disruptions**, demonstrating your ability to see around corners and guide your team or department through uncertainty with confidence, clarity, and focus.

- **Enhance your standing and reputation** as someone who can navigate challenges and lead others with confidence when situations demand more than just conventional thinking.

- **Strengthen your career prospects** by showing that you can lead, adapt, and inspire teams to thrive in unpredictable environments.

If you are self-employed:

- **Lead your business through uncertainty,** showing your command of chaos and empowering your team to make decisions in your absence.

- **Identify opportunities in disruption**, recognizing different levels of chaos as either stepping stones toward success or early warnings to adjust your course.

- **Build resilience into your business** by fostering adaptability and staying focused on the deeper purpose that drives your team forward.

If you are focused on personal growth:

- **Rewire your mindset to thrive in chaos**, reframing

challenges as opportunities for both personal and professional growth.

- **Strengthen your adaptability**, becoming more responsive to life's twists and turns while maintaining control over your direction, even in unpredictable environments.

- **Cultivate self-awareness and emotional resilience**, recognizing your natural tendencies and learning to grow by embracing, rather than resisting, uncertainty.

The "Strong" Leader

Let me share a story with you. It illustrates the common reactions of hardworking people operating in chaos without fully understanding their situation—or the opportunities it holds. I encourage you to view it through my perspective as an outside observer. While this story may read like fiction, it happened. Many of you will likely recognize it and think, "Yep, I've seen that before," or even, "I've seen worse."

This story highlights one specific type of chaos: its destructive form. It shows the resilience of people trying to do the right thing, but the harsh reality remains: damage was done, and it could have been avoided with a deeper understanding of chaos.

The Case of Veronica

Veronica chuckled with a mix of dry amusement and disbelief. After only a year as the Senior Director of Operations—a direct report to the Chief Operating Officer (COO) of a $200 million company—she received the company's newest honor: the

"Strong Leader" award. The irony was hard to ignore; she had just learned she was nearly fired—twice in the past year. Her first boss had aggressively campaigned to get rid of her, smearing her name to the executive leadership team. Her second boss saw no reason to keep her. Strangely enough, both were let go, and here she remained.

With nearly 20 years of project management experience across startups and Fortune 1000 companies, Veronica was no stranger to challenges. When her previous employer was acquired, she quickly found a new role as an Information Technology (IT) project manager at a rapidly growing software company. She quickly demonstrated a real talent to unite people across all departments. Senior leadership took notice.

So did Sarah, the newly appointed Chief Operating Officer (COO). Recognizing Veronica's talent, Sarah, like any good, industrious executive worth their salary, stole her. She immediately promoted Veronica to Senior Director of Operations. So, within eight months of being hired, Veronica now answered to the number two person in this 200-person company.

This wasn't necessarily an occasion for celebration; the timing couldn't have been more critical. Sarah had inherited a mess: Sales, Marketing, and Product Development were all operating in silos and not working together proactively. So, money, time, and opportunities were being wasted. The friendly, easy-going Chief Executive Officer (CEO) felt immense pressure from the board to resolve these issues. He needed to steer the company back on track. This is where Operations would come in.

At first, it seemed that Sarah and Veronica made a formidable team. Sarah was likable but also aggressive, intense, and mission-driven—traits the CEO had specifically sought when hiring her. Veronica, a more people-oriented leader, excelled in a supporting role, complementing Sarah's style perfectly. This was their time to shine and bring order to the current mess.

A Lack of Unified Direction

The first sign of trouble came with the delay of a major product rollout. The company had been working on launching a new software program for months, but miscommunication and competing priorities led to repeated delays. Marketing was distracted and sales had its own agenda. In other words, no one seemed to be on the same page.

The CEO, frustrated by the setbacks and the continued pressure from the board, directed Sarah to fix the issues—like, yesterday. Given Sarah's take-charge personality, the CEO once again delegated to Sarah, seemingly assuming she would rally the team and get everyone aligned with the company's goals. But instead of taking the reins herself, Sarah pushed the responsibility down to Veronica.

"Veronica," Sarah instructed, "you need to get everyone on board, now. We can get this rollout done without further delays." Her tone was much more telling than selling.

Veronica was taken aback. She had never been invited to senior leadership meetings before. Was she now expected to lead them? Wasn't this the COO's responsibility? Sarah had the authority to align the team and ensure compliance—not her. Besides, Sarah had the direct backing of the CEO.

Despite her concerns, Veronica followed orders. She began scheduling meeting after meeting with different departments. At first, the senior vice presidents (SVP) showed up. But that didn't last long. Soon, they stopped showing up and sent their direct reports instead. Each meeting felt more futile and frustrating than the last. Veronica relayed plans and sought approvals from mid-level managers who had no authority to commit one way or another. But they did promise to talk with their bosses...

It became evident that Sarah was not fulfilling her

responsibilities as COO. The teams were not working with one another despite Veronica's effort.

The Next Challenge

The second major issue surfaced when Veronica suggested that the company needed a comprehensive strategy. Despite the CEO's inspirational speeches, it was obvious there was no clear direction. Everyone seemed to be moving along according to the needs of the day. Worse, teams were operating with competing priorities, and the disaster of the last product rollout had left a bitter taste in everyone's mouth.

"The teams aren't cooperating because there's no common direction," said an exasperated Veronica. It was clear the company needed a roadmap forward, and leading this initiative would have been the perfect chance for Sarah to redeem herself. " This could be our opportunity to align the organization around a clear strategy," Veronica suggested to Sarah.

"I know we need a strategy!" Sarah snapped. "What do you think I'm working on?!" Her frustration was palpable. She immediately demanded that Veronica refocus on holding more meetings. Then, in a nasty tone, Sarah added, "I'm the head of operations for a reason: remember that."

Several weeks passed before Sarah finally shared her "strategy" with Veronica. It turned out to be nothing more than an extended to-do list. It was clearly lacking the depth and clarity expected from a senior executive at the very top of the company. Unsurprisingly, the document was quickly forgotten. Veronica later discovered that it never even shared with other senior leaders.

The stress began to take its toll on Veronica. Her role had been reduced to simply doing her boss's bidding. Disillusioned, she found herself going through the motions in her work, counting down the days until the weekend.

Meanwhile, Sarah's shortcomings were becoming obvious—to everyone, including the CEO. There was still no clear direction for the company, and teams continued operating in silos. Deadlines slipped. Complaints about confusion and unclear priorities grew louder every week. Executive leadership meetings, once tight and focused, now dragged on for hours.

Finally, the CEO—normally reluctant to offend—lost his cool. In front of the team, he confronted Sarah directly. He warned her to get her act together. He reminded her why he had brought her in: to bring order to chaos. And she wasn't doing it.

But instead of taking responsibility, Sarah doubled down. She started blaming Veronica openly in front of the team. The chaos, she claimed, was her subordinate's fault. Veronica must not have been following instructions.

A vicious cycle began between the two women. Veronica's growing resentment led to further alienation from Sarah, who only used Veronica's lack of presence—or better yet, her avoidance of conflict—as justification to micromanage her even more. Sarah's communication became increasingly short, terse, and task-oriented. She gradually commandeered Veronica's workload, taking on even the most menial tasks herself. "I got this," she'd say curtly whenever a new task or project came in.

Veronica read the tea leaves: her position in the company was untenable. "They're going to fire me," she confided to a friend. The stress was taking its toll. Besides losing sleep, Veronica noticed she was also losing her hair. It was too much. She eventually hired a consultant to help her update her resume and prepare for job interviews.

Fortunately, and just in time, the executive leadership team saw through Sarah's incompetence and deceit. After eight tumultuous and emotionally draining months, Sarah was fired. Jerry, the ambitious and self-assured Chief Technology Officer, had been quietly maneuvering himself into the role. His efforts paid off: he was now the acting COO.

Jerry's tenure was short-lived. Despite bold promises to get the company back on track, he overpromised and underdelivered. From day one, he inserted himself into the smallest projects, even micromanaging junior project managers. His only real accomplishment was uniting the entire company against him. Within five months, Jerry was fired. Eight employees—yes, eight—from four different departments, resigned in just four weeks after his promotion.

But what ultimately sealed his fate wasn't the talent exodus—it was signing an outrageously expensive contract with a subpar supplier. The board couldn't ignore that.

Veronica, who had genuinely tried to support Jerry, found herself sidelined again. Once a bundle of nerves, she now felt a dull indifference taking over. The stress, sleepless nights, and constant frustrations had drained her to the point where even anger or resentment felt out of reach. Her hair continued falling out. Apathy set in, along with the quiet acceptance that her time at the company might be over.

Just as she was ready to walk away for good, the CEO reached out personally. He thanked her for her dedication and assured her they were actively searching for the right person to fill the COO role.

After some serious soul-searching, Veronica decided to stay. And just in time, too. Apparently, the company had a brand-new award waiting for her.

The Costs of Ignoring Chaos

As the dust settled, the company's senior leadership team started pointing fingers. The Senior Director of IT blamed the lack of a comprehensive strategy. The SVP of Marketing pointed at Sales for being uncooperative. The Chairperson of the Board claimed the CEO should've been fired months ago. The HR manager cited the company's culture as the root cause.

Each of them had a point—but none saw the bigger picture. Veronica's experience wasn't just a string of unfortunate events. It was a predictable disaster—a textbook example of what happens when leaders and their teams are unprepared for chaos.

The truth is, none of these incidents were isolated or accidental. They were the result of failing to understand that chaos has a system—an underlying, logical order that can be observed, anticipated, and even managed... if you know how.

They didn't. But you can.

What you're about to learn is that chaos isn't some formless, vague, unsolvable problem. It's a logical system—orderly, observable, and ready to be leveraged to your advantage. And once you understand it, you'll gain a decisive edge in how you lead, manage, and win.

That's the paradox: chaos punishes those who ignore it but rewards those who learn to work with it.

The Chaos Paradox

Chaos isn't a pit. Chaos is a ladder.
— *Game of Thrones*, Season 3, Episode 6

Veronica's story vividly illustrates the dangers of failing to understand chaos—not just on a personal level, but across an entire organization. Without proper management, chaos produces destructive outcomes that hinder both individual and collective success:

- **Reduced Productivity**: Persistent disruptions stall projects, causing missed deadlines and wasted effort.

- **High Turnover**: Chronic uncertainty and confusion breed frustration, prompting valuable talent to seek stability elsewhere.

- **Eroded Trust**: Inconsistent decisions and unpredictable direction erode morale, weakening employee loyalty.

- **Stifled Innovation**: Constant crisis management consumes attention, draining energy away from creativity and progress.

- **Damaged Reputation**: Internal discord and visible failures tarnish the organization's credibility, eroding client and stakeholder trust.

- **Missed Opportunities**: low, ineffective responses allow competitors to seize market share and revenue streams.

- **Financial Loss**: Prolonged disorder magnifies inefficiencies, drives up costs, and jeopardizes profitability.

Viewing chaos solely as a disruptive force obscures its full potential. Properly managed, chaos becomes a powerful driver of success. Leaders and teams that harness chaos achieve results that any organization would eagerly invest millions to replicate:

- **Deep Leader Bench-Strength**: Chaos demands preparation, training, and education, developing capable leaders—both current and emerging—ready to step up in turbulent times.

- **Operational Efficiency**: Chaos uncovers hidden

inefficiencies, forcing leaders to rapidly simplify, prioritize, and streamline operations.

- **Market Leadership**: Teams that swiftly adapt to chaos seize opportunities, capturing market share and outpacing competitors.

- **Accelerated Innovation**: The urgency of chaos sparks creativity, generating innovative solutions rarely discovered under ordinary conditions.

- **Sustained Resilience**: While chaos breeds distraction, resilient teams remain laser-focused on strategic objectives, effectively navigating volatility to achieve long-term success.

- **Adaptive Capability**: Chaos requires rapid, decisive responses, equipping leaders to quickly recover from setbacks and proactively enhance future performance.

- **Optimized Resources**: Chaos tempts impulsive decisions and wasteful spending. Prepared teams resist these urges, strategically conserving resources to sustain success through future disruptions.

Rethinking "Strength" in Leadership

Strength is too often mistaken for mere endurance, as if simply withstanding hardship were a virtue in itself. This book takes a different stance. Drawing on Ancient Greek philosophy, particularly the virtue of Aretê, I define strength as the relentless pursuit of excellence—achieving one's potential despite adversity. In leadership, strength means exceeding expectations in the face of chaos. In my experience, serious, results-driven people respect leaders who strive for greatness rather than those who settle for mediocrity.

Leading effectively in chaos requires a fundamental shift in perspective. We must recognize chaos as both a natural and inevitable part of life—something to embrace, not fear. This paradigm shift moves us from merely enduring chaos to actively engaging with it. Leaders must do more than withstand disorder; they must proactively shape events with purpose, charting a clear path forward despite the obstacles and surprises along the way. This mindset empowers leaders like Veronica to thrive, not just survive, even amid the feeling of losing control.

This book invites you to rethink chaos—not as a threat, but as an opportunity. By gaining strength in chaos, you unlock a deeper, more potent form of leadership that anticipates change, harnesses unpredictability, and fosters an environment where people and ideas flourish. Adopting this mindset will elevate your professional value, boost your self-confidence, and position your organization for greater success.

Ultimately, strength in chaos means consistently excelling in areas where most leaders falter under pressure. Your ability to master the uncontrollable elements of leadership will define your legacy and actively shape your organization's future.

But how do we measure something as elusive as chaos? That's the next step. In the following chapter, you'll discover a practical model designed precisely for this purpose.

Chapter 2
Measuring Chaos

In Chapter One, we faced the harsh reality that most leaders are unprepared for chaos. Now, it's time to shift from problem to solution. In this chapter, I'll introduce you to the Chaos Model—a tool designed to help leaders not just survive chaos but master it.

But before we dive into the model itself, let's explore how it came to be. The Chaos Model wasn't born from theory alone. It's the product of real-world observation, built on the hard truths faced by leaders and teams when the unpredictable strikes. My goal here is simple: to show you not just what the model is, but why it works.

We'll begin by examining the expectations we place on teams. From there, we'll explore the Four Impact Areas—key components that determine whether a team rises to meet expectations or struggles to perform. These areas reveal two distinct paths: Constructive Chaos, where teams grow stronger, and Destructive Chaos, where they falter. Next, we'll explore the Control Factor, the pivotal element of leadership that dictates both the type and level of chaos a team experiences. Finally, we'll integrate these elements to form the Chaos Model, your framework for mastering chaos in any team setting.

By the end of this chapter, you'll not only understand this tool but also be equipped to transform your leadership approach with a practical, measurable framework that helps your team succeed where others stumble.

The Starting Point

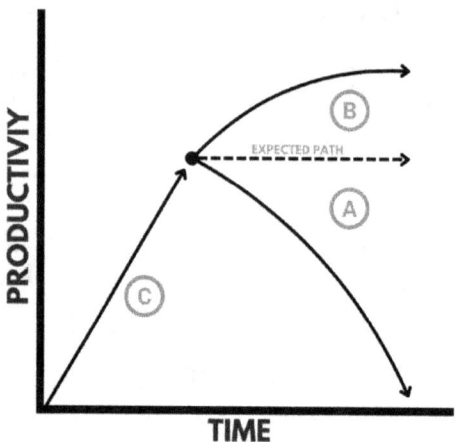

Figure 1. Ascending and Descending the Expected Path
Some teams fall short (A), others defy expectations (B). The challenge is identifying the path that builds strength under pressure, positioning the team for peak performance in chaos (C).

Generally speaking, we all have broad assumptions about how teams will perform. We expect them to meet our standards and timelines with minimal friction. This unspoken assumption is what I call the *expected path*. It represents a stable trajectory of performance that measures two key elements: Productivity (the balance of effectiveness and efficiency) and Time (the duration a team can sustain that performance).

Our reasoning is simple. We've seen the team members in action—their strengths and weaknesses. The leader has a history of success. And, of course, our directions are clear (or so we think).

Therefore, we assume the team will continue to deliver on time and meet our standards.

But as we all know, success is rarely a straight line.

Some teams fall short of expectations, struggling to cope with the mounting pressure to deliver. Their performance may lag behind schedule, or their results fail to meet the mark. Not all disappointments are equal—some teams fall further than others, and the deeper the descent, the harder it is to recover.

Conversely, some teams exceed expectations despite the increasing pressure. They deliver more value than anticipated, often ahead of schedule. These are the teams we call "strong"— they rise above the noise and chaos to deliver results that outshine the rest.

Why such a discrepancy? In my experience, factors like leadership quality, team culture, and clarity of expectations play a role, but there's a common, deeper thread: chaos.

Chaos acts like gravity, pulling some teams downward, away from expected performance. Yet, some teams don't just resist— they grow stronger. Just as weightlifters build strength by pushing against resistance, these teams develop resilience and adaptability, thriving under conditions where others falter.

For senior leaders, the critical question is: *How do I build teams that remain strong under pressure?*

For team leaders, the challenge becomes: *How do I help my people exceed expectations despite the chaos they face?*

The first step in answering these questions lies in identifying the key elements that drive team performance. I call these the Four Impact Areas. They provide a framework to measure how well a team navigates chaos—whether they rise above it or succumb to its weight.

The Four Impact Areas

After working with countless teams, I've noticed several essential trends that consistently indicate whether a team will be successful or not. They are:

> *A professional team sets aside petty, non-essential differences to work together effectively. They have a clear direction and operate like a well-oiled machine. The team is flexible in thought and action, prepared and ready to pivot or adjust when obstacles arise. Resources are managed to enable extended periods of work, and the team continually develops and grows, becoming more reliable and capable of repeating past successes.*

From this, several key patterns emerge—each exerting a direct impact on a team's ability to function, adapt, and succeed. I call them the **Impact Areas**.

To thrive, a team must first prioritize its *People*, ensuring cohesion and alignment. They must then establish *Direction + Order*: a deliberate pairing of two essential elements that must function as one, just as hydrogen and oxygen, when combined, form something greater than the sum of their parts: water. In this case, direction sets the path while order ensures disciplined movement along it. The team must be guided by another unique pairing: *Leadership + Management*. This fusion is critical: leadership guarantees resilience for the people facing chaos; management enables sustained success through smart decision-making and resource distribution. And finally, the team must demonstrate *Reliability*: the ability to consistently deliver under pressure.

Each Impact Area is essential, and together, they form the foundation of every successful team. If even one is compromised, it weakens the team's ability to meet its basic expectations. Let's explore each.

People

Success is delivered by teams, and teams are made up of people. A team's overall success depends on its members' willingness to come together and work as a unified force. But unity doesn't happen naturally. Teams consist of individuals with different personalities, backgrounds, and priorities. Left unmanaged, these differences create internal friction that leads to bickering, finger-pointing, and lingering grudges. The effect is to pull teams apart rather than bring them together into one cohesive whole. *Unity* is the foundation of resilience and durability—qualities essential in chaos. Without it, *disunity* takes hold. And when pressure mounts, the team fractures, then breaks.

Direction + Order

A professional team must know both where it's going and how to move as one. Think of an orchestra performing a complex symphony. Each musician follows the conductor's lead while adapting to the ensemble. Direction defines the path and the final destination, giving the team flexibility to adjust course as long as they reach that end point. Order ensures efficiency, helping the team manage time, energy, and resources for sustained operations. Team success depends on the leader *integrating* strategy, structure, systems, and culture into a unified whole. Without this integration, teams become *disoriented* and drift off course.

Leadership + Management

A team must be both led and managed if it is going to pivot, adjust, and improvise successfully. Consider a film director on set, balancing clear direction with trust in the cast and crew to adapt as scenes unfold. The leader must fully understand their dual roles—not just inspiring and guiding people, but also effectively managing resources, schedules, processes, and logistics. Their job isn't to be the hero, but to empower the team, channeling individual strengths into collective success. The real challenge lies in *relinquishing control* while preserving enough oversight to keep everyone aligned and engaged. Without striking this balance, *turmoil* emerges, creating internal dysfunction and seriously reducing team effectiveness to meet their obligations.

Reliability

Teams must be trusted to repeat success. Consider a sports team that, after winning a championship, must maintain its performance in subsequent seasons. The pressure to repeat is immense, testing the resilience of both players and coaches. The stress of competition strains relationships, disrupts established practices, and erodes confidence in leadership. As teams adapt, they must also evolve, becoming stronger, more efficient, and increasingly adaptable. Leaders must ensure the team heals its wounds and emerges better prepared for the next challenge. Ultimately, reliability is about *trust*. Once that is established, the team is positioned to exceed expectations in the face of chaos. Conversely, *a lack of trust* is devastating to both the team and its organization, potentially leading to long-term decline.

A Pattern Emerges

Through my work with teams in chaotic environments, a clear pattern emerged: teams experience the Four Impact Areas in a specific order—whether they are ascending toward high performance or descending into dysfunction. This reveals two distinct paths: one upward, toward meeting or even exceeding expectations, and the other downward, leading to failure. These are called **Constructive Chaos** and **Destructive Chaos**, respectively.

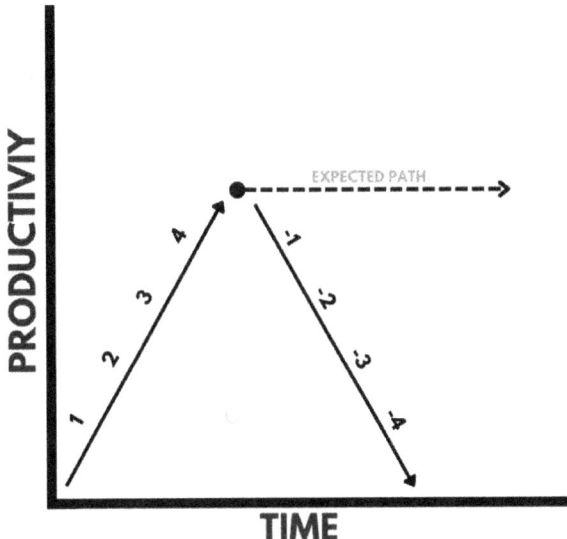

Figure 2. A Pattern Emerges.
Teams ascend or descend by moving through the four Impact Areas, in the same order.

Table 1. Constructive and Destructive Chaos Across the Four Impact Areas

Impact Areas	Constructive Chaos	Destructive Chaos
People	1 Unity	-1 Disunity
Direction + Order	2 Forward Integration	-2 Disorientation
Leadership + Management	3 Mission Command	-3 Turmoil
Reliability	4 Trust	-4 Distrust

Constructive Chaos turns challenges into opportunities by strengthening unity, sharpening direction, enhancing leadership, and building trust. Destructive Chaos follows the same sequence of Impact Areas but in reverse, leading to disunity, confusion, leadership breakdowns, and a loss of trust.

Each path mirrors the other—teams either climb or collapse through the same four stages. Understanding this pattern is critical for leaders because it allows them to diagnose where their team stands and anticipate what's coming next. There is no standing still—teams are always moving, either toward growth or decline.

By identifying where your team stands within the **Four Impact Areas**, you can assess whether they are on the **path to growth or decline**. Leaders who recognize early warning signs can intervene before challenges escalate to the point where chaos becomes overwhelming. In the next chapter, we'll break down both paths in detail, exploring how teams either rise or unravel—and how you can steer yours toward the right outcome.

Let's break down how each Impact Area manifests along these two paths:

- **People**: *Unity* reflects a team working cohesively toward a common goal in Constructive Chaos. In Destructive Chaos, *Disunity* reveals fragmentation, interpersonal conflict, and a collapse of cooperation that prevents the team from functioning under pressure.

- **Direction + Order**: In Constructive Chaos, *Forward Integration* means teams align their strategies, structures, systems, and a resilience-oriented culture toward a unified goal, no matter the uncertainty. In Destructive Chaos, the absence of any one of these elements leads to *Disorientation*, where confusion breeds inefficiency and ineffectiveness.

- **Leadership + Management**: *Mission Command*, a philosophy of decentralization and relinquished control, represents a balanced and empowering approach to leadership needed in Constructive Chaos. In Destructive Chaos, *Turmoil* reflects incompetent leadership that leads to poor execution and operational bottlenecks, potentially turning the team into a strategic liability.

- **Reliability**: In Constructive Chaos, *Trust* emerges from consistently high performance, making the team both dependable and predictable under pressure. In Destructive Chaos, *Distrust* arises from broken promises, perceived betrayals, and self-serving behaviors that undermine the organization's ability to function and deliver as intended.

Something is missing....

If these patterns are so clear, it raises an obvious question: Why don't all teams choose the path of Constructive Chaos? Why would any leader or team member tolerate disunity, disorientation, or turmoil—especially when the consequences are so destructive?

That's when I realized something critical was missing.

The issue isn't just about strategy or intent—those are the products of conscious decisions. The real issue lies in how people respond to control—how they experience it, resist it, or attempt to exert it. Through my work in behavioral profiling, I discovered that this response is often instinctive, not intentional. It's shaped more by automatic tendencies than deliberate choice.

Control is the final piece of the chaos puzzle.

It's not just another factor—it's the essential one. How people respond to it determines whether they harness chaos for growth or collapse under its weight. Some embrace control. Others instinctively resist it—unless they're the ones exerting it.

Understanding control as the missing variable for measuring chaos reframes everything. It raises critical questions: how does control fit into leadership, if at all? Does it contradict popular philosophies that emphasize humility, servant leadership, and empowering others? Isn't control inherently at odds with these ideals, or have we misunderstood what it truly means?

In this context, we'll soon see that control isn't about dominance or micromanagement. Rather, it's about mastering the balance that allows leaders to guide teams through chaos while enabling autonomy and growth.

We'll dive deeper into the role of control in chaos later in the book. For now, let's explore its essential place in life and leadership.

The Control Factor

Control is a fundamental human need, essential for independent, self-reliant beings. Because humans can choose their purpose in life, we must be able to shape our environment to our advantage. That requires exerting direct influence over the factors that support or hinder us. This ability to shape our surroundings lets us take our destinies into our own hands and bring order to a world full of uncertainty and surprises.

Consider the following areas—not as life hacks, but as levers of control. Each one represents a domain in which we exert influence to navigate uncertainty, assert autonomy, and create stability in our own lives:

- **Financial independence** grants us the freedom to make decisions and take actions that align with personal goals, reducing dependence on external factors.

- **Strategizing and planning** enables us to choose the direction of our lives and outline our paths forward rather than letting others determine our destinies.

- **Continuous learning** ensures adaptability and resilience, enabling us to recover from setbacks with certainty and confidence rather than being permanently derailed by outdated assumptions and a limited perspective.

- **Time management** increases the chances of success by keeping priorities clear and energy focused, while preventing progress from being derailed by distractions and non-essential tasks.

- **Emotion management** helps us stay composed and make thoughtful decisions precisely when impulsivity threatens to derail us.

- **Environmental control** means shaping, or at least influencing, our surroundings in a way to minimize distractions and foster an environment conducive to achieving our goals.

Another way to understand the value of control is by observing those who lack it. Think of someone who is "spinning out of control." Their life is often marked by stress, anxiety, and even depression. The infamous "midlife crisis" is a prime example. Often portrayed as a middle-aged man grappling with a lack of identity or purpose, this crisis reveals the painful truth: he has failed, for whatever reason, to take control of his destiny and instead allowed external factors to determine it. It's a stark reminder of what happens when control slips away at the most personal level. We feel lost, powerless, and adrift in a world of constant change. The result robs us of the motivation and confidence to face life's uncertainties, making every challenge feel overwhelming and insurmountable.

Control in Leadership

Leadership and control go hand in hand. The moment someone steps into a position of authority—whether in an executive suite or on the front lines—they take on the burden of translating vision into execution. That role demands accountability, decisive judgment, and, above all, the ability to ensure others carry out what must be done. Without control, that responsibility becomes impossible.

Consider a typical manager in a company. Their job isn't to define the mission; it's to deliver it. That might mean speaking hard truths, making tough calls, and, when necessary, replacing those who can't perform. It's not personal; it's a matter of survival. If the manager doesn't retain control over the team, the team won't deliver. When that happens, the company suffers. And when the company suffers, the team may not survive at all.

Even in politics, the pattern holds. A politician asking for your vote is, in truth, asking for control: control over how you are governed, how your resources are spent, and what future is prioritized. Once elected, they wield that power—often without your ongoing input.

In politics or business, leadership always requires control. Control over direction, over standards, and ultimately, over results. Even those who downplay control in favor of humility or servant leadership can't escape this reality. Without control, "leaders" are nothing more powerless influencers.

The Challenge of Control

Yet leadership is not about absolute control. It cannot be. **People, by nature, are largely uncontrollable**. Even with clear instructions, individuals will act according to their own judgment, values, and instincts. The challenge for any leader is to respect that innate drive for autonomy while still channeling it toward shared success.

The real skill of leadership lies in balancing control: directing others without smothering initiative, guiding performance without micromanaging. Too much of it: you either suppress engagement or invite resentment. Too little: you create inefficiencies and invite power struggles. Both kill trust. Both kill teams.

At the heart of leadership is a constant tension I call the **Control Factor**—the quiet struggle between the one who is expected take charge and lead and those within the team who feel compelled to take control themselves.

Embracing the Control Factor

Every individual within a team holds on to a sense of personal control. Some naturally want to lead. Others resist being led. As you'll see later, these tendencies can be measured using the right behavioral tools.

The Control Factor is a critical yet often overlooked element of leadership. Most traditional models assume that people will simply follow—but that's a mistake. In reality, people differ widely in how they experience control and how willing they are to yield it. Some resist outright, interpreting orders through their own lens because it feels safer. Others follow too rigidly, afraid to adapt or speak up even when circumstances demand it.

I've seen this play out personally. As a young junior officer in the Army, I often resisted orders—not out of defiance, but because I genuinely believed I had a better solution. And sometimes I did. To their credit, a few of my superiors adjusted course based on my input. It was uncomfortable for them, but the results often made them look good to *their* bosses. That experience taught me something essential: leadership isn't about blind obedience or rigid control. It's about guiding the team while staying open to ground truth—especially when it comes from those closest to the action.

This brings us to the central lesson of The Control Factor: Someone is going to take control of the team. As the leader, it better be you.

The Chaos Model

If control is the primary source of chaos, then the next step is understanding how it determines the path a team takes—either toward Constructive Chaos or Destructive Chaos. Enter the Chaos Model.

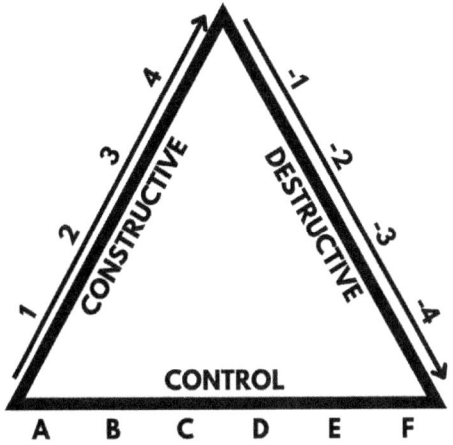

Figure 3. The Chaos Model

The Chaos Model gives leaders a practical way to measure chaos. It links how control is experienced within a team to the real-world outcomes that determine the team's overall health—specifically, their ability to operate at full optimization.

The model delivers three key practical benefits to teams and organizations.

- First, by identifying the specific control outcome a team is experiencing, you can **pinpoint** where they are on the chaos spectrum by intersecting it to its corresponding level of chaos.

- Second, knowing where you stand enables you to **predict** what level of chaos is coming next on your current trajectory.

- Third, the levels, and their fixed order, provide a developmental blueprint to **prepare** your team to grow stronger, exceed expectations, and avoid the traps that lead to destructive descent.

To make this actionable, the Chaos Model is structured into three interrelated scales: the Control Scale, the Constructive Chaos Scale, and the Destructive Chaos Scale. Each scale is provided to you in detail in the book.

The Control Scale

At the base of the model lies the **Control Scale**. It represents six distinct outcomes that reflect the type of response between the team and the leader at a given point in time. Each outcome indicates not only the type of chaos the team is experiencing, but also their general proximity to a specific level along its path.

The Control Scale is a vital tool for diagnosing team behavior in relation to leadership. Each outcome highlights not just how the team responds to control, but also the root causes driving dysfunction or success.

This scale is explored in depth in the chapter *How Chaos Unfolds in a Team*. There, we break down each outcome, illustrating how it plays out in real-world scenarios and offering actionable strategies for leaders to navigate these dynamics.

Table 2. Control Outcomes on the Control Scale

Control Outcome	Description
A: Anarchy	**The struggle for control.** Leadership has failed to take charge, leaving a vacuum for control-oriented team members to step up and attempt to fill.
B: Undisciplined Initiative	**Delegation without adequate oversight.** The leader's uneven focus creates gaps, forcing team members to step in and compensate. This leads to inefficiency and misaligned efforts.
C: Disciplined Initiative	**The optimal balance between empowerment and control.** The team operates with discipline, taking the initiative while ensuring their actions align with clear goals and guidelines.
D: Mechanical Compliance	**Rigid obedience to control.** Restrictions are tightened, and the team executes orders without engagement or adaptability. The result is uninspired and inflexible performance.
E: Malicious Compliance	**Compliance becomes self-sabotaging.** Team members feel powerless, to the point of following misguided directives that undermine authority or sabotage outcomes. Loyalties fracture, leaving the team divided and dysfunctional.
F: Deliberate Resistance	**Disillusionment turns into rebellion.** Feeling betrayed by leadership and the institutions that protect them, individuals launch active, deliberate opposition to inflict severe damage.

Constructive Chaos Scale

The team overcomes the stress of the challenges they face, evolving into a high-performing unit capable of exceeding expectations despite the obstacles and friction ahead. The four levels develop in the following sequence:

- **Level 1 Unity**. A group of people becomes a professional team. Unity is a seamless integration of different people who set aside their non-essential differences and voluntarily work together to achieve common goals. They adhere to a social contract between follower and leader and vice versa. They reinforce rank discipline to ensure the team can perform as expected. They develop an identity that they jealously protect.

- **Level 2 Forward Integration (FINT)**. The team becomes a well-oiled machine with a purpose. They have a clear strategy that permits flexibility in execution. Their organizational structure directly aligns with the needs of the mission. They have internal systems that enable intelligent and efficient work. Finally, they adopt a "forward" mindset that reinforces the resilience and adaptability necessary to succeed in chaos.

- **Level 3 Mission Command**. The team is maneuvered by a competent leader who has mastered the art of relinquishing control. Contrary to its military origins, this leadership and management philosophy is characterized by empowerment, flexibility, and individual initiative. Its products are agile leaders and team members who remain unified under stress, maintain FINT under pressure, and constantly strengthen themselves for the next assignment.

- **Level 4 Trust**. The team is reliable. Because they steadily adhere to the three previous levels, senior leaders have a high degree of confidence that they can be counted on to deliver, no matter what. The bonds of trust are strong internally. Team members exert discretionary effort and demonstrate personal initiative as needed because they are convinced their leadership has their back.

Destructive Chaos Scale

As pressure intensifies, the team's focus shifts from achieving success to simply surviving. Energy that should be directed toward shared goals is instead diverted to personal concerns. Silos form as team members retreat into self-preservation. If left unchecked, these conditions cause the team's effectiveness to deteriorate and, ultimately, collapse under the strain. The four levels occur in the following sequence:

- **Level -1 Disunity**. The team fractures as cooperation and mutual support begin to fade. Members operate more like a collection of individuals than a cohesive unit. The leader fails to manage personalities, resolve tension, or build the sense of trust and cohesion needed to hold the group together.

- **Level -2 Disorientation**. Confusion sets in as key elements of FINT break down or are neglected. Team members lose clarity about their direction, roles, and how to collaborate effectively. In response, the leader tightens control to suppress dissent. As a result, energy and resources are wasted. People show up to collect a paycheck with no motivation to go beyond the bare minimum.

- **Level -3 Turmoil**. Leadership becomes the central

obstacle to success. Turmoil marks incompetent leadership—leaders either refuse to fix the situation or worsen it by doubling down on misguided decisions. The team fractures as members retreat into silos for self-preservation. Morale plummets, engagement collapses, and the team becomes both inefficient and ineffective.

- **Level -4 Distrust**. At this final level, leadership crosses a delicate line from incompetence to corruption. Distrust signifies a breakdown of trust among the team, its leaders, and the organization as a whole. As a result, the team can no longer be relied upon to act independently or go above and beyond because they no longer believe leadership has their back.

How to Use the Model

A senior vice president of human resources at a $150M company reached out to me. Over a virtual coffee, she shared that three of their senior executives needed executive coaching. After some probing, she revealed that one of them was the CEO. "They're facing some real challenges," she said. Her goal was to support them by strengthening their communication skills and helping them work more effectively as a team.

However, the issues she described seemed to go beyond communication. I sensed something deeper was at play. I asked about how the executive leadership team communicated internally and how their messages carried through the rest of the organization. What were they saying to each other? What were they saying to everyone else?

Her responses pointed to major gaps in alignment and, in some cases, conflicting priorities. More tellingly, the way she described the executives—their personas and goals—suggested they were under significant stress. These were hardworking, well-meaning individuals, but the challenges they faced were triggering negative reactions and causing internal friction.

I shifted the conversation and asked if they had a strategy. She looked at me as if I had insider knowledge.

"Well..." she confessed, "I'm not sure we do."

"There's your issue," I replied. "It seems the issue among your executives isn't about communication—it's that they don't know *what* to communicate, because there's no established direction. Without a clear strategy, some of the individuals you mentioned are probably pushing their own agendas, which clash with senior leadership's unspoken expectations."

Sensing I had touched on a delicate truth, I lightened the mood. "It's probably like herding cats in a house on fire." She chuckled.

As we continued, it became increasingly clear that their executive team was experiencing **Undisciplined Initiative**, the second Control Outcome on the Control Scale. People wanted to contribute, but their efforts were unfocused, inefficient, and increasingly disruptive.

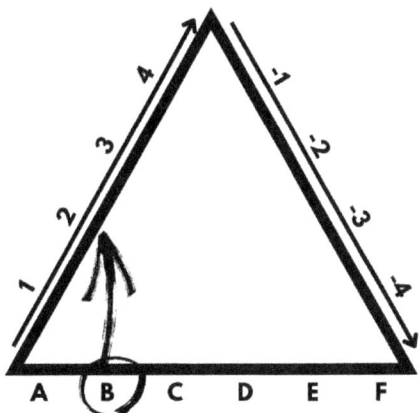

Figure 4. How to Apply the Chaos Model

They didn't just need executive coaching. What they truly needed was **Forward Integration**—and they needed it immediately. "You need to establish a strategy first," I advised. "Once that's in place, I bet you'll see a drastic improvement in leadership performance across the board." She seemed intrigued.

The conversation shifted toward how I could help. I was excited by the opportunity—it sounded like a wonderful company, and the challenge was clear: they were in Constructive Chaos.

She remained engaged, asking thoughtful follow-up questions. But in the end, the company didn't commit. It's possible they brought in an executive coach, but I'm fairly certain they never developed a strategy. In fact, I'd wager they lapsed into Destructive Chaos, likely falling into Disorientation and maybe even Turmoil. I'd also bet they lost key talent and missed some major opportunities for growth. Chances are, their senior leaders were constantly distracted by the latest crisis, as happens with many promising but unprepared companies.

A year later, I found out the VP left the company.

Without an objective tool to measure chaos, its causes can be difficult to pinpoint and its symptoms often lead to misguided diagnoses. The Chaos Model is your solution. Whether you lead a team of four or forty, it helps you isolate the core challenges your team is facing. Use it to predict what's coming, develop your leaders, and hire the right ones—so you can gain strength in chaos.

Applying the Chaos Model in Practice

The Chaos Model is not just a one-time diagnostic tool. Use it continuously. Assess your team's dynamics by identifying where your team currently stands on the Control Continuum. Ask yourself: Are you seeing signs of Anarchy, Undisciplined Initiative, or perhaps Mechanical Compliance? Pinpointing your team's state allows you to understand the underlying challenges more clearly and strategize your next moves accordingly.

By regularly revisiting the Chaos Model, you can monitor progress, anticipate potential pitfalls, and adjust your approach to ensure ongoing advancement. Use it not only to diagnose issues, but to stay proactive in steering your team toward high performance. The ultimate goal is to move beyond just surviving in chaos—to thrive in it, turning challenges into opportunities for growth and success.

Now that you have the tool to measure chaos, it's time to confront the deeper question: What, exactly, are you measuring? Before you can lead through chaos, you must understand its true nature—not the vague, overused buzzword, but the real, definable force driving behavior and breakdowns alike. The next chapter takes you there. If you're serious about mastering chaos, this isn't just important. It's non-negotiable.

PART II

UNDERSTANDING CHAOS

Chapter 3
The Metaphysics of Chaos

Metaphysics is a branch of philosophy that helps us understand the nature of existence. It's fundamental to a thriving life because it shapes how we interpret everything around us. It also underpins other branches of philosophy: from epistemology, the science of how we know things, to ethics, the science of the values we choose to live by. For example, if you believe in two distinct realms—heaven and earth—that belief will shape how you prioritize reason versus faith in your decisions. In turn, it will influence the kinds of values you pursue, whether material or spiritual.

Chaos has its own kind of metaphysics—an underlying framework that shapes how we perceive it and how we respond. Understanding that framework is essential because chaos touches nearly every aspect of leadership, teamwork, and decision-making. If you see chaos as purely destructive, you'll spend your energy fighting it—always reacting, always behind. But if you view it as neither good nor bad, but as a natural process, you can shift from reactive to proactive, learning to adapt and even shape outcomes before they happen. When leaders understand chaos on this deeper, philosophical level, they stop fearing unpredictability and start working with it.

In this chapter, we'll break down chaos beginning at the individual level. We'll define it and identify its core elements to show why it's inevitable. Along the way, we'll explore chaos's ancient roots and how thinkers throughout history have sought to understand it. In the next chapter, we'll dive into specifics to explore why people react differently to chaotic situations. For now, let's focus on the basics.

The Evolution of Chaos

In the beginning there was chaos.

In his poem "Theogony" (8 BCE), the Ancient Greek poet Hesiod was one of the first to discuss the subject. He described chaos as a formless chasm—the genesis of creation. Chaos was understood to be the source of the universe, the very thing from which gods, people, and the rules governing existence emerged.[2]

The philosopher Heraclitus contributed to our understanding of chaos too, albeit indirectly. He declared that change, symbolized by fire rather than water or earth, was the fundamental force connecting everything in the universe. His world was one of constant flux, captured in his central metaphysical insight: "You cannot step into the same river twice." The world of Heraclitus was unpredictable, filled with contradiction and therefore beyond our control. It was a world of chaos.[3]

As Western civilization evolved, the uncontrollable essence of chaos remained largely unchanged until the Renaissance. This period of intellectual and spiritual rebirth in the West marked the beginning of a deeper exploration of the universe and its mysteries. Thinkers of the time debated the nature of the cosmos and the values we should pursue within it.

In the 19th century, philosopher Friedrich Nietzsche offered a groundbreaking perspective on chaos. He saw it as essential to a fulfilled life—one defined by autonomy, freedom, and creativity. Nietzsche famously declared, "One must still have chaos in oneself to be able to give birth to a dancing star."[4] His view is fascinating because it reversed the traditional perception of chaos from something completely uncontrollable, and thus to be feared, to something beneficial—a force to be harnessed rather than avoided.

Today, our understanding of chaos has advanced beyond the philosophical into the scientific realm. Chaos theory, a specialized field in mathematics and physics, reveals that seemingly random behavior can still be governed by deterministic laws.[5] A key concept within this theory is the Butterfly Effect, which illustrates how small changes in initial conditions can lead to vastly different outcomes.[6] The metaphorical example of a butterfly flapping its wings in Brazil causing a tornado in Texas underscores the sensitivity of systems to initial conditions, revealing the underlying structure within what appears to be randomness.

This insight has profound implications for leadership and strategy. While we may never fully control chaos and its effects on individuals, with the right data and information, we can predict its general trajectory and its impact on team performance and productivity. In other words, we can gain a degree of control over what was once considered uncontrollable.

Understanding the Butterfly Effect helps leaders see how even seemingly minor decisions or actions can lead to significant consequences for the team. For example, tightening restrictions on a team that already feels things are spiraling out of control can cause people to shut down. Worse, they may sabotage the leader over a decision they see as unnecessary or harmful—even if, in reality, it was harmless and simply not essential.

The evolution from viewing chaos as pure, uncontrollable

disorder to understanding it as a dynamic system governed by deterministic laws allows us to approach it not as a force to be feared and avoided, but instead as one to be studied, understood, and strategically managed.

A Modern Take on Chaos

The objective lens used by the hard sciences to measure chaos can now be applied to the soft sciences, including leadership and management. **The challenge lies in understanding how people respond to the perception of losing control**, which ultimately determines the impact of chaos on themselves and those around them.

The essence of chaos is unpredictability. Think about it: we expect people to behave consistently, just as we assume the systems we rely on will function reliably. When they don't, we become thrown off—distracted, confused, and discouraged. How can we perform effectively when the world around us refuses to operate as it should? This frustration pulls our focus away from what matters, and erodes our ability to lead and execute with precision.

Chaos drains our energy and disrupts our focus. Left unchecked, it traps us in the immediate moment, eroding our ability to think beyond the now. We become fixated on the present—a state known as cognitive myopia—reacting to our surroundings instead of adjusting them to our will.[7] Without reorienting ourselves to the bigger picture, we become slaves to every new crisis, ruled by urgency rather than strategy.

Deadlines and obligations intensify the effects of chaos. As pressure mounts, people lose focus on what matters and become more susceptible to distractions that ultimately undermine performance. Over time, our energy dwindles and our frustration builds. And, if left unchecked, that tension spreads to those around us, straining cooperation and killing momentum. Eventually, we lose the drive to push forward, and the team's ability to deliver as expected weakens.

Before we examine how chaos affects leaders and teams—and why—we must begin at the foundation: the individual.

Chaos Defined

Chaos is a state of progressive disorder. It emerges when a series of events, situations, or personalities increasingly contradict our expectations. As these contradictions pile up—and reality refuses to align with what we thought or believed should happen—confusion and frustration take hold. The result? A diminished ability to think with clarity of purpose and act with sound judgment, even self-control.

Control—or more precisely, the perception of losing it—is the source of chaos. A lack of control over our environment can quickly spiral into a sense of powerlessness. Yet, our responses to it vary. One person might panic at the sight of a sudden kitchen fire, while another treats the situation as a dangerous but manageable problem to solve. These contrasting reactions reveal a fundamental truth: chaos is not just about what happens—it's about how we each perceive and respond to it.

The driver of chaos is personality, which shapes how individuals interpret and respond to unpredictability and volatility. While personality itself is broad and complex, one critical element of it can be scientifically measured and has practical value: **natural behaviors**. Understanding them provides valuable insights into how people are likely to react when they perceive a loss of control. In the next chapter, *The Driver of Chaos*, we will dive deep into these behaviors.

Crisis vs. Chaos

To fully grasp chaos, we must distinguish it from a commonly misused term: **crisis**. While both involve unpredictability, their nature and outcomes are fundamentally different.

A crisis is a single, high-stress event, whereas chaos unfolds through a sequence of disruptive events, often containing multiple crises.

Though crises are typically associated with disaster, chaos is not inherently negative. In fact, it can drive success by shaking up the status quo. By exposing weaknesses and vulnerabilities, chaos forces individuals, teams, and organizations to adapt, cut what isn't working, and re-center on their strengths and core purpose.

A crisis brings only negative stress, while chaos can generate both negative and positive forms of it. The positive fuels resilience, adaptability, and heightened awareness, strengthening rather than solely depleting those who embrace it.

A crisis has a binary outcome: disaster or the avoidance of one. Chaos, however, produces a spectrum of results—from exceeding expectations to just meeting them, and from falling short to complete failure.

Crises are easy to recognize, with clear beginnings and endings. Chaos, on the other hand, is continuous. Its effects are subjective, and its impact varies from person to person.

Unlike a crisis, which has a definitive endpoint, chaos never fully disappears. It's a constant that ebbs and flows in intensity and remains present as long as the team exists.

Differentiating Between Disorder and Crisis

Chaos is not simply disorder but an avalanche of it. It feels like one disruptive event piling onto another. The result is compounding stress and uncertainty, triggering immediate and seemingly instinctual reactions.

Take Samantha, a senior executive who works from home. Her husband, Jeff, also has a home office on the other side of their house. Samantha is a workaholic, and her desk looks like a tornado hit a stationery store—piles of paperwork, documents, and books laid out everywhere.

It's 4:30 p.m., the tail end of a long workday. Just as she's considering closing her laptop, her boss calls. He's in full panic mode—he needs a crucial document now, before 5 p.m. The document is late, and if it's not found, the company could be in deep trouble. Samantha starts to sweat. Her boss's anxiety is felt through his voice. She begins to frantically dig through the paper jungle on her desk.

As if on cue, the doorbell rings. It's the FedEx guy delivering a check Samantha's been waiting on for days—the one she desperately needs to deposit. Right on schedule, the doorbell sets off the family's three German Shepherds, who erupt into a symphony of howls and barks that could wake the dead.

Across the house, Jeff, who's on a critical conference call, shouts at Samantha to "shut those dogs up!" Apparently neither he nor his clients appreciate the background canine entertainment.

At this moment, and given her personality, Samantha has two likely reactions:

- **Reaction #1:** She can take a deep breath, tell her boss she'll call him right back, dash through the house like a woman possessed, shush the dogs with her best alpha voice, and sign for the package like a pro—all while somehow managing to look completely in control. Crisis averted! She even has time to grab a calming cup of tea before getting back to the task at hand.

- **Reaction #2:** She stays on the phone, screaming at the dogs like a banshee and yelling at Jeff that she should've listened to her mother and married that quiet accountant instead. She races to the front door, fumbling to sign for the package with the phone wedged awkwardly between her shoulder and ear, papers spilling everywhere as she curses under her breath. The dogs continue their howling concert, Jeff's clients are horrified, and Samantha's boss is still waiting—stunned by her PhD in profanity—and very much still document-less.

Good and Bad Chaos

In leadership—just like in Samantha's scenario—chaos can take one of two paths: it can be a force for growth or a spiral into dysfunction.

- **Constructive Chaos:** This path builds resilience, which is critical for adapting to uncertainty and ever-changing conditions. It comes with stress, but a positive kind: **eustress**. Think of the discomfort from running or lifting weights: your muscles ache because they've been broken down, but they recover and grow stronger over time, increasing your capacity to take on even greater demands.

- **Destructive Chaos:** This form of chaos is overwhelming and draining. As disorder builds, it triggers **distress**—the negative stress that depletes energy, clouds judgment, and erodes willpower. Patience wears thin, tolerance fades, and motivation collapses. The deeper one descends into Destructive Chaos, the harder it is to recover.

Both Constructive and Destructive Chaos are ever-present

possibilities for leaders and teams. The determining factor? How they react to the perception of losing control. No matter how well-prepared a team may be, they will certainly face chaos. But why? Because chaos isn't just a possibility or accident—it's built into how we operate as humans and goal-driven beings.

Chaos Is Inevitable

Three fundamental aspects of human nature make chaos unavoidable. First, we can think beyond the immediate present, allowing us to strategize and plan for the future. Second, the lack of real-time information creates a gap between our expectations of the future and current reality. Finally, we attempt to bridge that gap through improvisation. Each of these aspects introduces uncertainty and risk, making us feel—even slightly—that we've lost control in the pursuit of our goals.

Now, let's break these aspects down to better understand why chaos is inevitable, and why it's something we must actively engage with rather than resist.

#1 - The Conceptual Mind

The key to understanding chaos dates back to the Ancient Greeks. In *On the Soul* (Book III, Chapter 2), Aristotle identified a hierarchy of consciousness that explains how living beings perceive the external world. Animals react instinctively to their surroundings, but humans are different. We anticipate, plan, and form expectations about the future—all because of our distinct attribute: the conceptual mind.

The most basic level of awareness is sensation: the automatic grasp of our surroundings through the five senses. There's no cognitive thought involved—touch a hot stove, and you'll feel pain instantly, whether you want to or not. Simple life forms, like plants and microorganisms, exist at this level. Animals, however, progress beyond sensation early in life to the perceptual level, where the differences become stark.

Imagine this: You and your friends are camping in the mountains at night, gathered around a fire, your loyal dog beside you. The dog perceives the campfire's flickering flames, feels its heat, and smells the smoke. It also notices a distant glow on the horizon—a forest fire you've been hearing about all day. Then it sees the glow of the cigar you just lit.

To the dog, these are three completely separate things: the campfire, the distant fire, and the cigar. But you? You see the common denominator, fire. You're not distracted by size, shape, or color. No, you strip away the non-essential details of perception—the immediate surface differences—and recognize the essence: the underlying connection that links them all, no matter how different they appear. This ability is the hallmark of the Conceptual Mind.

Essentials and Expectations

Our ability to look past surface details and focus on what's essential is the defining trait that sets humans apart from the rest of the animal kingdom.

First, thinking in essentials compensates for the inconvenient fact that the mind has finite capacity. We all have a limited amount of bandwidth before we mentally overload. By reducing complexity to its core, distinct elements, we can retain only the most important information. This helps us stay focused on what matters most, no matter the barrage of noise and distractions we encounter on a daily basis.

Essentials, then, become the building blocks of our knowledge.

Not only do they help us focus, but they also enable us to categorize, prioritize, and integrate what we learn into a larger, usable framework.[8]

Equally important is the fact that thinking in essentials allows us to recognize patterns. By focusing on what remains constant across changing conditions, we're able to detect patterns that would otherwise be hidden by surface noise. For example, our experiences with fire—across different situations, environments, and periods of time—show us that it behaves consistently. This consistency gives us confidence that fire will act the same way in the future, regardless of context. In effect, thinking in essentials provides us with a model for how we build reliable expectations.

This understanding extends to other enduring forces that govern the world: gravity, the changing of seasons, the fundamental drive of living creatures to survive, and even human nature. We then use this foundation of knowledge, this predictability of our surroundings, as the basis for decision-making in both the present and the future.

Similarly, this foresight applies to human behavior. While emotions like excitement or sadness are universal, certain traits—such as perfectionism or introversion—manifest more prominently in some individuals than others. By recognizing essential patterns in both the physical world and human nature, we build a logical framework for prediction. In effect, we can reasonably anticipate specific behavioral responses in certain conditions before they happen.

For example, before assigning a mission to William, I ask myself, "How do I know I can count on him?" The answer lies in his consistent past performance in similar circumstances. No matter the task, the mission, or the people he has worked with, every assignment he has led has been a success. His track record—despite differences in people, organizations, and cultures—forms the basis of my confidence that he will overcome challenges and still deliver.

Why the Conceptual Mind is Essential for Leadership

Our ability to think conceptually allows leaders to make sense of complexity, connect seemingly unrelated events, identify root causes, and devise holistic strategies for navigating a volatile world. Without it, leaders are reduced to reacting to events as they unfold, rather than proactively shaping them to their benefit.

Here are some of the critical capabilities the conceptual mind provides:

- **Analysis**: Applying critical thinking to break down complex issues, determine what matters most, and prioritize actions—even when faced with multiple alternatives.

- **Synthesis**: Seeing the big picture and understanding how people, processes, and systems interconnect.

- **Talent Alignment**: Evaluating people based on their true capabilities rather than personality traits or superficial quirks.

- **Goal Selection**: Selecting goals that align with strengths and thereby increasing the probability of success despite times of uncertainty.

- **Planning**: Creating a flexible, well-defined path forward that corresponds with available resources, including contingency plans that help stay on course despite sudden changes.

- **Character Strengthening**: Building moral resilience

by maintaining focus under pressure, reinforcing will-power to succeed, and adapting to change without compromising core principles.

When Chaos Appears

When our expectations are contradicted—when reliable systems fail or trusted individuals falter—the balance between what we expect and what actually happens collapses. This clash creates a sudden and unsettling realization: we are no longer in control. The result is often profound emotional and psychological consequences.

People who don't think conceptually default to a purely perceptual level of awareness. Much like the dog in the earlier example, they see everything as separate and distinct. With no clear hierarchy of importance, they treat all issues as equally urgent, reacting to everything instead of prioritizing their responses. Not surprisingly, they become stuck putting out one fire after another, unable to pull back from the tree in front of them to see the whole forest.

This inability to see the bigger picture makes chaos even harder to detect. It doesn't always appear in obvious, perceptual forms like a tornado or earthquake. More often, it operates as a subtle undercurrent beneath a calm surface, creeping in unnoticed.

Perception-bound people fail to recognize the early warning signs. When chaos finally hits, it can feel sudden and overwhelming, catching them completely off guard. Unable to process what's happening, they internalize the stress without realizing it. As weak assumptions go unchallenged, cracks in self-confidence begin to form.

The personal impact of not seeing chaos is profound. When a leader's decisions clash with reality, the effect isn't just temporary disorientation, but possible long-term psychological strain. Self-confidence—so essential when leading others into the unknown—begins to erode, fueling a growing sense of insecurity. As errors in judgment occur, self-doubt takes root. Leaders may start to question their core strengths.

Imposter syndrome can even set in. This internal conflict gradually results in a loss of belief in one's ability to lead effectively. Left unchecked, this emotional toll compounds, leaving leaders vulnerable to challenges from team members or peers who now perceive them as weaker or less capable.

This emotional and psychological toll sets the stage for understanding why this critical gap between expectation and reality exists—what military leaders have long referred to as the "Fog of War" and "Friction." These natural forces distort judgment and amplify the effects of chaos, making even the most seasoned leaders susceptible to further missteps and disappointments.

#2 - The Fog of War + Friction

The future is inherently uncertain because countless variables— weather, markets, politics, and human decision-making under pressure—create unpredictable conditions. No matter how much we prepare, we will never have complete or entirely accurate information about what lies ahead.

Two forces primarily drive this unpredictability: the Fog of War and Friction. These universal forces are unavoidable.

- The **Fog of War** represents the gap between expectation and reality—what we think will happen versus what actually occurs.

- **Friction** refers to the unforeseen obstacles and complications that slow us down and frustrate progress.

Together, these forces ensure that even the best-laid plans face resistance, exposing flaws in our thinking and often triggering fear and self-doubt.

The Fog of War

The term "Fog of War" was coined in the early 19th century by Carl von Clausewitz, arguably the West's most famous war philosopher. In his seminal work On War, Clausewitz wrote:

> *"All action takes place, so to speak, in a kind of twilight, which, like fog or moonlight, often tends to make things seem grotesque and larger than they really are."*[9]

This "twilight" represents the uncertainty that amplifies fear of the unknown, clouding and distorting decision-making. Clausewitz observed that while all armies face uncertainty, those that manage it best are the ones most likely to prevail.

Napoleon Bonaparte is Clausewitz's premier case study. The French general-turned-emperor masterfully leveraged the Fog of War to his advantage. By masking his army's movements in enemy territory, he concealed his true intentions, sowing confusion in enemy ranks. He knew that under pressure, conventional opponents would struggle to respond effectively—and in doing so, they would likely make critical mistakes he could exploit.

But the Fog of War isn't limited to battlefields—it affects anyone required to make decisions under uncertainty.

Consider an attorney at trial. He stands before the jury, making his best case, but their silent, expressionless faces reveal nothing about his progress in persuading them. His experience tells him the argument is solid, but he can't be sure. What are they thinking? he wonders. He searches for the slightest hint— an expression, a raised eyebrow, a smirk—but finds nothing.

Should he stick to his strategy or adjust? He's operating blindly, with no feedback from his environment—only his training, judgment, and instincts to guide him. Will his decisions pay off? He can't know for certain. All he can do is move forward, trusting his preparation amid high stakes.

Or, think of the sales executive overseeing five regional offices across the country. Every day, she receives reports on the team's progress. But how much does she really know about what's happening on the ground? She's been in offices before—she knows how employees behave when management isn't around. Is her team following through, or is a disaster quietly unfolding?

She wrestles with a decision: should she make an unannounced visit, risking backlash and the perception that she's a micromanager? Or should she trust that everything is under control—knowing that if she's wrong, the fallout could damage her career?

The Fog of War affects everyone to some degree. Whether it's missing an important call by seconds or the pressure of a high-stakes job interview, the fog fuels fear and self-doubt, eroding confidence and even making us question our ability to lead in uncertainty.

The Fog of War makes chaos inevitable. But it rarely arrives alone. Its counterpart, Friction, adds drag to every decision and disrupts even the best-laid plans.

Friction

Friction is the accumulation of obstacles that disrupt progress and create frustration. It can be as small as a traffic jam when you're in a hurry or as major as a key subordinate leaving in the middle of a critical project.

Regardless of scale, Friction slows momentum, derails plans, and increases stress. It comes in two forms: external and internal.

External Friction consists of forces beyond your control. These can range from macro-level disruptions, like a global pandemic crippling international supply chains, to micro-level setbacks, such as corporate leadership slashing your budget at the worst possible time. For military leaders, it might be an unexpected enemy maneuver that renders their strategy useless. For politicians, it could be a sudden shift in public opinion that forces them to defend an unpopular stance.

In daily life, external friction might take the form of a power outage during a critical meeting or a storm shutting down your child's school on the one day you absolutely need to be in the office.

Examples of it in teams:

- **Delayed decisions or unclear directives** from senior leadership.

- **Burdensome policies** mandated by government or corporate headquarters.

- **Supply chain disruptions** or unexpected vendor delays.

- **Economic downturns** forcing budget cuts or resource constraints.

- **Regulatory changes** or legal shifts that disrupt operations.

- **Rapid market changes** that demand immediate response.

- **Internal Friction** arises from forces within your control. It could be as simple as a car breaking down due to neglected maintenance or as costly as losing a critical job opportunity because of poor interview preparation.

For leaders, internal friction often stems from ineffective communication or a failure to build trust with the team. In daily life, it can result from poor time management or failing to delegate tasks properly.

Examples of it in teams:

- **Personality conflicts** disrupt collaboration.

- **Breakdowns in communication** between team members or departments.

- **Missed deadlines** due to procrastination or lack of follow-up.

- **Withholding critical information** from peers or stakeholders.

- **Self-serving decisions** that put personal interests ahead of team goals.

- **Poor prioritization** leading to missed deadlines and burnout.

Fog and Friction are inevitable, forcing leaders to stay focused on their goals despite doubt and mounting obstacles. Some panic and make rash decisions, while others freeze, halting progress altogether. But those who are comfortable with chaos understand that the gap between expectations and reality will always exist.

The real question is: how do they navigate it?

#3 - *The Necessity of Improvisation*

Improvisation bridges the gap between reality and expectations. It goes beyond mere adaptability, which is simply adjusting to external conditions. True improvisation demands creativity and quick thinking to generate time-sensitive solutions. It's the act of reasserting control the moment it starts slipping away.

For example, if a teammate says, "The road forward is blocked," the right response is, "No problem. Let's go around. If that doesn't work, we'll have to build a bridge ourselves."

Improvisation rests on conceptual thinking. While the challenges we face may seem unique, we must look inward and recognize that we've encountered similar obstacles before. By reflecting on past experiences and focusing on the core challenges created by the Fog of War and Friction, we can confidently apply hard-earned lessons to the present—regardless of superficial differences.

Improvisation takes many forms:

- It could be a salesperson who ditches the formal meeting and sketches a proposal on a cocktail napkin at a networking event—securing a sought-out customer's commitment on the spot.

- It might be the keynote speaker who, upon spotting high-profile VIPs in the audience, shifts her presentation minutes before stepping on stage.

- It could even be a project leader who, frustrated by stalled progress, reassigns roles mid-project to reignite momentum.

Despite its value, improvisation is often wrongly dismissed as carelessness or a lack of preparation. But in reality, it's a critical skill set.

Improvisation is about adapting on the fly—changing course with minimal loss of time and resources while still meeting expectations. It's not a desperate last resort for poor planning, but an essential skill for competitive organizations.

When executed by a competent, confident leader, improvisation isn't just a response to the unexpected—it's a decisive advantage, especially when speed and agility are critical.

What Makes Good Improvisation?

Successfully deviating from an intended path while still reaching the final destination requires four key elements:

- **A Clear Vision of Success**: The central objective for the team must be clear—it serves as the guiding star for decision-making. When everyone knows what success looks like—defined by specific metrics—they can adjust the route as needed with confidence, whether by taking detours, adding tasks, or eliminating unnecessary steps, all without losing sight of the goal.

- **A Flexible Path Forward**: The path forward should resemble a multi-lane highway, not a narrow, single-lane road. Flexibility allows for multiple approaches, while the leader's level of control acts as guardrails, keeping the team on track and aligned with their purpose. Clear objectives serve as signposts, ensuring the team remains oriented, even if a detour becomes necessary.

- **Freedom to Maneuver**: People must have the autonomy to exercise judgment without constantly seeking permission. This freedom depends on clearly defined responsibilities and a strong sense of accountability, ensuring that individuals know when to act independently and when to consult others.

- **Competency Above All**: Technical skill, problem-solving ability, and self-awareness form the foundation of effective improvisation. A competent team shares a common problem-solving framework, allowing them to anticipate decisions and quickly align with new directions. In high-pressure situations, skilled team members can step up, fill gaps, and help realign the group—ensuring clarity in both intent and execution.

Of course, improvisation is not easy and can feel unnatural. The fear of it stems from discomfort with uncertainty, leading to hesitation or avoidance. Some leaders embrace change too aggressively, creating unease among those who prefer stability. Others cling to structure, fearing that even small changes could unravel the entire strategy, plan, or team.

But here's the reality: the stress of losing control—and being responsible for regaining it—makes chaos inevitable. No matter how well you plan, uncertainty will emerge, expectations will be challenged, and disruptions will occur. Leaders who resist improvisation won't avoid chaos; they'll be unprepared when it strikes.

Nevertheless, improvisation is a necessity in any goal-oriented pursuit. Be ready to do it, or don't plan to lead. The best leaders don't just accept that plans will fail—they expect it. They prepare for the unexpected. The ability to generate solutions on the fly while staying focused on the larger goal is the hallmark of strength in chaos.

The Human Element in Chaos

The Metaphysics of Chaos has shown that chaos is inevitable. No matter how much we plan, prepare, or attempt to control our environment, uncertainty will always persist. But while no one can escape chaos, not everyone responds to it the same way. Some thrive under pressure, while others struggle to keep up.

This raises an important question: why do people react so differently? The answer lies in personality in general, and natural behaviors in particular.

In the next chapter, we'll explore how natural behaviors shape the way we adapt, lead, and respond to uncertainty—revealing why each person's path through chaos is as unique as their personality.

Chapter 4
The Driver of Chaos

In Chaos Theory, the Butterfly Effect shows how a small, seemingly insignificant action—like the flap of a butterfly's wings—can set off a chain reaction, ultimately leading to massive, unpredictable outcomes, such as a hurricane or tsunami on the other side of the world.[10]

The same principle applies to human behavior: our responses to chaos, even when seemingly harmless, can ripple through a team and cause effects—positive or negative—far greater than we expect.

Consider a control-oriented leader under increasing pressure. It's fair to expect their communication to become more direct—possibly even abrupt—when time is working against them. Their terse reactions unintentionally create tension within the team, especially among those who avoid confrontation. In response, these team members may disengage, shut down, or stop contributing altogether.

Most of the time, the leader's response to chaos isn't deliberate or calculated. They are automatic, like a reflex when a doctor taps your knee. Why do they happen? The answer goes beyond experience or maturity.

In the previous chapter, we explored chaos as an inevitable force that affects everyone. Now, we take the next step by examining why it affects each of us differently. Natural behaviors are the answer. They're the key driver of chaos.

In this chapter, you'll learn why natural behaviors—not personality as a whole—are the *practical* key to understanding how people respond to chaos. You'll see how these behaviors shape leadership, influencing both focus and style. And finally, we'll break down the specific traits that explain why people react so differently when control begins to slip.

A Cautionary Note

This chapter is meant to raise your awareness of how specific behavioral traits influence our responses to chaos. **It is not designed to help you accurately identify your own behaviors.** In other words, it's not a substitute for expert profiling. While you may notice parallels in your own experience—and you likely will—resist the urge to profile yourself or others. Behavioral profiles can be very complex. Producing accurate, meaningful insights requires tools and guidance beyond what this book provides.

There's no shortage of so-called "personality" tools out there, but this chapter isn't about endorsing any particular one. My aim is to show that natural behaviors currently offer a more reliable and practical lens than broad personality categories. If you're interested in finding the best tool, I offer guidance on what to look for in the final chapter.

That said, the insights you gain about behaviors should still resonate—regardless of which tool you use in the future.

Personality and Human Complexity

Chaos is a deeply personal experience that varies from person to person. Why? It comes down to human complexity—specifically, personality.

Personality encompasses the traits, qualities, and characteristics that make each of us unique. It's so central to our lives that it shapes how we perceive the world and interact with others. But personality is broad—so broad that it's often difficult to pinpoint what drives someone's actions in chaotic situations. It's like listening to a booming orchestra and trying to detect the sound of a single instrument.

Think of personality as a layered cake, with each layer representing a different aspect of what makes us who we are:

- **Worldview**: The foundation of how you perceive and interpret the world, shaping how you see yourself and your place in it. This perspective is rooted in your deeply-held beliefs and values.

- **Life Experience**: The events and challenges you've faced, which build your willpower, resilience, judgment, and ability to form relationships. These experiences shape how you overcome adversity and maintain meaningful connections.

- **Work Experience**: The practical knowledge and wisdom gained from your professional life. This layer impacts how you support leadership, contribute to team unity, and respond under pressure.

- **Personal Values**: The inner motivations that guide your decisions, whether driven by goals like financial success, recognition, or stability. These values matter because they shape how you prioritize, how you approach challenges, and how you judge what's right or wrong. Ultimately, your values define what long-term success and satisfaction look like to you.

- **Intellectual Mindset**: How you interpret complexity, solve problems, and adapt to uncertainty—especially under pressure. Some people stop learning early, relying on fixed beliefs and familiar patterns. Others are constantly refining their understanding and expanding their worldview.

- **Maturity**: The ability to make balanced, rational decisions rooted in life experience. Maturity shows up most in high-stress or delicate situations, where sound judgment and emotional control directly impact long-term outcomes.

- **Psychology**: The deeper thread that ties together all aspects of your personality, revealing the underlying motivations behind your actions and decisions.

While these insights into personality are valuable, the bad news is that they're often impractical, at least in a business setting. Think about the time, number of tools, and costs required to profile just one frontline manager—let alone a hundred. And for what? Maybe it makes sense to invest that effort in a professional athlete who brings in millions a season. But in the high churn of the business world, such investments rarely justify the expense— especially when that person might leave in a year or two.

The good news? There is an alternative. Within personality lies a practical, scientifically measurable element: natural behaviors.

The Power of Natural Behaviors

Personality explains *why* a person acts; natural behaviors reveal *how* they do it. Behaviors are the visible, outward actions that others clearly observe. Think of them as the icing of the personality cake—it's the thing everyone sees and notices.

Each person has a behavioral profile—a unique combination of traits formed early in life that tends to remain stable over time. For example, some people are naturally extroverted and energized by social interaction, while others are fast-paced and impatient, thriving on change more than those who prefer predictability and harmony.

While these traits rarely change, people can learn to manage how they express them through reflection and maturity. An extrovert with few close friends hasn't lost their sociability—they've just become more selective about their relationships. The drive to engage is still there, but they've learned to apply it with more intention. Likewise, the control-oriented person who feels the need to take over holds back and lets her coworker lead—not because the impulse is gone, but because she's learned the cost of not appearing as a team player.

Your behavioral profile is as ingrained in you as writing with your dominant hand. Likewise, when you go against your natural self, the experience is like writing with your non-dominant hand. It's hard, frustrating, and ultimately unsustainable. It's how burnout occurs.

Not surprisingly, leveraging natural behaviors is critical to effective leadership. When you know whether someone is risk-averse or thrives under pressure, you gain real insight into how they'll respond in chaos. That awareness helps you anticipate reactions, adjust your approach, and drive stronger performance across the team.

Leaders who understand and apply behavioral profiles make

better decisions in team placement, coaching, and development. Aligning individuals' natural talents with job demands—whether it's pacing, risk tolerance, or relationship management—increases the odds of success. In high-pressure situations, this understanding becomes essential for ensuring people remain dependable and adaptive. Ignore these behavioral cues, and you risk setting unfair expectations or introducing bias that hurts performance more than helps.

Natural Behaviors and Leadership

As an army officer, I was taught that leadership is built on two fundamental pillars: mission and people. I still believe that to this day. Upon closer examination, those pillars—whether by coincidence or not—perfectly align with natural behaviors. In fact, each reflects a distinct orientation toward leadership, with its own priorities, focus areas, and style.

Mission-oriented behaviors focus on achieving outcomes above all else. People with these traits emphasize execution and feel a deep need for control—whether it's the big picture or the perfection of the outcome. For them, success is measured by results, and the team is a means to achieve that end. Obstacles are simply barriers to overcome. The two mission-oriented traits are **Vision** and **Task**.

Conversely, **people-oriented behaviors** emphasize the human side of leadership. These individuals focus on fostering strong relationships and setting the team up for success before tackling an assignment. They prioritize morale and cohesion over perfection or victory. The two primary people-oriented traits are **Relationship** and **Team**.

By understanding the behavioral traits aligned with these pillars, leaders can better leverage their team's strengths. This awareness helps them anticipate reactions under pressure and proactively adjust their approach. For example, a vision-oriented leader may excel at setting direction but struggle with personal connection. Recognizing this imbalance allows them to take deliberate steps to improve engagement, such as seeking feedback or building stronger interpersonal bonds.

This understanding also enables leaders to assign tasks that match team members' natural strengths. A task-oriented leader might delegate quality-critical work to those who thrive on precision, while tapping relationship-driven team members to sustain collaboration and morale. By tailoring their approach, leaders can maximize effectiveness and preempt potential behavioral challenges.

Behavioral Adaptability

Adaptability is the ability to adjust to new conditions in pursuit of a goal. **Behavioral adaptability refers to how easily we make those adjustments, based on our unique set of natural behavioral traits.** These traits don't just form our behavioral profile—they define our comfort zones.

In leadership, behavioral adaptability translates into tolerance—specifically, the ability to accept situations or personalities that trigger our stress of potentially losing control. Some moments and people, usually a combination of both, require us to step back, breathe deeply, and resist the urge to do or say what our gut is screaming for. That restraint—intentional, disciplined, goal-oriented—is what separates a reactive leader from an adaptive one. Behavioral adaptability is the difference between reacting instinctively and responding intentionally.

For example, consider an intensely people-oriented leader who thrives on bringing positive energy into the workspace.

They'll tell you they love making sure everyone feels valued. For this type of leader, holding subordinates accountable—especially when it might lead to confrontation—feels unnatural and deeply uncomfortable. And yet, for the team to function effectively, the leader must overcome it. They must learn to override the force in their throat and heart that holds them back from saying what they don't want to—but know they must—in order to address performance issues directly, even if it risks upsetting the subordinate.

Highly adaptable individuals excel at this. They've learned to prevent instinctual reactions from overriding conscious decisions. They developed the self-control to work effectively with people they may not personally like, masking their personal discomfort while projecting a clear focus on unified success. This ability to prioritize the larger goal over personal comfort makes them not only resilient, but incredibly valuable. They can engage the full range of strengths and talents available to the team—no matter how trivial the distractions may seem, or how real they feel in the moment.

Individuals with low adaptability, by contrast, lack the maturity or ability to recognize how their impulses impact the team, the mission, or their own reputation. Instead, they allow their dominant traits to dictate their responses, regardless of the situation or appropriateness. For example, a vocal, assertive person might argue when they should listen to critical feedback, signaling to leadership that they're uncoachable. Similarly, a perfectionist might say, "I told you this wouldn't work" after a failed plan, implying they'll only cooperate if things are done their way. In both cases, the lack of adaptability not only stunts their growth but also hinders the team's progress.

Developing behavioral adaptability takes time, patience, and deliberate reflection. It's a deep people-skill, honed by processing experiences through a lens of self-awareness. Leaders and team members must objectively review how they behaved during moments of stress or challenge. They need to ask themselves how they responded to a given situation, and how much of that response reflected their natural preferences versus the needs of the team and the situation. Most of all, they must learn to step into the shoes of others and consider why someone reacted to them the way they did, given that person's behavioral profile.

The bottom line is that behavioral adaptability is non-negotiable for effective leadership in chaos. Leaders who adjust their approach based on the moment's demands—not just their default tendencies—are better equipped to coalesce their teams into a cohesive, purposeful body capable of succeeding in the face of chaos.

The Complexities of Natural Behaviors

Behavioral profiling can feel like a powerful shortcut to understanding how people operate. It's tempting to categorize others and believe we can predict their actions, almost like a modern-day Sherlock Holmes or an FBI profiler who sees what others miss. And it makes sense—spotting behavioral patterns is fascinating, and it gives us a sense of power in anticipating what someone will do before they do it.

But here's the catch: this can be a dangerous oversimplification. Trying to profile people without the proper knowledge or expertise often leads to costly mistakes and misjudgments. You might think you've got someone figured out, only to realize you were way off. Misunderstanding someone's behavior leads to unrealistic expectations, which can cause unneeded friction, strain relationships, and harm the team's overall performance.

Let's dive into why natural behaviors are more complex than they seem:

First, **behavioral profiles are multi-dimensional**. People should never be defined by a single trait; rather, they embody a blend of traits that can vary significantly in degree. Think of a behavioral profile like a manual gear shift in a car: while most people operate primarily within their dominant trait, they can comfortably shift to their second or third most dominant trait when the situation demands it.

For example, take a results-driven leader who's highly competitive. Normally, he relentlessly pushes his team toward a goal, prioritizing performance above all else. His second-highest trait is extroversion. When a crisis hits and morale plummets, he shifts into an inspirational mode, rallying his team and rebuilding their confidence. While this might appear empathetic, it's ultimately his way of satisfying his most dominant need: to win.

Second, **people often adapt their behaviors to fit their environment**. This adjustment—sometimes called "masquerading" or role-playing—can be both misleading and self-destructive. Under pressure, individuals may act in ways that don't align with their true nature. Instead, they modify their natural strengths to influence others by projecting how *they want to be perceived.*

Take, for example, a free-spirited, impatient marketing executive applying for a role as head of operations. Knowing the job demands meticulous care, she presents herself in the interview as methodical, detail-oriented, and, above all, patient. While this mask might land her the job, it's rarely sustainable. Eventually, her true nature surfaces, causing surprise and irritation among her colleagues. Worse, those who hired her now risk losing face and political capital with their superiors.

Third, **behavioral traits vary in intensity and don't always show up in obvious ways**. Some remain hidden, only surfacing in unique circumstances. I once worked with a young scientist in a medical device lab who was very quiet and unassuming. Yet her teammates frequently complained about her. She regularly ignored lab protocols, leading to errors and delays that hurt the team's overall performance rating. They labeled her as "selfish" and even a "troublemaker."

How could someone so reserved cause such issues? After profiling her, we discovered the root cause wasn't malice but a hidden need for control. While this trait wasn't immediately visible, it explained her reluctance to follow protocols. To her, she was following protocols—just the ones she deemed necessary. Uncovering this didn't excuse her behavior, but it reframed the problem: the issue was a lack of self-awareness, not a lack of character.

As you can see, behavioral profiling is an extraordinarily powerful tool for understanding people—especially how to work with them.[11] Frankly, I wish I'd had this knowledge as a junior officer in the Army; it would have clarified much of the self-induced chaos I created. If nothing else, I hope you recognize that this tool demands expertise, caution, and respect. Used properly, it helps you avoid misjudging others and, most importantly, fully leverage their strengths.

Now, let's dive deeper into natural behaviors, keeping all their complexities in mind.

The Four Behavioral Traits

Figure 5. Linking Natural Behaviors to Leadership

Mission Oriented Traits: Vision and Task

The Vision Trait (V) is all about winning. Vision-oriented individuals thrive on taking control and leading their team toward a larger mission. Their focus is on the big picture and execution. This highly competitive mission trait will accept casualties as long as ultimate victory is secured. Their greatest fear is losing.

Vision-oriented leaders feel a strong need to be in charge—whether it's over people, a project, or a process. In a room full of people, they're the first to raise their hand when they hear, "Who wants to lead this project?" The intensity of their trait can be seen in their unwavering eye contact and body language, signaling that they are the right person to lead.

Their communication style is direct and frank, with little tolerance for repetition or unnecessary details. Non-verbal cues, such as their posture and tone, often reinforce their message. It's not just *what* they say but *how* they say it that leaves a lasting impression.

To maintain control, vision-oriented leaders aggressively avoid distractions, including small talk or details they consider non-essential. For them, success is about achieving strategic goals, and every moment not spent moving forward is viewed as an unnecessary delay.

Their leadership style is direct—often bordering on authoritarian. They expect others to follow their lead without hesitation, trusting their team to handle the details as long as the mission is accomplished. Those who hesitate or seem unsure of their ability to deliver risk being sidelined.

For vision-oriented leaders, chaos is a nuisance—a temporary impediment to overcome at all costs. They expect everyone to be ready, willing, and capable of navigating it, improvising as needed. If they had a mantra, it would be: "Don't wait for orders—just make it happen and drive on."

Response to Chaos:

Highly adaptive vision-oriented leaders inspire their team's determination to win, no matter the chaos. They unite people with diverse approaches and mindsets, expecting everyone to step up and contribute ideas—even unconventional ones—on how to achieve the team's primary goal. Decisive and unafraid of confrontation, they quickly quash negativity that could harm morale. Vision-oriented leaders act independently, often solving problems without input from their superiors. Give them a mission, and they'll execute it—frequently exceeding expectations.

Low-adaptive vision-oriented leaders create chaos when their confidence exceeds their competence to deliver effectively. They can come across as imposters, issuing arbitrary directives or demanding action without a clear plan. Under pressure, they instinctively intervene in both minor and major matters, taking on others' work because they don't trust the team to deliver. If they feel the team is off course, their response is to tighten controls. Dissent is treated as a personal challenge to their authority.

In extreme cases, low-adaptive team members with a strong Vision trait may override respect for authority and directly challenge the leader, regardless of seniority. They might initiate hostile takeovers through subtle manipulation, such as convincing others that current leadership is failing, or through overt confrontation. In the worst scenarios, an inexperienced team member could publicly undermine the leader, forcing a showdown.

How to Work with the Vision Trait:

- Get to the point; avoid small talk, and don't sugarcoat bad news.

- Don't let minor details overshadow larger goals.

- Speak of challenges, not problems, and show readiness to tackle them.

- Offer solutions that are already planned, coordinated and ready for implementation.

- Demonstrate control over your responsibilities, regardless of the chaos around you.

The Task Trait (T) is focused on perfecting outcomes. Individuals with this trait are perfectionists, driven by a deep-seated need to produce work of the highest quality. For those with the task trait, their work must be synonymous with excellence. Their greatest fear is being exposed as not being the subject matter experts they strive so hard to be.

Task-oriented leaders focus on getting things exactly right. Unlike Vision-oriented leaders, who naturally want to take charge, Task-driven individuals may also seek control. The perfect opportunity for them is when they feel compelled to step in when they perceive a threat to the quality of the work—especially when they detect inaccuracies or carelessness from others. The more intense their task-oriented trait, the sharper their critical eye becomes, and the more vocal they are about their concerns. Intense task-oriented individuals often resist change, preferring established systems and procedures that have proven reliable in the past.

In communication, task-oriented individuals have a deep respect for precision and detail. You can expect them to cite policies verbatim and scrutinize every aspect of a discussion to ensure accuracy. They may take time to process new information—even when they're impatient to move forward. Everything about the task must align with their high standards—everything.

Their leadership style is methodical, leaning more toward the principles of management than influencing leadership. They focus on enforcing systems and ensuring people adhere to standards. In communication, they demand *precise* feedback. Also, they generally prefer written communication. Writing allows them time to process ideas thoroughly, ensuring their thoughts are articulate and accurate.

Response to Chaos:

Highly adaptive task-oriented leaders are invaluable assets for teams focused on delivering top-quality products or services. In chaotic situations, they provide much-needed clarity by breaking down complex strategies into manageable, measurable steps and precise metrics. They also help reorient teams to focus on what can be controlled in the moment, ensuring that each task is completed with exactness despite the distractions around them.

Low-adaptive task-oriented leaders can stifle creativity and teamwork. Their air of intellectual superiority often intimidates subordinates, making them hesitant to offer ideas for fear of being judged incompetent or simply wrong. As deadlines loom and stress levels rise, this trait becomes increasingly defensive, interpreting even mild criticism or setbacks as personal attacks. Under pressure, they overwhelm others with data and facts, insisting on their approach while dismissing equally valid alternatives. Their need for perfection fosters a climate of fear, discouraging team members from taking risks or suggesting innovative solutions, ultimately eroding morale.

Low-adaptive team members with this trait can quickly become cynical and defeatist if they feel their advice or suggestions are ignored. Instead of contributing to solutions, they fixate on potential failures, creating a negative and demotivating atmosphere. Under stress, they often hyper-focus on proving why an idea won't work, rather than seeking creative alternatives.

How to Work with the Task Trait:

- Be ready to discuss specifics and details; vagueness won't sit well.

- Provide concrete evidence to support your stance or suggestion.

- Present solutions that are backed by sound reasoning and logic.

- Involve them in problem-solving by asking for their expert opinion: "What do you think?"

- Clearly define expectations to give them the time they need for precision and thoroughness.

People Oriented Traits: Relationship and Team

The Relationship Trait (R) is quintessentially people-oriented, centered on developing and nurturing human connections. Individuals with this trait bring immense value by creating strong bonds that can withstand the pressures of everyday business. They emotionally energize their teams, helping to orient, unify, and engage everyone with the task at hand. It's clear they genuinely want those around them to feel engaged, happy, and eager to be part of something meaningful. Their greatest fear? Falling out of favor with others.

Teammates often describe individuals with this trait as motivational, optimistic, and empathetic. The stronger this trait, the more outgoing and talkative they become. They're easy to spot— at social gatherings, for example, they're the ones mingling, shaking hands, laughing loudly, and striking up conversations with strangers.

This extroverted trait *thrives* on human interaction. Working in isolation, whether in a solitary room or cubicle, isn't just uncomfortable for them—it's emotionally draining. Also, their natural ability to connect with others can be a double-edged sword.

While they're comfortable around people and eager to make others happy, this can lead to oversharing or trusting strangers too quickly. Their desire to help often results in overextending themselves, sometimes to their own detriment.

Their communication style focuses on selling ideas, energizing others to get on board with enthusiasm. They prefer emotionally charged, inspiring language over detailed explanations and absolutely need real-time interactions, where they can read people and respond to them instantly.

In leadership roles, those with the relationship trait favor a participative, almost democratic style. They strive for inclusivity, ensuring that every team member feels heard. The idea of exerting too much control over others is anathema to them. They gain energy from giving and receiving recognition—a simple pat on the back or a "good job" can reinvigorate them during tough times.

Chaos threatens the positivity they strive to cultivate. As frustration sets in, the risk of disengagement and disunity grows. Relationship-oriented leaders often find themselves unprepared to manage conflicts that escalate into bickering and infighting, turning the workplace into a far less pleasant environment.

Response to Chaos:

Highly adaptive relationship-oriented leaders inject adrenaline into team morale. They rally the troops with motivational speeches that reignite the spirit needed to push through adversity. Their unique ability to encourage quieter, more reserved team members to speak up fosters honest feedback—something mission-oriented leaders can struggle to draw out.

Conversely, low-adaptive relationship-oriented leaders struggle to hold underperforming team members accountable, fearing that confrontation could damage relationships. I've worked with highly extroverted entrepreneurs who even hesitate to send invoices, saying, "I've done great work for the client; they know it. I don't need to burden them by asking for payment. They'll pay eventually, right?" This avoidance of difficult conversations often leaves issues unresolved, allowing them to fester and grow.

Low-adaptive team members similarly prioritize personal comfort and preserving relationships over embracing necessary change. Their reluctance to confront challenges can manifest as passive resistance when new strategies or structures are introduced. This aversion to disrupting the status quo or making tough decisions can lead to stagnation. Over time, their unwillingness to adapt creates tension within the team, as others perceive them as obstacles to progress and innovation.

How to Work with the Relationship Trait:

- Focus on the level of engagement and participation of others.

- Try to be optimistic and not just "all business."

- Welcome brainstorming sessions to encourage creative input.

- Ask for their opinion on how to better align people with the task.

- Emphasize your appreciation for their hard work and dedication.

The Team Trait (TM) serves as a bridge between mission and people-oriented traits. Team-oriented individuals excel at creating coherent strategies by clarifying goals and metrics set by mission-oriented leaders and organizing the team for effective execution. Their greatest fear? Letting the team down through poor planning or preparation.

This trait is instrumental in establishing direction, order, and predictability—essential conditions for successful and efficient teamwork. Team-oriented leaders gather data for planning sessions, design organizational structures, and define processes that ensure consistency and reliability in the team's work. Most importantly, they emphasize collaboration and build consensus within the team. Their approach relies on thorough, deliberate planning, avoiding decisions that seem hasty or off-the-cuff.

Unlike the Relationship trait, which focuses on personal connections, the team trait views individuals as integral components of a productive unit. In this dynamic, trust must be earned through active and enthusiastic participation; those who fail to engage risk being sidelined or potentially excluded from the team.

Team-oriented leaders communicate carefully and procedurally, striving to avoid conflict. They believe that collaboration brings out the best ideas. In meetings, they are often seen meticulously taking notes, ensuring every detail is captured for future planning and improvement.

Their leadership style blends pacesetting with participation. They create plans, implement control measures to track progress, and step back to observe execution, ready to adjust when necessary. By involving the team in the planning process, they prepare everyone for changes and pivots.

Chaos poses a significant threat to the Team trait, disrupting the predictability they struggle hard to establish. When chaos strikes, team-oriented leaders often face pressure to act quickly, which can lead to hasty decisions that undermine their carefully laid plans. If they hesitate to act, they risk pushback from more impatient, control-oriented individuals eager for immediate solutions.

Response to Chaos:

Highly adaptive team-oriented leaders balance speed with caution. They recognize that while planning is essential, time for reflection is often a luxury. To address this, they implement processes that enable ongoing improvement as the team progresses. Although this trait typically avoids conflict, highly adaptive leaders overcome this tendency. They've developed the resolve to confront difficult situations when necessary, refusing to compromise their standards. By speaking up—even at the risk of conflict—they ensure the team stays aligned and on track.

Low-adaptive team-oriented leaders often delay decisions due to incomplete information. To their more impatient, control-oriented colleagues, this hesitation can appear as insecurity or indecision, which frequently leads to conflict. Control-oriented personalities may pressure these leaders into making premature decisions, exploiting their discomfort with confrontation. This dynamic fosters resentment and disunity, as more reserved team members may withdraw further, feeling their quieter contributions are unnoticed or overshadowed by dominant voices.

Low-adaptive team members with the team trait often hesitate to contribute effectively. They may withhold valuable feedback or ideas out of fear of creating conflict, limiting their impact on the team. Others may delay their input until they feel confident that all processes are firmly in place, which can stall progress and reduce their overall contribution.

How to Work with the Team Trait:

- Avoid vague, general talk; be prepared to get down to business of doing things right the first time around.

- Demonstrate commitment to the agreed-upon plan and processes.

- Speak up and contribute meaningfully—bring something valuable to the table.

- Show that you are organized and prepared for in-depth discussions.

- Don't rush them into making decisions; give them the time they need to process thoroughly.

Bridging Behaviors to Success

In this chapter, we've explored the driver of chaos: natural behaviors—a practical, measurable subset of personality. To lead effectively in chaotic environments, leaders and teams must learn to adapt their natural inclinations to meet the demands of the moment.

Behaviors shape leadership in profound ways. Mission-oriented traits drive goal achievement and execution, while people-oriented traits focus on building relationships and preparing the team for success. Understanding how these traits interact—and how to balance them—is critical to leading effectively in chaos.

In the next chapter, we'll shift focus to cultivating behavioral adaptability—the key to navigating uncertainty with strength. By developing this skill, leaders can build resilience, sharpen effectiveness, and exceed expectations, even in the most challenging conditions.

PART III

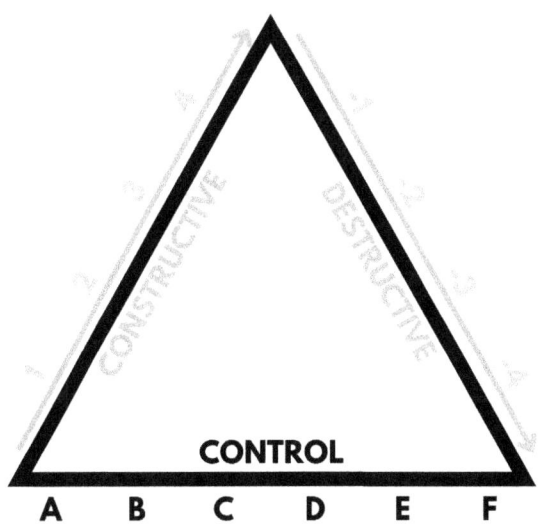

Chapter 5
Leadership in Chaos

So far, we've examined chaos through the lens of individual experience—specifically, how it challenges and shapes us personally. Now, we turn to leadership, where chaos shifts from a solitary trial to a shared experience. Here, chaos becomes the ultimate test of a leader: to align and guide their people toward a common goal while navigating the stress caused by the perception of losing control. In these moments, chaos doesn't just expose weaknesses—it reveals the strengths that determine whether a team will meet basic expectations or exceed them.

In this chapter, we tackle this complex subject with a focused lens. Over years of observation and study, I've uncovered several key patterns among the most successful leaders and teams. These aren't specific traits, qualities, or behaviors that a leader needs to be successful. Rather, they are foundational assumptions about the role. From these, I've distilled three core principles that, in my experience, are essential for any leader striving to exceed expectations in the face of chaos.

The three principles are:

- Leadership Is Measured by **Team Performance**

- Success in chaos requires **balancing human ends and means**

- Leadership in chaos is **the art of relinquishing control**

Leaders who embrace these principles don't just endure chaos; they transform it into an engine for growth. Under their guidance, teams emerge from the friction of daily work not only intact but stronger, more adaptable, and better prepared for the challenges ahead.

Now, let's explore what it takes to turn chaos from a looming threat into your greatest ally.

Leadership Is Measured by Team Performance

Leadership isn't about standing out as the most valuable player, rather, it's about making sure the team succeeds. Strong leadership is measured by the outcomes the team achieves, not the leader's personal style or individual contribution. When leaders focus on themselves—on being charismatic, liked, or indispensable—they risk losing sight of their primary role: enabling the team to deliver results.

Leadership is a means, not an end. It's an input—the force that drives team success—not an output or a product of individual brilliance. Leaders who treat leadership as a platform to showcase themselves often end up prioritizing image over responsibility. That shallow approach doesn't just weaken the team but erodes the very foundation needed for sustained success.

To succeed in chaos, we need a definition of leadership that reflects its true purpose. It must acknowledge chaos as a constant, stress the need for independent decision-making in the leader's absence, and reject the notion of a one-size-fits-all style.

It must also demand flexibility—the ability to adapt and pivot while staying aligned with the team's ultimate goal.

The following definition captures these requirements:

Leadership is the art and science of influencing others to actualize a vision in the most constructive and practical manner.

Notice its four key elements. Let's break each one down to better understand a leader's responsibilities in elevating and maintaining a team's performance in chaos:

The Art and Science

Mastering leadership requires learning, reflection, and experience. While the principles of leadership and management are timeless, how people apply them varies. That's why leadership is both an art and a science.

The science of leadership has roots over 2,000 years deep. Across history, leaders have faced conflict and uncertainty. These lessons—regardless of era—remind us that the core challenges of leadership, especially in chaos, haven't changed. From Homer's epics exploring the tension between emotion and intellect, to Thucydides' analysis of hubris and judgment, to Machiavelli's playbook on power and manipulation, history has long served as a practical teacher. Today's leadership development builds on those foundations with frameworks to sharpen decision-making, manage risk, and guide teams more effectively.

The art of leadership lies in how each leader interprets and applies those principles based on their unique style. A leader's behavioral profile determines which lessons resonate and how they're put into practice. A vision-oriented leader, for instance, may prioritize strategy and tolerate setbacks, so long as the mission succeeds. A relationship-driven project manager, by contrast, may insist on direct contact with their team, even when digital tools allow for distant oversight.

The best leaders strike a balance between art and science. They adjust their knowledge and style to meet the demands of the mission. It's not about them; it's about using the full strength of the team the best way they know how.

Influencing Others

In leadership, influence isn't about persuasion. It's about creating conditions where people follow your direction while acting on their own—without needing reminders, pressure, or hand-holding.

To be clear, influence is not the same as democracy. Just because people are trusted to act on their own doesn't mean they get to decide where the team is going. Input should be encouraged, and disagreement allowed—but once the leader makes a decision, that decision stands. Execution requires alignment, not consensus. That's why the chain of command exists. It's not just structural: it's the agreement that when it's time to move, we move as one.

Picture a ship navigating turbulent seas. Steering it is easy. The captain's value lies in preparing the crew for the storms that will inevitably come. That means every crew member feels a personal stake in the mission. Each one knows what's expected of them when the moment comes.

This kind of ownership doesn't come from blind obedience or force. It comes when each person accepts responsibility for their role within the team. Influence is what inspires people to take initiative—to do what they must, not just what they're told. It's not a luxury; it's a necessity.

In chaos, influence is indispensable if a team is to be adaptable and resilient. The willingness to engage voluntarily—driven by trust and shared purpose—is the surest way to overcome the friction and uncertainty teams face in chaos. When people take ownership, they make better decisions, move faster, and anticipate challenges before they escalate.

Actualizing a Vision

Future success rarely comes from a rigid plan based on today's information.

Success begins with a vision—a mental image of the desired future. That vision doesn't dictate a single route but opens multiple paths forward, allowing for change along the way.

Vision demands adaptability. The moment the team begins execution, the landscape may already have shifted. So instead of following outdated checklists or rigid taskings, teams must make real-time, situational decisions that align with the broader goal, adjusting and improvising as needed.

In both corporate and military settings, the senior leader provides the vision of success first. It is the responsibility of subordinate leaders and teams to bring it to life. Clarity is needed: What is the leader's intent? What are the metrics of success? When do we know we're done? Where is there freedom to act, and where isn't there?

With this understanding, teams prepare themselves to stay focused and agile, capable of achieving the objective regardless of the obstacles ahead.

The Most Constructive and Practical Means

Perfection is a myth. There is no such thing as a flawless plan nor spotless execution. There are too many unknowns, too many variables. A leader's job is to make the best possible decisions with the resources and information at hand.

The most constructive and practical approach is to focus on what can realistically be achieved given current knowledge, capabilities, and resources. Leaders who stay flexible and adjust expectations as conditions shift keep their teams moving forward. As George C. Marshall said, "When a thing is done, it's done. Don't look back. Look forward to your next objective."[12]

This approach frees teams from chasing perfection and keeps them focused on what matters most: meaningful progress under real-world conditions. It gives them the confidence to act in uncertainty and the resolve to keep going when the path is messy or unclear.

Balancing Human Ends and Means

Success in chaos requires understanding human nature. People aren't cogs in a machine. They don't show enthusiasm or initiative by blindly following orders. They respond best when personal incentives are clear, and in a team environment, they work together in a way that directly satisfies those incentives.

In my experience, the strongest leaders ensure their teams have two essential traits. First, a personal sense of purpose that aligns with the team's mission. Second, a mindset that channels their energy toward achieving both personal and collective goals with clarity and precision.

Together, these two elements form the foundation of

effective leadership in chaos: **Productive Purpose** and **Instrumentality**.

Understanding Purpose

Teleology is the philosophical idea that all things in the universe have an innate purpose and order. Consider the eye: its purpose is to see, and its structure is ideally suited to this function, allowing a living creature to observe its surroundings. Or think about the tooth: its purpose is to chew food, facilitating digestion for survival. Its design enables cutting and crushing, perfectly aligned with its function.

Teleology traces back to Aristotle, who argued that all living things are inherently goal-oriented. Each is driven by a natural impulse to fulfill its *final cause*—its ultimate purpose (telos). In his work *Physics*, he laid out four types of causes, placing special emphasis on the final cause as essential to understanding nature.

Take the daisy, for example. Its purpose is to grow and bloom. Even when a concrete slab covers it, the plant spends its energy seeking out openings, crevices—any path of least resistance to reach sunlight. This drive for fulfillment shows how all living beings are instinctively oriented toward their purpose, whether in helpful or hostile conditions.

Humans, however, are more complicated. Unlike animals or plants, we don't have instincts for survival. We have free will—the ability to choose our goals and values. And there's no guarantee we'll act in our own best interest. In fact, sometimes we make harmful decisions or engage in self-destructive behavior. But even then, we're still driven by something. Whether it's the pursuit of instant gratification, fleeting pleasure, or a long-term ambition, people are always acting toward some goal.

Purpose gives our energy direction. Whether or not people

have clearly identified their personal goals, one thing remains true: they are reservoirs of unspent energy. Every experienced leader knows that their subordinates will spend that energy somehow, somewhere. And if it isn't guided intentionally, it will likely get channeled into places you didn't anticipate—and probably didn't want.

How can you direct your people's energy in a way that not only meets the mission's goals but also encourages them to willingly tackle the obstacles chaos presents? The solution is counterintuitive: collective success as a team lies in appealing to the rational self-interest of each team member. They must believe that they gain something personally valuable from their contributions, beyond a paycheck.

Productive Purpose

Unlike animals, humans are stirred by deeper motivations than simple survival. Our awareness of the past fuels a belief that we can shape a successful future—no matter how long the journey. This sense of purpose, sometimes called a "calling," drives us to realize our potential: to become what we should and ought to be. Whether through creating, building, or achieving, it's about leaving a meaningful mark in the world.

Purpose becomes an invaluable asset in chaos. Like a flower pushing through concrete to reach the sun, a person with purpose doesn't avoid difficulty—they move toward it. Obstacles don't intimidate them because they see hardship as part of the path to something greater. Challenges aren't proof of weakness or limitations; they're simply temporary impediments that *must* be overcome. Nietzsche said it best: "If you have your *why* for life, you can get by with almost any *how*."[13]

Not surprisingly, those who lack purpose default to survival.

They focus on now, not next. Priorities shift. Distractions multiply. Hard decisions get kicked down the road because, "Who knows what'll happen anyway?"

They wait to be told what to do. They don't think ahead. They don't take the initiative. They move only when pushed. And so, the burden falls on you.

You: not just leading the mission, but carrying their weight too.

You: slowing momentum to remind them what matters—again and again.

You: splitting your focus between pushing them forward and steering the ship.

It's not sustainable. And in chaos, it's a recipe for failure.

But a leader who aligns a person's individual purpose with their role on the team gains a major advantage. Their people go the extra mile. They face challenges head-on and endure stress without complaint because they believe the team's success serves their own. They stay focused because it personally benefits them to do so.

This alignment of personal and collective goals is what I call Productive Purpose.

> **Productive Purpose = Calling + Career**

Productive Purpose is the alignment between a person's individual goals and the mission of the team. When it exists, something powerful happens: people stop working to live and start living to work. That means they no longer see their job as a list of tasks to complete for someone else, but as a personal pathway to something meaningful. They want to win personally—and to do that, they understand the team has to win first.

Productive Purpose is what sets high performers apart. They

don't need external motivation to push them; they are self-driven, ready to unleash their talents. That's why they push harder, last longer, and adapt faster in chaos than other teams that simply come to work to collect a paycheck.

It's in your rational self-interest to help your team members achieve their Productive Purpose. Remember, you're not their life coach or best friend, and this isn't about making them more fulfilled people, per se. Rather, it's about building a strong, durable, and capable team.

Productive Purpose in Action

Take Heather R., a 25-year-old rising star in a medical device company. She wasn't sure what she wanted long-term in life, but she was very passionate about design and problem-solving. However, she was seen as disruptive by her teammates. They complained she always wanted to go her own way instead of following the team's priorities. After analyzing her behavioral profile, it became clear that while she loved the industry, she didn't like being confined by tradition. She was creative, a natural innovator, and eager to contribute in new ways.

Once her boss understood her strengths and her genuine desire to build, she adjusted her approach by giving Heather more freedom. "Fulfill your role without any more complaints, and I'll give you time to experiment." Heather agreed. Three months later, she introduced a refinement to one of their products that saved the company $2–3 million a year. By aligning her strengths with her role, Heather discovered her Productive Purpose, benefiting both herself and the company.

Then there's Daniel S., a 31-year-old scientist making an enviable salary for his age. Despite his success as a lab technician, he too had become a source of stress for his team and boss: he was overpromising and under-delivering as a new team leader. Daniel indicated that he wanted to be a "people leader." Yet, this wasn't where he was most comfortable, behaviorally speaking. His natural strengths leaned toward independent work, where he had previously excelled.

When asked why he wanted to lead people rather than continue in his independent work, Daniel explained, "The most successful executives here manage large teams." He was equating professional success with leadership roles. Although he had the potential to develop his leadership skills, this path would have required significant preparation and coaching. Instead, Daniel dove in, taking on responsibilities that didn't align with his natural strengths. This decision not only led to unnecessary errors and delays but also strained his relationships with coworkers, potentially jeopardizing his career. By basing his path on a flawed perception of success, Daniel risked undermining both his current reputation and future opportunities.

Productive Purpose isn't always obvious and it's not always present. It's your responsibility to help team members discover, confirm, or refine theirs. When individuals' strengths align with their roles, as with Heather, the results can be extraordinary. When misaligned, as with Daniel, frustration and underperformance follow. Leaders shouldn't force people into a mold but should guide them toward roles where their talents thrive, strengthening both the individual and the team. Do that, and people will want to be a part of your team.

Fostering Productive Purpose in your team

The first step to fostering Productive Purpose is helping each team member identify their individual purpose. Talk to them about their long-term goals. Many won't have a clear answer yet—and that's fine. Think of it like heading toward a general destination. They may not know the exact address, but they should at least know the city or region. As they gain experience and self-awareness, the path becomes clearer. They begin to recognize where they're strong, what excites them, and where they want to go.

Start with sharp, pointed questions: What are their long-term goals? What are they passionate about? Where do they excel? Use these insights to draw a line between their current role and their future path.

Then, connect the dots. Show them how today's work isn't just a task—it's a stepping stone to something greater. Help them see how performing well now builds the skills, trust, and momentum needed to reach their personal ambitions. When people connect their daily responsibilities to their bigger purpose, their energy shifts. They don't just show up—they engage to win.

Instrumentality

If Productive Purpose is what drives you, Instrumentality is what disciplines you.

Instrumentality is the focused commitment of all available skill, energy, and willpower to fulfill the mission in the quickest, most effective manner possible. It means temporarily setting aside your personal ambition, your discomfort, even your preferences so that nothing stands between you and accomplishing the mission. In that moment, you're not thinking about how you feel or what you deserve. You become an instrument—sharpened, laser-focused, and ready to absorb all the friction needed to ensure victory.

In a team context, Instrumentality means every member operates as part of a cohesive unit. It is seamless alignment, the type that significantly improves the team's ability to respond quickly without losing ground. Staying efficient and purposeful helps them bounce back fast—even after a pivot.

A Race Car Analogy

Think of a high-performance race car. Built for maximum performance, every part—the engine, tires, suspension—is designed to function optimally under extreme conditions. This potential is only realized however when all components work in harmony with the driver's intent. If one wheel pulls in a different direction, thinking it knows a better path, or if the engine holds back, doubting the importance of speed, the car's performance falters, and victory slips away.

Similarly, teams must operate as unified instruments of the organization. Unlike a race car, though, people are not lifeless parts that automatically align. Each team member must actively choose to work as one, fully committed to the mission. Any division of effort—whether through hesitation, holding back, or prioritizing individual goals over the mission—undermines the team's strength and ability to succeed.

In Instrumentality, there can be no selective resilience. When the car faces intense pressure, no individual part decides to give only partial effort; each component performs at its best, regardless of strain. Likewise, team members must ensure that obstacles or setbacks do not needlessly reduce their commitment or performance.

Instrumentality as a Mindset

For Instrumentality to work, it must be adopted as a mindset across the entire team. This outlook translates into clear, practical behaviors and performance standards:

- **Full Utilization of Skills:** Every team member's talent must be fully leveraged; no strength should be left untapped. Any underutilization delays success and brings problems.

- **High Expectations:** Team members must strive to exceed expectations. Holding back isn't an option; every person must give their best effort, no matter how challenging the situation. Those who don't give their all have no place in the team.

- **Decisive Action:** Once a decision is made, every team member must fully commit, in mind and spirit, even if they might disagree with the leader's decision. There can be no room for half-efforts.

- **Resilience:** Mistakes and setbacks are inevitable. What matters is the rebound. The team must commit to getting up quickly and re-engaging with the same energy, focus, and determination as before.

- **Results-Oriented Focus:** While processes matter, success is ultimately measured by tangible results. Team members must stay focused on outcomes, even if it means sacrificing perfection, minor details, or occasionally ruffling feathers. Feelings heal, but damaged reputations are harder to repair.

- **Delayed Gratification:** People must learn to subordinate their desire for immediate recognition or validation to the ultimate success of the team. Individual wins will be recognized once the team triumphs. No one remembers the most successful person on a sinking ship.

- **Alignment with the Organization's Vision:** Success is not just about completing tasks—it's about aligning work with the organization's broader goals. Every tactical action should contribute to strategic long-term success.

Instrumentality and Productive Purpose in Practice

Consider two employees tasked with presenting a product to potential clients. The first employee is a new hire and works for a paycheck and waits for weekends. He follows a standard approach to selling: he explains the product's features, outlines advantages, and provides technical information. While he is articulate, it is clear he's going through the motions. He secures some sales, but the relationships with customers remain transactional, with minimal long-term impact.

Now, the second employee is motivated by prestige, recognition, and promotion. He goes the extra mile to learn how to sell and communicate, so much so that he transforms into a product evangelist. His goal isn't just to sell the product, but to build a fanbase and get them to sell it for him. So, he learns how to engage his audience with passion, projecting a sincere commitment to their success. He not only discusses the benefits to their businesses but addresses how it will affect them personally. His enthusiasm becomes convincing and contagious. Even when faced with skepticism, he persists with confidence and certainty.

The evangelist doesn't just make sales—he's created new opportunities. His pipeline practically runs on autopilot, with referrals now coming to him. In fact, he's built a safety buffer for the company: this continuous revenue stream should provide some financial stability if and when turbulent times arise.

The Foundation for Weathering Future Storms

Aligning personal incentive with the team's success is the foundation of strong, proactive teams in chaos. People with Productive Purpose aren't just willing to adapt to chaos—they're eager to. Through Instrumentality, they channel that drive into the team, converting personal ambition into focused, decisive execution. The result is a cohesive unit—fast, effective, and ready to exceed expectations at a sustained, optimal momentum.

Learning the Art of Relinquishing Control

Leadership in chaos requires knowing how to empower the team to act autonomously while still holding them to high standards. By relinquishing control thoughtfully, leaders foster initiative and accountability. Just as important, they prevent the rigidity that leads to Destructive Chaos. The key is learning to lead through **influence**, not **obedience**.

Control by Influence

Influence is the ability to guide others toward a desired outcome by relying on their voluntary participation. It creates an environment where people willingly contribute to the mission, understanding that their personal success is tied to the success of the team. Influence is a form of indirect control—it works by empowering people to take initiative and stay aligned, especially when no one is watching.

Influence fosters initiative and encourages ownership. When plans unravel, you must rely on your team to act without direct oversight. That only works when people feel trusted. When they're trusted to use their best judgment, they become personally invested in the outcome. The result? Smarter decisions, stronger commitment, and a more accountable team. That independence doesn't weaken cohesion—it reinforces it.

Influence reinforces discipline. When subordinates are given discretion to act, they understand that autonomy is earned—and fragile. That awareness keeps them sharp. They avoid shortcuts, stay within intent, and meet high standards, knowing that any lapse could jeopardize the trust they've earned.

Influence builds trust. When a leader is considered reliable, their decisions can be executed with minimal explanation, which speeds up response times and maximizes effort. That trust, built over time through mutual accountability and discipline, lets the team operate fluidly amid chaos, knowing that their judgment will be supported, and that their actions will contribute meaningfully to the mission.

Control by Obedience

Obedience is the act of following orders out of fear, pressure, or threat of punishment. It creates an environment where people comply, not because they're committed, but because they feel they have no choice. Obedience is a product of excessive control—it strips people of the freedom to act on their own judgment or initiative.

Obedience is the refuge of leaders who fear chaos.

To them, anything outside their immediate span of control is a direct threat to their authority. Therefore, they must control everything around them. That means systems, processes, and of course, people. Team members are expected to follow any directive given, to the letter, regardless of circumstances.

Obedience prevents adaptability. Over-controlling leaders dread initiative and improvisation because surprises threaten their illusion of control. In their minds, anything produced outside their line of sight is a threat, not a win. So they tighten their grip and eliminate discretion altogether. You're expected to follow instructions to the letter—no matter how tactical, unnecessary, or out of touch they are.

Obedience stifles creativity and initiative. In non-military settings, where people can leave bad managers, rigid obedience becomes a liability. Imagine a manufacturing plant where a worker sees a defect but feels powerless to stop production. That hesitation can lead to disaster—costly mistakes, lost revenue, and sometimes even lawsuits or criminal charges.

Obedience destroys resiliency. Team members stop caring. They show up to collect a paycheck, not to contribute. As control tightens, engagement collapses, and resentment builds.

The contrast between influence and obedience is stark. Leaders who rely on obedience create rigid teams that are brittle and hypersensitive to minor disruptions. Those who lead by influence foster flexibility, initiative, and durability. In chaos, the difference isn't academic: one breaks under the slightest pressure, the other bends under the worst and still wins.

Learning to Relinquish Control

Strong leaders take charge, but they also know when to step back. Learning to relinquish control prudently is essential to leading in chaos. Too much control stifles initiative, too little leads to inefficiencies.

To strike the right balance, you'll need to address three key areas:

1. **Personal Comfort Zone:** Understanding your comfort level with control is essential to fostering team adaptability. Striking the right balance often requires knowing when to step back and allow team members the freedom to adapt independently. Leaders who hesitate to give up control risk letting dominant personalities shape team priorities. Conversely, those who enforce rigid controls on creative teams may stifle innovation and erode morale. Effective control is about knowing where oversight genuinely adds value and where granting autonomy strengthens the team.

2. **Motivation for Control:** Leaders must ensure their control measures reflect the mission's demands and standards for success, not their personal bias or insecurities. Setting strict deadlines to meet critical market needs can create necessary pressure. When those deadlines are clearly tied to mission success, teams tend to accept them. But when control feels arbitrary—like deadlines set to soothe a leader's anxiety rather than match the realities of the mission—it damages credibility and discourages initiative.

3. **Professional Knowledge:** In chaos, control isn't about micromanaging; it's about applying the right tools with precision, offering guidance without suffocating independence. Here, leaders must delve into the field of management to understand the types of control measures

available, such as prioritized information requirements, reporting guidelines, and standardized planning templates. These tools create a sense of internal order, empowering the team to operate with clarity and direction even as chaos unfolds around them.

The Subordinate's Role

For relinquished control to work, subordinates must actively engage in the process. While they defer to the leader's authority, they share responsibility for team outcomes. This dynamic requires subordinates to balance respect for the leader's direction with the exercise of their own judgment in three key areas:

1. **Clarifying Boundaries:** Subordinates must take the initiative to clarify the limits of their autonomy. Uncertainty is not an excuse to hesitate. If unsure about their authority to act, they must seek clarity to prevent delays, confusion, or bottlenecks.

2. **The Duty to Speak Up:** Subordinates must communicate information the leader may not have. Leaders are not omniscient, and strong teams don't wait to be asked— they proactively surface updates, raise issues, and offer solutions. This keeps the leader informed without forcing them to micromanage.

3. **Navigating Leadership Transitions:** When a peer is promoted, former relationship dynamics must shift. Subordinates must mature professionally, replacing informal or unfiltered habits with disciplined support. They serve the role, not the person. The new leader deserves the same objective feedback that would be offered to any

leader, with no expectation of preferential treatment, regardless of past history.

Relinquished control only works when both sides participate. Leaders must empower subordinates to act within clear limits. Subordinates must seek guidance when needed and fully own their responsibilities. When that balance is struck, teams stay aligned and become agile.

The Dynamics of Control

Control in leadership isn't about exerting authority for its own sake; it's about creating the conditions that empower others to act independently and confidently, in alignment with your intent. When leaders strike the right balance between control and autonomy, they unlock a performance mindset—one where personal drive and organizational goals move in the same direction.

But balance isn't always achieved. In chaos, leaders often overcorrect—gripping too tightly or letting go too soon. The result? Teams drift, stall, or break down entirely.

In the next chapter, we'll examine how these imbalances reveal themselves in six distinct control outcomes. Each one signals a deeper pattern—one that tells you exactly what level of chaos your team is facing, and what must change to regain momentum.

Chapter 6

How Chaos
Unfolds in a Team

In this chapter, we examine the subtle interplay between leaders and their teams, where a powerful dynamic emerges—one that is central to understanding how chaos unfolds. This exploration is divided into two parts.

The first introduces the **Chaos Dynamic**, a unique exchange between leader and team that centers on one issue: control. Through perception, action, and reaction, it reveals how chaos moves from an abstract feeling into a measurable pattern of behavior. It also shows why the same team can either fragment under pressure or emerge stronger from it.

The second presents the **Control Scale**, which measures the Chaos Dynamic in action. It defines six distinct outcomes—each shaped by how control is exercised and perceived. These range from the instability of Anarchy, where leadership is absent and power struggles erupt, to the open defiance of Deliberate Resistance, where teams rebel against perceived betrayal. This scale becomes a critical tool for identifying both the level and type of chaos a leader and team are experiencing at any given time.

Let's begin by breaking down the interactions that shape a team's response to perceived chaos.

The Chaos Dynamic

The Chaos Dynamic represents the emotional exchange between a leader and their subordinates that determines whether they function as a cohesive, productive team.

The core issue is control—specifically, how it is wielded and accepted. As we've discovered, not all team members respond to control the same way. When behavioral adaptability is low, instinctual reactions dominate, escalating tensions within the team. When adaptability is high, even uncomfortable situations are managed calmly—reducing tension before it spreads. The result is a delicate emotional chemistry—one that decides whether the team becomes strong in chaos or spirals into dysfunction and eventual failure.

Chaos doesn't *just* happen in a team. It unfolds through a unique dynamic defined by three stages:

- **Perception:** Team members sense a loss of control, somewhere or somehow. They believe that one or more critical ingredients for success—such as unity, clarity, direction, or resources—may be missing.

Figure 6. The Chaos Dynamic. A repeating cycle of emotional responses to control that reveals a team's position on the Control Scale.

- **Action:** The leader responds to the perceived void by either implementing change or doing nothing.

- **Reaction:** The team responds. They either regain confidence in leadership and mission success, or they fall deeper into frustration and disengagement.

Each stage feeds into the next, creating a perpetual cycle that continues as long as the team functions together. This is the Chaos Dynamic. Understanding how it unfolds depends on the level of behavioral adaptability within both the leader and the team.

Let's take a closer look at each stage:

The First Stage: Perception

The Chaos Dynamic begins when a team senses that something critical is missing—something that prevents them from operating at their full potential. Team members experience a growing frustration as they recognize the following typical warning signs:

- **Communication Breakdowns:** Crucial information isn't shared, leaving some team members uninformed and unprepared.

- **Unrelenting Crises:** Daily work devolves into a series of emergencies that funnel everyone's attention and energy.

- **Role Misalignment:** Critical roles are filled by the wrong people, causing delays, creating bottlenecks, and slowing progress.

- **Neglected Systems:** Standardized processes meant to facilitate smooth and efficient operations are either missing, poorly designed, or ignored.

- **Absent Leadership:** Leaders avoid making tough decisions, leaving the team to feel powerless in a sea of directionless activity.

- **Loose Restrictions:** Team members frequently over-step boundaries, crossing into each other's responsi-bilities. The result is bickering, duplicated efforts, and turf wars.

- **Tight Restrictions:** Team members lack the autonomy to address issues that should be within their control.

- **Lack of Reliability:** Promises made are not kept.

The result of these observations? Frustration mounts, and team members react. Some vocalize their concerns, offering solutions to combat the growing chaos. Others withdraw, slip-ping into survival mode. A few openly criticize leadership for their lack of attention.

At this critical juncture, the leader faces a defining moment: How will they respond?

The Second Stage: Action

The leader becomes aware of the perceived chaos and is com-pelled to act. Behavioral adaptability determines their response.

Highly adaptive leaders acknowledge the issue and take full ownership. They understand that mission success depends on a focused, engaged team.

These leaders move quickly to identify and resolve root caus-es. They aren't afraid to make difficult, even disruptive but neces-sary changes. This may involve dismantling ineffective systems, addressing personnel issues, or challenging entrenched ways of working—if so, so be it. What matters most is that the team sees the leader is serious about equipping them for success.

Highly adaptive leaders actively engage the team, soliciting feedback from all members and ensuring even the quieter voices are heard. They ask thoughtful questions and expect thoughtful, informed answers. Most importantly, they empower the team to self-regulate. They encourage A-players to step up, take initiative, and assert their influence to help actualize the leader's intent and uphold professional standards.

Moderately adaptive leaders want to do the right thing, but they struggle to regulate their emotions under pressure. Their most common tendency is to focus on surface symptoms rather than root causes. The result is an imbalance of outcomes.

Their erratic performance creates confusion across the team.

Sometimes their control is too loose. For example, they might roll out a new tool or process to improve team performance but fail to drive full adoption. They assume people will follow through on their own. The result? They don't. The original problem remains—and now the team is stuck with another one layered on top.

Other times, their control is too tight. They impose strict oversight in an effort to prevent chaos from taking hold—such as insisting on being included in even the smallest tactical decisions. What sounds like a request to be "kept in the loop" is really a signal: they don't trust things to run without their involvement.

Their inconsistency often stems from an inability to balance the mission and people pillars of leadership. Under pressure, they revert to their natural tendencies. They usually realize—after the fact—that they've gone too far. But they lack the behavioral control to catch and correct it in real time. The damage is done before they recover.

Low-adaptive leaders allow emotion—not competence—to drive their decisions. Under pressure, they become consumed by the fear of losing control. Their instincts say, "control harder," when the situation actually demands openness, delegation, and engagement. The irony is striking: they desperately crave order, but their actions accelerate disorder.

Many respond by tightening their grip until the team becomes nothing more than an extension of their will. They act like chess masters, expecting everyone around them to behave like inanimate pieces—waiting silently for orders.

Others deny the presence of chaos altogether. But this always backfires. By shutting down discussion and hoarding control, they render the team powerless. Problems fester. Initiative dies. Morale collapses.

Low-adaptive leaders know neither how to build strong teams nor how to function as team players. Burdened with the responsibility of doing everything themselves, they quickly burn out—overwhelmed by the very weight they created. So they retreat into self-isolation, mirroring the very behavior they must fix to create a unified team. In that retreat, they surround themselves with a few loyalists—people who flatter them and offer no resistance or honest feedback. It feels safe, but the effect is corrosive. The team fractures further into an "us versus them" dynamic.

Regardless of their level of adaptability, how a leader responds to the team's perception of chaos reshapes the emotional atmosphere. Every action—or inaction—sends a signal about the future. The team is watching closely, consciously or not, to determine what's safe, what's expected, and whether they can still trust the mission. In the next stage of the Chaos Dynamic, we'll see how those signals land—whether the team re-engages, hesitates, or begins to check out.

The Third Stage: Reaction

This final stage of the Chaos Dynamic reveals how the team interprets and responds to the leader's actions. This is the moment of decision: do they re-engage as a team, or do they start checking out?

Highly Adaptive Teams

High-adaptive teams can be counted on to respond construc-tively. They've earned a reputation for adjusting quickly and functioning as a responsive, flexible unit—even with a mix of experience and skill. Stronger members step up, take informal leadership roles, and actively support others. They fill gaps, cre-ate shared awareness, and drive the team forward.

When the leader's response to chaos is clear and credible, high-adaptive teams not only align with it but they actively help implement changes. Their default posture is, "Let's do this."

But sometimes, the leader is less experienced or new to the role, and their recommendations are not clear. They may even seem counterproductive. This is where high-adaptive teams rise to the occasion. They offer honest feedback, share perspective, and provide recommendations or solutions based on their expe-riences. They deliver this feedback discreetly and do everything they can to ensure the leader succeeds—because when the leader wins, everyone wins. In doing so, they help the team course cor-rect as well as accelerate the leader's growth and competence.

High-adaptive teams almost always operate within Constructive Chaos—as long as the leader is intellectually hon-est and receptive to feedback. The mindset of this team is clear: "We believe in you, and we're here to make this work—as long as you let us."

Moderately Adaptive Teams

Moderately-adaptive teams are a mixed bag. They can adjust to new challenges, but their results are often uneven. Strong con-tributors lean in but their efforts are offset by others who hesitate or disengage. In effect, there's no internal force in the team that pulls the group together as a cohesive unit. These teams aren't necessarily dysfunctional, but their reaction time lags—costing resources, time, and momentum.

Not surprisingly, their response to their leader's corrective measures can be unpredictable. They may initially commit and signal all is well, but then hesitate when changes feel uncomfortable or unclear. Their support often appears cautious, as if they're waiting to be told—guided step-by-step—through the adjustment process.

If the leader fails to take charge, or is overly controlling, expect these teams to stall. Feedback is rarely provided to the leader unless they directly request it.

However, moderately-adaptive teams can shift toward Constructive Chaos. They need strong and consistent leadership that clearly articulates expectations, enforces accountability, and shows a seriousness about addressing root issues. Once that occurs, the team will slowly begin making adjustments on their own, without waiting for prodding to do so.

The determining factor in whether a moderately-adaptive team responds positively to a leader's corrective measures is the leader's ability to shift the team from a reactive posture to an actively engaged one. If that shift doesn't happen, the team will drift steadily toward low-adaptability—responding more with hesitation than initiative.

Low Adaptive Teams

Low-adaptive teams cannot be counted on to adjust effectively. This doesn't mean the people are incompetent; rather, they're no longer functioning as a team. A-level talent might be in the room, but they are disconnected. There's no coordination, no contribution, no collective effort. People work to survive, not thrive.

Individuals in these teams have become overwhelmed, confused, or emotionally disengaged due to poor leadership. In many cases, controls over them have been so restrictive that they've been conditioned not to take initiative without permission.

Not surprisingly, these teams struggle to respond to the leader's efforts to restore order. Many remain skeptical, disengaged, or quietly resistant. Some wait passively to be told exactly what to do. Others withhold effort or subtly undermine decisions they don't trust or simply disagree with.

Instead of aligning to help restore order, the team fragments further. People self-sort: some align with the leader to protect their standing, others form informal cliques in anticipation of a leadership change, and a few disappear into stealth mode to avoid drawing any attention at all.

Low-adaptive teams will never fully execute a leader's attempt to fix chaos until they believe the environment is both safe and worth investing in. Without that, the likely outcome is failure—for both the team and its leader.

The Control Scale

The Chaos Dynamic produces six distinct outcomes, forming a spectrum of alignment—or misalignment—between leaders and their teams. At one end of the scale lies Anarchy, where team members seize control in the absence of clear leadership. At the other end is Deliberate Resistance, where teams actively rebel against leaders they perceive as betraying them.

This spectrum is captured in the Control Scale. Half of the Control Outcomes (A–C) fall within Constructive Chaos, where the leader's primary control mechanism is influence. The other half (D–F) fall within Destructive Chaos, where control is defined by obedience.

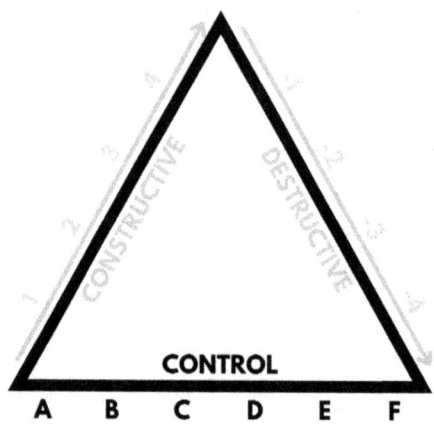

Figure 7. The Control Scale

Table 3. Definitions of the Six Control Outcomes

Control Outcome	Description
A: Anarchy	Control established through internal power struggles.
B: Undisciplined Initiative	Delegation without sufficient control or oversight.
C: Disciplined Initiative	Empowerment balanced with appropriate controls.
D: Mechanical Compliance	Strict obedience to direct control.
E: Malicious Compliance	Contemptuous obedience to an overcontrolling leader.
F: Deliberate Resistance	Destructive opposition to unethical leadership.

Each Control Outcome points you to both the type and level the team is experiencing. For example, Disciplined Initiative suggests the team is operating at either Level 3 or 4 of Constructive Chaos—Mission Command or Trust, respectively. From there, it's up to the leader to investigate further and determine the specific level based on context, behavior, and team dynamics.

Table 4. The Relationship Between Control Outcomes and Chaos Levels

Control Outcome	Corresponding Level of Chaos
A: Anarchy	Unity (1) and Forward Integration (2)
B: Undisciplined Initiative	Forward Integration (2) and Mission Command (3)
C: Disciplined Initiative	Mission Command (3) and Trust (4)
D: Mechanical Compliance	Disunity (-1) and Disorientation (-2)
E: Malicious Compliance	Disorientation (-2) and Turmoil (-3)
F: Deliberate Resistance	Turmoil (-3) and Distrust (-4)

Use the Control Outcomes to guide your leadership approach. They reveal whether you're encouraging autonomy and initiative or pushing the team toward powerlessness and resistance.

Consider these guiding questions:

- What is the prevailing mood within the team?

- Do they feel free to exercise judgment?

- Is too much control stifling initiative and creativity?

- Is too little control leading to fragmented efforts and inefficiencies?

Table 5. Typical Emotional Responses to Control Outcomes

Control Outcome	General Feelings About Leadership
Anarchy	"No one is in charge."
Undisciplined Initiative	"Good but messy."
Disciplined Initiative	"Tough but fair."
Mechanical Compliance	"Controlling" or "It's just a job."
Malicious Compliance	"A tyrant" or "A coward."
Deliberate Resistance	"I don't trust [the leader] or this place at all."

The Control Scale isn't just for diagnosing chaos—it's a tool for adjusting your leadership in real time.

Use it to reflect on how you lead. Are you relying on influence or obedience? How is the team reacting? Their behavior will tell you whether your current approach is building initiative or triggering resistance.

Adjust accordingly. If your team is drifting toward Anarchy or Undisciplined Initiative, tighten coordination without choking autonomy. If they're stuck in Malicious Compliance, you'll need to step back and seriously examine your style and systems before you can expect to lead effectively.

Whatever the case, treat the Control Scale as a snapshot, not a definitive verdict. Your challenge is to adapt your leadership to match the team's needs as they evolve.

Leadership in chaos requires understanding how control evolves. It's rarely static: it shifts with the environment, and so do the responses to it. To lead effectively, you must recognize how control moves within a team and what each stage of that shift looks like.

The Flow of Control

Control in a team is fluid, continuously shifting in ways that can either strengthen a team's engagement or suppress it, pushing members from personal initiative into mindless compliance.

This brings us to the **Control Continuum**—a sequence of evolving outcomes that reflect the changing relationship between a leader's authority and the team's response to it. At its core, the continuum represents a progression of restriction over people and processes. Understanding how this escalation works, and where healthy control gives way to dysfunction, is key to steering chaos in a productive direction.

The continuum begins with Anarchy, where the leader has no effective presence. In this stage, control-oriented subordinates—those with a strong impulse to take charge—compete with one another to fill an obvious leadership void.

As the leader begins to reassert authority, the team enters Undisciplined Initiative. Here, management is loose and laissez-faire. The leader exercises some control but delegates major decisions to subordinates. While this can produce moments of success, it is often marked by inefficiency and inconsistency.

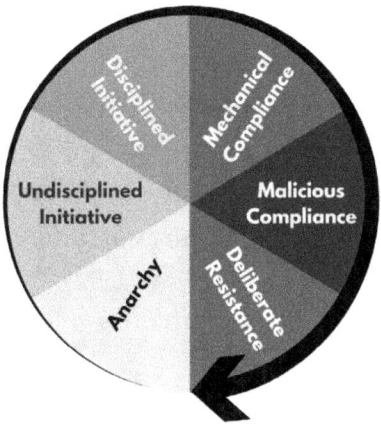

Figure 8. The Control Continuum

The ideal outcome is Disciplined Initiative, where the leader strikes the right balance between control and autonomy. Subordinates are empowered to take calculated risks within a clear, structured framework. At this level, the team becomes self-regulating and holds itself to high standards.

The team crosses a threshold into dysfunction when control becomes too rigid.

The first outcome is Mechanical Compliance. In an effort to prevent chaos, the leader imposes strict rules that stifle creativity and ownership. Frustration builds. Team members disengage, going through the motions with little concern for outcomes.

When control suffocates initiative—along with any genuine interest in making the team succeed—the group slips into Malicious Compliance. Frustration turns into resentment. Team members follow orders in ways they know will fail, using obedience to expose flawed leadership.

The continuum reaches its final stage in Deliberate Resistance, where leadership is seen as dishonest and unethical. Resentment turns into revenge, sometimes expressed through sabotage or retaliation. The goal is not just to remove corrupt leadership, but to force radical change within the organization that protects and promotes them.

When that drastic change occurs, the cycle resets. The old guard is removed, and a leadership vacuum emerges. The team reenters Anarchy, where control is once again contested until a new leader earns the team's confidence and willingness to follow.

With the cycle complete, the six outcomes of control can now be examined in full.

The Six Control Outcomes

A - Anarchy

Anarchy arises when there is a noticeable absence of effective leadership—even if someone is officially in charge. It becomes obvious that no one is steering the ship, prompting certain team members to step up and take the wheel.

Anarchy means the person in charge isn't actually in control. This usually happens for two reasons: the leader hasn't learned to take charge—or more often—they can't manage their control-oriented subordinates.

That doesn't mean the team is falling apart. In fact, Anarchy can produce short-term gains. But it also risks empowering the wrong individuals and creating a shadow chain of command.

The core danger of Anarchy is what it signals: if the leader can be ignored, what else can? Priorities, policies, expectations. In effect, everything becomes negotiable and malleable, and thus inconsistent and unpredictable.

Take the example of Sandy M., a supervisor at a solar panel manufacturer. A technical expert with 15 years of experience, Sandy is soft-spoken and avoids confrontation. As a result, she's routinely overshadowed by assertive subordinates like Mark and Steve. On high-pressure projects, they compete for control—personally directing coworkers and openly contradicting Sandy's instructions. When asked what she'll say, they wave it off: "Don't worry about it. I'll take care of it. Just do what I ask."

In situations like this, the leader is perceived as weak—either due to a lack of confidence or an inability to assert authority. Sometimes, they try to compensate by "reminding" the team that they're in charge. But it doesn't work. Their directives land like suggestions.

The result is a divided team. People are forced to choose sides: follow the ineffective leader with the title, or follow the more competent subordinate without the authority.

Either way, energy is wasted managing tension instead of solving problems. Interpersonal conflict replaces productive work.

Still, Anarchy isn't all bad: it signals engagement, not apathy. When someone steps into the vacuum—even clumsily—it reveals that people still care. They're trying to restore order in their own way. But this is not sustainable.

The official leader must reassert control. If they can't, they need to be replaced—fast. Senior leaders who act decisively can harness that energy, reset expectations, and redirect the team toward productive outcomes before the level of chaos becomes a destructive force.

B - Undisciplined Initiative

This level of control is marked by inefficiency. While the leader's authority is acknowledged, their control is loose and selective. They focus on areas where they feel most comfortable, leaving subordinates to cover the gaps—often without adequate preparation or clear direction. These team members—essential to success—are often neglected and left to shoulder disproportionate burdens.

The distinctive feature of Undisciplined Initiative is individuals or small groups taking independent action without the clarity, coordination, or alignment needed for sustained success. The initiative is real—people are trying—but it's scattered, uneven, and often counterproductive. Team successes are consistently overshadowed by inefficiencies. Performance suffers because the leader fails to unify team efforts toward a shared direction. Despite these challenges, the team endures, driven by their commitment to succeed as a unit.

Undisciplined Initiative stems from selective focus. For example, a sales executive promoted to CEO may continue prioritizing sales above all else, overlooking their responsibility for the entire organization. Non-sales functions, such as Corporate Communications or Technology, are left to subordinate leaders with little oversight, under the assumption that they will "just make things happen" to support sales.

Team performance at this stage is characterized by scattered successes. Some areas may excel, but achievements are inconsistent and lack coordination. Without a unified direction, individual efforts are misaligned, and the team's overall potential remains unrealized.

Several types of leaders contribute to the inefficiencies of Undisciplined Initiative:

- **The Subject Matter Expert** focuses narrowly on their area of expertise, dedicating most of their attention to technical or specialized tasks. This siloed approach leaves other areas of the team unsupported and disconnected.

- **The Intensely Reserved Leader** avoids confrontation, providing minimal oversight and allowing team members to work independently as long as essential tasks are completed. This lack of engagement enables team members to pursue their own agendas or priorities, often leveraging collective resources in ways that may not align with the team's goals.

- **The Generalist** provides broad, visionary guidance but fails to provide the specifics needed to align the team. While they delegate responsibilities, they also expect subordinates to fill in gaps and work toward shared goals without offering clear direction or actionable plans.

Despite its challenges, Undisciplined Initiative reflects a team's underlying drive to succeed.

C - Disciplined Initiative

Disciplined Initiative represents the ideal level of control. Here, control shifts from loosely applied to deliberately exercised. The team is both prepared and equipped to deliver results without direct supervision.

Trust flows both ways in Disciplined Initiative. The leader develops the team to act independently and take initiative when needed. During execution, the leader supports them by removing obstacles, aligning resources, and doing whatever is necessary to ensure success. In return, the team willingly follows the leader's direction. Their discipline and thoughtful engagement—especially their willingness to ask questions in pursuit of the best solution—reinforce the leader's confidence to step back and trust their judgment in the moment. This mutual trust becomes the foundation of shared accountability and sustained high performance.

At its core, Disciplined Initiative is driven by clarity. The leader provides the what and the why. The team owns the how. Control is present, but it isn't stifling. Teams don't freelance; they operate through agreed-on structure, systems, and techniques. They act with autonomy because they've been prepared to, and they know leadership stands behind them.

Key Competencies for Success in Chaos:

Leaders at this level develop the following capabilities:

- **Thinking in Essentials:** The ability to cut through complexity and isolate what truly matters. This enables clear priorities without overwhelming the team in chaotic conditions.

- **Purposeful Communication:** Leaders communicate intent with precision. Everyone understands the mission, their role, and the boundaries of flexibility during execution.

- **Flexible Planning:** Plans are clear, coordinated, and built with contingencies in mind. Leaders prepare the team to adapt seamlessly to changing circumstances, ensuring alignment with objectives.

- **Disciplined Execution:** Teams maintain high standards by acting with intention, not impulse. They communicate frequently, hold each other accountable, and rely on consistent routines that support precision and reliability.

Table 6. Emotional Responses for Influence-Based Control Outcomes

Control Outcome	Points of Friction	Emotional Responses
Anarchy	– Lack of clear leadership or conflicting direction – Constant conflict and power struggles – Unclear roles and responsibilities	– **Restlessness** from competing loyalties and inability to achieve goals effectively. – **Unease** due to instability and internal turmoil from competing factions. – **Apprehension** from feeling disconnected and unsupported by leadership.
Undisciplined Initiative	– Unclear tasks, roles and responsibilities – Overlapping efforts and misaligned goals – Mixed messages about priorities and expectations	– **Confusion** caused by unclear roles and expectations. – **Irritation** due to wasted efforts and inefficiencies. – **Skepticism** toward leadership's ability to provide clarity and order.
Disciplined Initiative	– High expectations for performance and accountability – Balancing autonomy with alignment to team goals – Pressure to innovate and take initiative	– **Empowered**, feeling encouraged to deliver positive outcomes. – **Fulfilled** from contributing and being trusted by leadership. – **Energized**, driven by the excitement of responsibility and autonomy.

Achieving Disciplined Initiative requires deliberate preparation. Leaders invest in developing their teams, identifying natural strengths, and fostering the judgment needed for calculated risk-taking. Continuous education and realistic training ensure the team is ready to handle uncertainty with confidence.

Performance at this level can be exceptional. Structured autonomy drives productivity, fast problem-solving, and innovation. Team culture becomes forward-looking, anchored in a shared commitment to excellence. Every member understands their role and takes pride in delivering on it.

Sustaining this outcome demands patience, focus, and constant reinforcement of trust. Leaders must ensure that team members feel confident acting independently while staying aligned with the mission. Through consistent engagement and a tolerance for trial and error, trust forms, becoming the foundation of high performance. The result is a team that doesn't just deliver—it becomes a strategic asset.

D - Mechanical Compliance

Mechanical Compliance marks the tipping point into Destructive Chaos. Here, the leader tightens their grip over the team as their way of preventing events spiraling out of their control. In doing so, though, their restrictive measures do more harm than good. Instead of establishing chaos-proof order, they end up handicapping the team when they need their situational judgment and initiative most.

The defining trait of Mechanical Compliance is the shift from engagement to indifference. Team members aren't asked to think—they're expected to obey. Their role becomes purely reactive: push the buttons, pull the levers, follow the checklist. They are treated as muscles, not brains. Not surprisingly, any incentive of an eager team member to go above and beyond disappears quickly.

The root cause of Mechanical Compliance? Fear.

The leader is afraid of losing control, or being seen as not being competent or worthy of the position. So they clamp down. Little can be done without their approval. They restrict communication to make sure they're kept in the loop for everything. They limit autonomy because subordinates taking the initiative feels like a one-way ticket to disaster.

Hard conversations are ignored. Some leaders avoid open, honest feedback—to do so will only highlight how they are hurting the team. Others treat honest questions or concerns about their control as challenges to their authority, even their competence. This is where defensiveness and veiled threats come in. "You don't like my rules," the leader says passive aggressively, "Go somewhere else—if they'll take you."

The result of this clampdown is a stale, seemingly "safe" environment—one where creativity is stifled, and ownership of success belongs only to the person handing out orders.

The team's reaction is predictable: they do the bare minimum—it's all they're allowed to do.

Take Jonathan T., a director of quality control at a manufacturing firm. A perfectionist, he creates task lists with hundreds of items per person and insists on approving every step. Progress stalls. Team members can't move without his signoff. Delays pile up. Trust in his leadership erodes. His obsession with control, though well-intentioned, suppresses the very outcomes he's trying to deliver.

Mechanical Compliance isn't a death sentence, but you're definitely heading in a direction you don't want to go. Recovery is still possible, but only if the leader stops hoarding decisions and starts empowering the team to act on their own. That means real conversations, clear handoffs, and giving people the freedom to solve problems without asking for permission. If that doesn't happen soon, valuable talent won't stick around for long.

E - Malicious Compliance

Malicious Compliance represents one of the most corrosive outcomes of control. Team members become so resentful of their leader's approach that they allow them to fail—deliberately. This response often stems not only from frustration and self-preservation, but a desire for retribution. It reflects the wisdom often attributed to Napoleon: "Never interfere with an enemy while he's destroying himself."

In this toxic environment, trust and collaboration have completely broken down. Subordinates feel powerless and alienated; their leaders, overwhelmed by their inability to control everything, either double down on restrictive measures or retreat into complete avoidance of conflict.

A vicious cycle sets in: the team, stripped of agency, disengages further, offering no feedback because they fear retribution. The leader interprets their silence as a lack of commitment, or even incompetence, thus justifying even tighter control in a misguided effort to prevent chaos from escalating.

Leaders at this stage typically fall into one of two categories:

- **The Bully Leader,** who dismisses criticism, tolerates no dissent, and enforces control through intimidation.

- **The Absentee Leader,** who avoids decision-making altogether, while preventing others from stepping in to correct course.

Both approaches stifle objective feedback, foster silos and echo chambers, and reward loyalty over merit. It's a retreat into a false sense of security—an attempt to avoid the painful reality they've created for themselves and everyone around them.

When people have had enough of being made to feel helpless and miserable, they begin executing the leader's misguided plans exactly as instructed, knowing they will fail. Some comply out of fear, others out of spite. Most, simply out of fatigue.

Team performance deteriorates quickly under Malicious Compliance. Communication breaks down, deadlines slip, and productivity stalls. These failures ripple outward, creating bottlenecks, damaging reputations, and straining relationships with customers and stakeholders. Over time, top talent walks away, and the organization's credibility suffers.

Consider the case of Tony D., a marketing superstar with 15 years of experience. Senior leadership kept him around for his exceptional talent—and out of fear he might join a competitor. But Tony's team despised him for his arrogance and habit of taking credit for their work. When Tony sent incorrect information to the board for a key presentation, the team knew it was wrong—but followed orders anyway. They hoped the mistake would expose his incompetence. And it did. The fallout ruined Tony's reputation and embarrassed the CEO, who was already on shaky ground with the board.

Recovery from Malicious Compliance demands a radical shift in the leader's behavior. They must acknowledge past failures, empower the team, and foster open communication. But this rarely happens. These leaders are usually unwilling to change.

If recovery isn't possible—and it usually isn't—the leader must be removed immediately. No hesitation. No more excuses. The organization must act decisively to rebuild trust with those who remain on the team. A clear message must follow: We see the damage. We take responsibility. And we will fix it.

F - Deliberate Resistance

A   B   C   D   E   F

Deliberate Resistance represents the team's most extreme response to control. A profound breakdown in leadership and institutional integrity has occurred. It's no longer a question of competence but rather of ethics. Subordinates feel deceived and no longer see leadership as legitimate. As a result, they purposefully sabotage them in order to cause drastic change to the status quo.

At the heart of Deliberate Resistance is a sense of betrayal. Leadership has presented one face publicly while operating with a very different agenda behind the scenes. People feel conned, manipulated, or used. Moreover, team members no longer believe the larger institution that breeds and protects these duplicitous leaders have their best interests at heart either.

Resistance takes two distinct forms. One group acts out of anger, feeling taken advantage of; they seek retaliation designed to cause lasting, even permanent damage. The other group takes a principled stand, exposing systemic failures to force major change. Their resistance isn't about destruction per se, it's about redemption. The institution has deviated from its original, mandated course, and their goal is to reveal the corruption and restore it to what it was meant to be. Regardless of motive, both groups aim for the same outcome: not only to replace the dishonest leader, but to fundamentally reshape the organization itself so this systematic betrayal never occurs again.

Leadership rarely recovers from Deliberate Resistance. Rather than reform, most double down on their treacherous course—purging those who refuse to play along and surrounding themselves with loyalists inside insulated echo chambers. Loyalty replaces competence. Scapegoating replaces accountability. Optics replace reality.

Deliberate Resistance isn't always a negative thing. Some acts are driven by a moral obligation to expose truths the public has a right to know. In 1971, Daniel Ellsberg, a former military analyst, leaked the Pentagon Papers. Though slightly outdated, the secret documents revealed the U.S. government's deliberate deception about its involvement in Vietnam. They exposed a war fought on false premises and on deliberate lies. The result: countless lives lost, and immense national treasure wasted.

The government's response to the leaks? Destroy the messenger. Ellsberg was prosecuted under the Espionage Act. Fortunately for him, the case quickly collapsed once it was revealed that the FBI had broken into his psychiatrist's office and stolen his medical records in a desperate attempt to discredit him.[14]

The government's treatment of Ellsberg only reinforced people's suspicions about it in the late 1960s and early 1970s. No longer was it the trusted institution that saved the world from tyranny in WWII. Now, it was a compromised bureaucracy—stained by scandal, secrecy, and self-preservation. The result? A deep, lasting skepticism toward political leadership that still lingers today.

Deliberate Resistance is often the point of no return in chaos. Once a team turns against its leadership, the damage is rarely reversible. The only path to survival demands radical, immediate action:

- Ruthlessly remove all toxic leaders, no matter how senior.

- Take real steps to rebuild trust among those who feel betrayed.

- Implement sweeping structural reforms that focus on merit and competency.

Without these changes, top talent will not only leave in droves but will enthusiastically tell their stories about why the organization or the institution cannot be trusted. When that happens, collapse becomes inevitable, and recovery nearly impossible.

Table 7. Emotional Responses for Obedience-Based Control Outcomes

Control Outcome	Points of Friction	Emotional Responses
Mechanical Compliance	– Lack of autonomy and decision-making power – Strict adherence to instructions without input – Micromanagement of even low-risk tasks	– **Boredom** from repetitive and unchallenging tasks. – **Dissatisfaction** from inability to change or influence outcomes. – **Apathy** due to lack of ownership and personal investment.
Malicious Compliance	– Forced adherence to counterproductive policies – Feedback is ignored or punished – Constructive dissent treated as disloyalty	– **Anger** at leadership for perceived unfairness. – **Resentment** from being made to feel powerless. – **Defiance**, acting out against policies and directives.
Deliberate Resistance	– Leadership promises one thing but doesn't deliver – Rewarding loyalty over competence – Retaliation against those who speak up	– **Anxiety** about following orders, especially those that demand risk. – **Hostility** toward leadership and policies. – **Vindictiveness**, a desire to retaliate or sabotage.

Turning Chaos into Real Power

In this chapter, we've broken down how chaos unfolds in a team. Through the Chaos Dynamic, we examined the ongoing interplay between the leader and team. With the Control Scale, we outlined six distinct outcomes that give leaders a clear picture of where their team stands on the spectrum between Constructive and Destructive Chaos.

Armed with this understanding, leaders can take decisive steps to turn chaos from a force of disruption into a catalyst for alignment, resilience, and adaptability.

But understanding chaos is only half the battle. The next step is harnessing it for maximum impact. In the next chapter, we'll explore Productive Power, the point where teams reach their full potential and crush expectations.

Chapter 7
What Success in Chaos Looks Like

Most teams survive chaos. Very few become stronger because of it. That rare outcome—when a team doesn't just endure pressure but grows stronger because of it—is what I call **Productive Power**.

Productive Power is what success in chaos actually looks like. It is the point where a team satisfies all four levels of Constructive Chaos and begins exceeding expectations in the middle of volatility, confusion, and risk.

To be clear, Productive Power is more than bouncing back from upsets or maintaining control in turbulent times. That's the bare minimum of satisfactory performance. No—Productive Power is a breakthrough in performance. Think of the difference between an airplane and a jet: once a jet breaks the sound barrier, it gains entirely new capabilities. The same is true of teams: they shift from being specialized units to strategic assets. They not only deliver ahead of schedule, but they contribute beyond the limits of their role.

But it's not a permanent state. Productive Power is an active point of performance. Teams can reach it—but they can also lose it. Chaos never lets up. It keeps pressing, destabilizing, and testing everything—systems, trust, alignment. That's why Productive Power must be re-earned over and over and over.

This chapter introduces Productive Power not just as an aspect of chaos, but as a new way to measure team effectiveness under pressure. You'll see how it works, what it takes to build, and how to apply it. Then we'll dissect a case study from over 2,000 years ago that shows exactly what Productive Power looks like in action.

There should be one lingering question about Productive Power: what does it look like, exactly? How do you know you've reached it? That's where the acronym DOING comes in.

How is Your Team DOING?

Success as a team goes beyond mere task completion and budget adherence. While important, these metrics don't capture the essence of an exceptional team or a true strategic partner. What does is a set of five elements captured in the acronym DOING:

- **D**iscretionary Effort

- **O**perational Duration

- **I**ndependence

- Co**N**tribution

- **G**rowth

These elements form the essence of Productive Power. Each one plays a critical role in transforming a team from a group of task completers into a powerhouse of innovation, resilience, and strategic value. Let's dive into them:

Discretionary Effort: The Above-and-Beyond Element

In any complex environment, success often hinges on the willingness of team members to go above and beyond their basic responsibilities.

Discretionary Effort refers to the voluntary exertion of energy that goes beyond what is explicitly required or expected. It is the element that turns a good team into a great one, as members willingly tap into their energy reserves to fill in the gaps where plans fall short.

However, Discretionary Effort is not something that can be demanded. It must be cultivated through leadership that inspires trust and confidence. Leaders who consistently demonstrate competence and integrity create an environment where team members feel motivated to contribute more than what's required. That trust is built on the belief that the leader genuinely cares about the team's well-being and success—and in return, team members choose to give more than they have to.

Strategies to Encourage Discretionary Effort:

- **Lead by Example**: By showing you're willing to go above and beyond, you normalize initiative and discretionary effort across the team.

- **Make Failure Safe**: Treat honest mistakes and failed calculated risks as learning opportunities, not as punishable offenses. When people aren't afraid to fail, they're more likely to step up.

- **Set Clear Expectations for Initiative**: Clearly define where and how team members are empowered to act.

People will go further when they know where the lines are, and that they won't be punished for going near the edge.

- **Maintain Open Communication Channels**: A feedback-rich environment shows that contributions matter. When people feel they're shaping the outcome—not just executing—they care more and give more.

- **Recognize and Reward Extra Effort**: Publicly acknowledge those who go above and beyond. This reinforces the value of Discretionary Effort and encourages others to follow suit.

Operational Duration: The Wear-and-Tear Element

In the strategic arena, success is not a short sprint but rather a marathon.

Operational Duration measures a team's ability to sustain high performance over extended periods without a reduction in quality.

Operational Duration requires a delicate balance of pushing teams to achieve peak performance while also integrating adequate rest and recovery into their regimen. A team that maintains excellence over time is far more valuable than one that burns out after a single big win. This type of endurance is what sets high-performing teams apart in competitive environments.

Steps to Build Operational Duration:

- **Conduct a Behavioral Energy Audit**: Everyone has specific energy levels and stress tolerance. Understanding these dynamics allows you to distribute workloads effectively, ensuring that no one is pushed to the point of burnout.

- **Lock In the Mission Boundaries**: Define exactly what success looks like—and what it doesn't. Be precise about timelines, deliverables, and scope. Ambiguity breeds fatigue. When teams are forced to operate in the grey, they burn energy managing uncertainty rather than delivering results.

- **Identify Critical Points**: Recognize *where* in the project the team's effort will be most decisive in ensuring success. Prepare them for those moments, confirming they're ready to exert Discretionary Effort when it matters most.

- **Implement Essential Routines**: Establish practices that streamline decision-making and focus the team's energy on what truly matters. Reducing unnecessary choices and distractions helps conserve energy for when it is needed most.

- **Prioritize Strategic Rest**: Build recovery into the schedule. Avoid the trap of constant urgency, which drains energy and leads to burnout. Sustained performance requires deliberate pauses, not just relentless pace.

Most of all, avoid Pyrrhic victories. The story of King Pyrrhus of Epirus is a classic example. After several, costly triumphs against Rome, Pyrrhus famously remarked, "If we are victorious in one more battle with the Romans, we shall be utterly ruined."[15]

In business, a Pyrrhic victory occurs when success in one project comes at such a high cost that it undermines the ability to accomplish the mission at hand. Leaders must be vigilant not to sacrifice long-term viability for short-term gains.

Independence: The Self-Sufficiency Element

High-performing teams not only generate their own ROI, but they also don't get in the way of leadership generating theirs, which is just as important.

Independence means trusting teams to think, decide, and act without constant oversight. It's about owning problems, making adjustments, and driving progress without needing senior leadership to step in, re-direct or rescue them. That kind of self-sufficiency frees them to focus on strategy instead of getting pulled into tactical work they shouldn't be doing.

Independence doesn't happen on its own. Leaders have to set the conditions for it, and teams have to rise to meet them. That means the leader articulates clear expectations up front, then steps back to let the team learn and adapt. That's when the team takes ownership—using their judgment, solving problems, and staying accountable for results.

Strategies for Fostering Independence:

- **Make the Why Clear.** Teams act independently when they understand *why* they've been given a task—not just what to do. When the leader's intent is fully grasped, team members feel empowered to make decisions without constant check-ins. Purpose gives them confidence to move, even when the situation shifts.

- **Define the Edges.** Spell out exactly which decisions the team owns, and where approval is required. This includes clarifying what information needs to be reported and when. Without these boundaries, people either hesitate when they should advance or overstep when they should have sought permission or at least clarification.

- **Develop Judgment Under Pressure.** Independence demands situational decision-making. Give your team opportunities to assess, choose, and act in real-time. Train it, pressure-test it, and reinforce it. The more they practice and reflect, the more reliable they'll be when it counts.

Contribution: The Added Value Element

Average teams complete their tasks; exceptional teams constantly look for ways to add value beyond their assigned responsibilities. **Contribution is about offering new ideas, solutions, and innovations that benefit the larger organization**. It reflects a team's ability to connect its efforts with the broader strategic objectives, ensuring that they are not just participants in the organization's success but active drivers of it.

Contribution is a uniquely leader-centric element of Productive Power. It requires leaders to step beyond the comfort of routine work and see the bigger picture. They must create an environment where team members are not just encouraged to innovate, but where their ideas are valued and their solutions are positioned for integration into the organization's strategy.

Key Elements for Fostering Contribution:

- **Understanding Positional Roles**: Recognizing the three levels of business operations helps your team understand where their work fits, how it supports broader goals, and how to tailor their contributions for maximum impact. The *tactical* level is on the ground floor, involving you and your team directly. The *operational* level involves broader functions, such as departments like sales and marketing or key areas like operations and finance.

The *strategic* level encompasses the entire company as a unified whole.

- **Objective Measurement of Success**: Use clear, simple metrics to evaluate contributions. Avoid vague qualifiers like "big," "good," or "strong." Define exactly what those words mean; quantify them when possible. Clarity eliminates ambiguity. It not only ensures the team's efforts are a meaningful use of time and energy, but also strengthens your case for acquiring extra resources.

- **Facilitate Idea Generation**: Push your team to think beyond daily tasks. Encourage them to identify ways to improve performance, increase efficiency, or better contribute to long-term goals. Host targeted brainstorms and ask, "If you were running this department, what would you change?"

- **Master Written Communication**: Capture your team's contributions in writing to make their value clear, lasting, and actionable. Well-crafted communication doesn't just document progress—it connects your team's work to the organization's goals. When done right, it builds alignment, earns trust, and strengthens your case when future opportunities or challenges arise.

Growth: The Update Element

Continuous development is an essential trait of any team striving to adapt to a constantly changing world.

Growth means continuously advancing skills, knowledge, and capabilities—not just to keep pace, but to seize new opportunities the moment they emerge. Growth powers progress.

It propels a team from good to great, keeping them ahead of the competition and relevant in an evolving world.

Growth is not a passive process; it requires a conscious, deliberate effort from both the leader and the team members. It demands a mindset that is open to learning, unafraid of challenges, and willing to step out of comfort zones. Leaders must foster an environment where growth is a core value, essential for exceeding expectations in the face of chaos.

Strategies to Cultivate Growth:

- **Promote Intellectual Honesty**: Encourage team members to be realistic about their strengths and weaknesses. Cultivate a culture where it's acceptable to admit mistakes and learn from them. This unbiased recognition of reality builds a foundation for continuous improvement.

- **Facilitate Continuous Learning**: Provide opportunities for team members to expand their knowledge and skills. This could involve formal training, mentoring, or hands-on experience with new challenges. Ensure that learning is seen as an integral part of daily operations, not just a random check-the-box activity.

- **Make Reflection Mandatory**: After every project or major task, require the team to pause and assess: What worked? What didn't? What should we change next time? Keep it structured, focused, and honest. The goal isn't just review—it's to extract lessons and apply them immediately.

- **Reward Adaptability and Growth**: Acknowledge team members who actively pursue development and respond well to change. Use promotions, public recognition, or new responsibilities to reinforce that growth-minded behavior is noticed—and valued.

- **Embrace Constant Change**: Condition your team to expect change, adapt fast, and stay effective under shifting conditions. Treat every disruption as a chance to evolve—not just survive. The goal is resilience with forward momentum.

When growth becomes a core behavior, teams don't just respond to change—they seek it out. In ever-evolving world of business, the ability to grow and adapt is what separates the average from the exceptional.

Productive Power in Action

Scipio Africanus (right) meets Hannibal (left) before the Battle of Zama. Scipio faces the man who nearly destroyed his nation and whose armies killed his father and uncle. Hannibal now defends the homeland against the Romans—the very people his father made him swear to destroy. (Photo: Courtesy of TheCollector.com)

Nowhere is Productive Power more vividly demonstrated than in the leadership of Scipio Africanus. The young Roman general secured Rome's dominion over the Mediterranean, reshaping the balance of power in the ancient world. In Chaos Studies, his success can be attributed to three critical elements: his command of all four levels of Constructive Chaos, his ability to twice lead his team to Productive Power, and his personal mastery of the uncontrollable.

October 19, 202 BCE. North Africa, near present-day Tunisia.

The sun cast long shadows over the arid plains. Two massive armies stood poised for battle—one Roman, the other Carthaginian. At their head, two legendary generals broke from their ranks to meet face-to-face.

Publius Cornelius Scipio, the 35-year-old Roman prodigy, had driven Carthage from Spain and Sicily. Opposite him stood Hannibal Barca—now 46, the most feared commander of his time, and the man who had come closer than anyone to toppling Rome itself.

Their eyes locked in silent assessment, the culmination of sixteen years of relentless warfare across the Mediterranean. The stakes were nothing less than the survival of their respective civilizations. Though little is known about what was said between them, it is recorded that Scipio, before turning back to return to his men, said to Hannibal, "Prepare for war, since you have been unable to endure a peace."[16]

This moment marked the pinnacle of Scipio's rise as Rome's savior. He had exemplified every level of Constructive Chaos, enabling him to consistently outmaneuver first-rate opponents. His army was a unified, resilient force, adept at executing unconventional strategies and continuously evolving in organization and tactics. Scipio's vision of success—what famed military theorist Liddell Hart later described as "a more perfect peace"— was to protect Rome's prosperity by compelling Carthage's submission at the least possible human and economic cost.[17]

Scipio's leadership was legendary, as was his management of his armies—each the size of a small city. His soldiers, inspired by their victories, trusted him wholeheartedly, as did the Roman people. The young general leveraged his popularity to persuade hesitant Roman politicians to back a bold new strategy: to abandon the defense in Italy and take the fight to Carthage in North Africa.

Now, two years later, on the battlefield of Zama, Scipio and his army stood as the last barrier between Carthage and its greatest general. On paper, the Romans were not in an ideal position. They were deep in enemy territory, surrounded by hostile populations and with limited options for retreat. While a typical Roman general might have acted cautiously, seeking only a battlefield victory, Scipio's vision extended further: he sought to end the war permanently, on Rome's terms—and did.

How did this young Roman achieve legendary results that continue to inspire leaders and strategists over 2,000 years later? Let's explore this powerful case study of leadership achieving Productive Power.

The Second Punic War (218 to 201 BCE)

In 218 BCE, Hannibal did the unthinkable: he led his battle-hardened army—war elephants and all—across the frozen Alps into Italy. The Carthaginians descended like a storm, marching south and leaving death and destruction in their wake.

Hannibal's military genius revealed itself through three

devastating victories. At the Trebbia River, he lured the Romans into a trap, inflicting over 20,000 casualties. The following year, at Lake Trasimene, he ambushed and annihilated a Roman army of 40,000. But it was at the Battle of Cannae in 216 BCE that his brilliance reached its apex. By provoking a Roman force nearly twice the size of his own into attacking, he executed a masterful double envelopment and, in just a few hours, slaughtered 50,000 Romans with sword and spear. To put that number into perspective, it's roughly equivalent to the total U.S. casualties during the decade-long Vietnam war.[18]

Rome's situation became dire. Within two years of Hannibal's invasion, total Roman military losses exceeded 125,000.[19] Decades of battlefield experience were wiped out. Even the political elite suffered: eighty senators who volunteered to fight at Cannae were killed.[20]

The once-mighty republic found itself not only on the strategic defensive but on the verge of collapse. Traditionally hostile barbarian tribes raced south to plunder and support Hannibal. Longstanding Roman allies in southern Italy began defecting.

By 216 BCE, Hannibal controlled the southern half of the Italian peninsula. For the next decade, he and his coalition would continue to harass, destabilize, and threaten Rome's survival.

Hannibal's Mastery, Scipio's Evolution

To fully appreciate Scipio's achievement, one must first understand why Hannibal was so successful. While Rome relied on disciplined infantry and predictable strategies, Hannibal mastered unconventional tactics. His weapon of choice was cavalry, which he used as a shock force to strike the rear of enemy formations mid-battle. The effect was decisive: it not only sowed chaos within Roman ranks but also shattered their reliance on the steady, methodical approach that had defined their way of war.

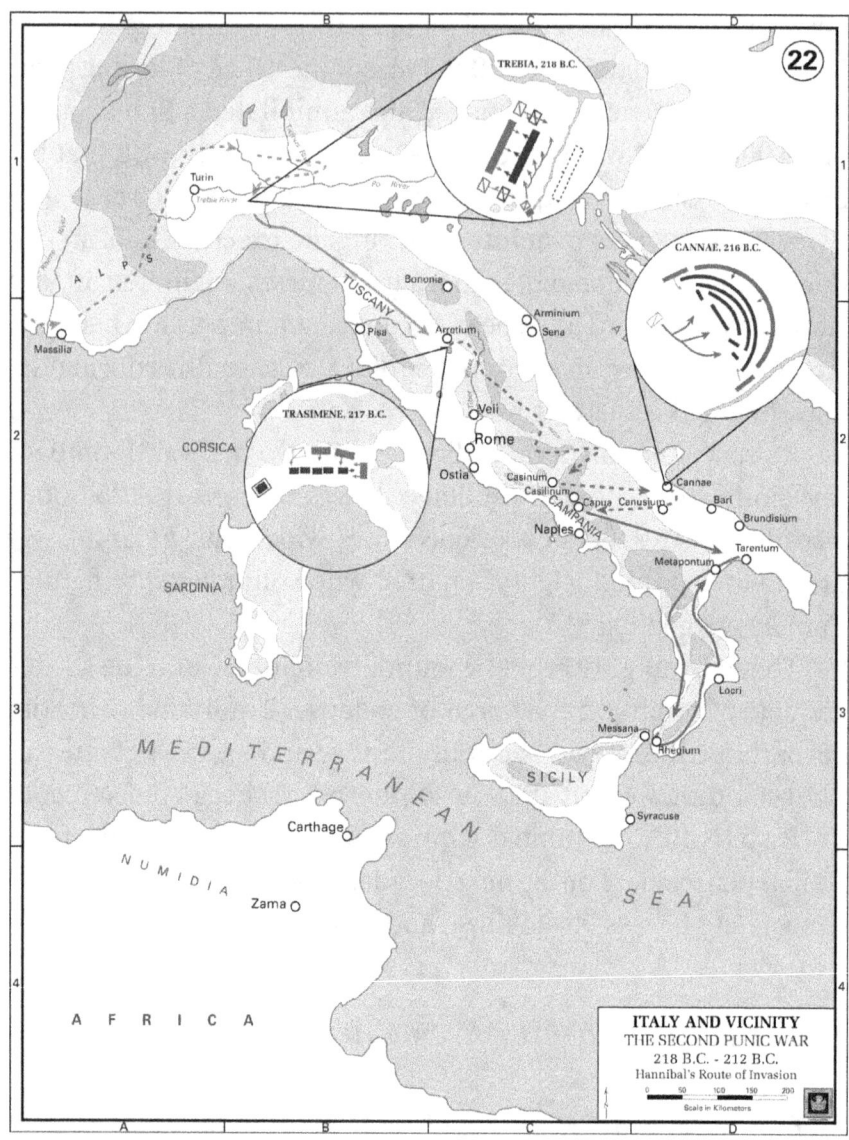

The Second Punic War. Despite three crushing victories, Hannibal was unable to take the capital of Rome, locking him into a prolonged campaign in southern Italy. Meanwhile, Rome's naval control around the peninsula and Sicily blocked Carthaginian reinforcements by sea, forcing them to travel overland through Spain. Scipio struck there—at the logistical jugular—severing Hannibal's lifeline at its source. (Map courtesy of the United States Military Academy Department of History).

Hannibal notably exploited the psychological side of war. His ruses, ambushes, and surprise maneuvers consistently caught the Romans off guard—tactics their own generals would never have used because they were considered dishonorable.

A young Scipio watched closely, studying how the Carthaginian commander dismantled one Roman army after another. His opportunity to prove himself came sooner than anyone expected.

Scipio's father and uncle were tasked with reclaiming Spain from the Carthaginians. Although they made progress, even defeating Hannibal's brother Hasdrubal at the Battle of Ebro River, both were killed in 211 BCE. Following their deaths, the Roman Senate elected 24-year-old Scipio to assume his father's command of the remaining Roman forces in Spain.[21]

In the years that followed, Scipio made a name for himself with a bold, seemingly un-Roman approach: he adopted his enemy's unconventional methods and stratagems, especially the use of cavalry. He would employ the very tactics and ruses that had nearly brought Rome to its knees.

The Spanish Campaign (210-206 BCE)

Scipio's Spanish campaign marked the beginning of his transformation into a master of Productive Power. Recognizing that Rome's direct clashes with Hannibal had ended in disaster, he took an indirect approach to fighting Hannibal. By targeting Spain—Carthage's foothold in Europe—he worked to cut off Hannibal's vital reinforcements and supplies to Italy.

Deep in enemy territory, Scipio and his army showcased remarkable *Independence* and *Operational Duration*. For years they remained self-sufficient, operating among friendly and hostile Spanish tribes, and gathering their own supplies and intelligence from local sources.

The pivotal moment of the campaign came with the capture of New Carthage, the Carthaginian capital and its primary logistical hub. Driven by confidence in his men and certainty in their capabilities, his troops launched a daring nighttime attack—an unconventional move for the time, especially for a Roman general. Their *Discretionary Effort* turned this high-risk strategy into a decisive victory, severing Hannibal's last major supply link from Europe.

Over the following years, Scipio defeated a series of first-class opponents using deception and psychological warfare. At the Battle of Ilipa in 206 BCE, he threw the Carthaginian army into disarray with a brilliant last-minute maneuver. Just before the battle, Scipio broke convention and repositioned his 50,000 troops, shifting his strongest units from the center to the flanks, targeting the Carthaginians' weaker troops. This was unheard of. Caught completely off guard, the Carthaginian flanks rapidly collapsed as their strongest forces in the center stood by, paralyzed by the uncertainty of what was happening around them. The 70,000-strong Carthaginian army suffered a devastating defeat. Only 6,500 survived.[22]

Carthage's foothold in Spain was over by 206 BCE. Scipio's *Contribution* was significant. In four years, "Scipio won a regular war, ended an irregular war, destroyed Hannibal's supply chain, and integrated the Spanish tribes into the greater Roman political and economic system in the Mediterranean."[23]

Internal Friction and Sicily

Scipio returned to Rome a hero and with a new, bold plan. He would invade North Africa and take the war to Carthage directly. The terrifying sight of Roman legions outside the walls of Carthage, he argued, would force them to recall their famed commander from Italy. The general understood the political ramifications of his plan. It would "undermine the foundations of Carthaginian power until the edifice itself collapsed in ruin."[24]

Scipio's proposal was met with distrust and skepticism from the Roman Senate. Envy and professional jealousy were clearly at work.[25] Senior senator Cato openly condemned the plan, calling it reckless to leave Italy vulnerable while Hannibal remained at Rome's doorstep. His objections quickly turned personal, attacking Scipio's youth and lack of experience.

Nonetheless, Scipio defended his strategy as bold and necessary: "He who brings danger upon another has more spirit than he who repels it."[26] His *Contribution* was to flip the strategic dynamic of the war, forcing Carthage on the defense. The Senate, fearing he might bypass them and appeal directly to the Roman people, offered a compromise. They granted him command of Sicily as a springboard for invasion but denied him the use of regular troops. Scipio would have to build his own volunteer army.

Scipio accepted their terms. He was going to be successful with or without the Senate's help.

Preparations

Over the next year, Scipio once again satisfied all levels of Constructive Chaos in Sicily as he did in Spain.

First, Scipio secured the island, clearing it of Carthaginian influence while preparing to launch his invasion.

Next, he began recruiting volunteers from the local population. In a half-hearted gesture of support—driven by Scipio's progress and growing popularity—the Senate grudgingly allowed him to enlist the remnants of the 5th and 6th legions: survivors of the catastrophic defeat at Cannae who had been living in dishonor for surviving the battle.[27]

Yet Scipio saw their potential. These men, shamed and cast

aside, were driven by a deep need for redemption. Their hunger to restore their honor would produce the kind of *Discretionary Effort* that only those with something to prove. As one account put it, these men were "burning to wipe off the unjust stigma of disgrace."[28]

Scipio then shifted focus to preparing his army for the mission ahead. They stocked up on supplies and intensified training—the kind of work that builds *Operational Duration, Growth,* and *Independence.*

Notably, Scipio also restructured the force based on his opponent. He focused on developing a premier cavalry unit—Hannibal's weapon of choice and Rome's most neglected arm. It would be his horsemen, not Rome's traditional legionnaires, who would carry the day on the plains of Africa.

The North African Campaign

In the summer of 204 BCE, roughly 30,000 Roman soldiers landed outside the city of Utica.[29] Scipio immediately laid siege, aiming to secure a strategic foothold for launching operations deeper into Carthaginian territory. His alliance with Masinissa—the Numidian king and bitter enemy of Carthage—proved invaluable. Masinissa's cavalry, among the finest in the ancient world, joined Scipio's forces and transformed Rome's mounted capabilities into a battlefield advantage.

The Carthaginians responded swiftly to Scipio's invasion—but he was ready. Upon learning of the approaching enemy cavalry, he repositioned his forces to intercept. With support from Masinissa's elite horsemen, the Roman cavalry executed a calculated ambush, drawing the enemy in and smashing the 4,000-man contingent.[30]

Shortly thereafter, two enemy armies—both larger than Scipio's—arrived outside Utica. Once again, the young Roman general was ready. Drawing on lessons from Spain, his troops displayed *Discretionary Effort* by launching another nighttime attack. They first set one of the enemy camps ablaze. African soldiers rushed from their wooden huts to fight what appeared to be an accidental fire—only to be ambushed by Roman troops lying in wait. Spotting the flames from a distance, the second Carthaginian camp rushed to assist their comrades, only to walk into the same Roman trap. The result was a crushing victory. Known as the Battle of Utica, Carthage suffered 45,000 casualties.[31]

Carthage grew desperate. They hastily assembled a fresh force of 30,000 troops, many of them raw recruits with little to no training. Scipio crushed it at the Battle of the Great Plains.[32] Reeling from the loss, Carthage did the only thing left: they recalled Hannibal from Italy.

With Carthage completely vulnerable, Scipio demonstrated *Independence* and *Contribution* by successfully negotiating a peace treaty to end the war. However, it was short-lived. Hannibal was back home with his army. The stage was set for the final confrontation.

The Battle of Zama

Scipio's 30,000-man force now stood between the Carthaginian capital and Hannibal's 40,000-man army. Outnumbered as usual, Scipio held a critical advantage: cavalry. His 6,000 horsemen—including Masinissa's elite contingent—faced just 4,000 on Hannibal's side.[33]

Hannibal opened the battle by unleashing 80 war elephants—ancient tanks designed to terrify and trample. They thundered toward the Roman lines, meant to break formations and unleash chaos. But the plan backfired spectacularly.

Scipio's *Growth* paid off. Anticipating the move, his soldiers were ready. As the Carthaginian elephants charged, the Romans blasted trumpets and pounded drums, creating a wall of sound that spooked the beasts. Many panicked and turned back, trampling Hannibal's own lines. The few that pressed forward were funneled through preplanned lanes opened by Roman infantry and cut down. In minutes, Hannibal's chaos-inducing assault had been completely neutralized.

The Battle of Zama. At a glance, Zama looks like pure chaos. In reality, it was the product of careful preparation and control. What appeared to be Hannibal's advantage—his charging elephants—was neutralized within minutes, stripping him of his last real hope for victory. (Photo: Courtesy Metropolitan Museum of Art)

Scipio's cavalry, sensing the opening, charged and drove the Carthaginian horsemen from the field. With the battlefield cleared of both horse and elephant, the infantry lines surged forward and collided in a brutal melee. Dust clouds rose, choking lungs and blinding eyes. The clash of iron, shouted commands, and the screams of the wounded filled the air. The fighting was savage—neither side willing to yield an inch.

The tide turned when the Roman cavalry, having routed the Carthaginian horsemen, returned to the field. They slammed into the rear of Hannibal's infantry—the same tactic he had so successfully used against so many Roman armies. The shock shattered Carthaginian cohesion and triggered a full-scale rout.

Hannibal's army disintegrated. The war was over.

According to the historian Polybius, the Romans suffered around 1,500 casualties, while Hannibal's forces endured a staggering 20,000 killed or wounded, with another 20,000 taken prisoner.[34]

The Battle of Zama was a monumental defeat for Carthage, marking the end of the Second Punic War and securing Rome's dominance over the Mediterranean. Scipio was later honored with the rare and prestigious title *Africanus*, becoming the first commander to be distinguished by the name of the land he had conquered.[35]

The Foundation of Success

What explains Scipio's success? How did he twice satisfy all levels of Constructive Chaos and twice demonstrate Productive Power, first in Spain and then in Africa? The simple answer is that he balanced tactical brilliance with strategic insight. Yet, there is a deeper explanation.

Mastering the Essentials of Chaos

First and foremost, **Scipio was a conceptual thinker**, skilled at reducing complexity to its bare essentials and forming

reasonable expectations about the future. This helped him identify root causes and recognize the underlying systems that shaped
them. As a result, he correctly determined that just as "Cartagena
was the key to Spain, and Spain was the key to Italy, so too was
Africa the key to the entire struggle."[36]

Scipio's conceptual thinking extended beyond the battlefield.
He understood that real success required integrating military,
political, and economic dimensions into a unified strategy. That
clarity allowed him to define victory in simple, precise terms—
not just winning battles, but securing a lasting peace. His vision
of success provided him and his subordinates with a reliable
framework for making decisions under pressure, no matter the
situation on the ground.

Then there was the matter of self-control: preventing emotion from overriding reason. After expelling the Carthaginians
from Spain, for example, Scipio faced a difficult choice: what
to do with the hostile Spanish tribes who had helped kill his father and uncle. He chose clemency over vengeance—not an easy
choice when he had every reason to retaliate. His decision, however, was not driven by altruism. No, it was strategic, calculated
self-interest. By showing mercy, Scipio secured new alliances,
stabilized the region, and eliminated the need for a long-term
Roman occupation—freeing up troops and resources for his true
objective: taking the war to North Africa.

The Continence of Scipio. Scipio stayed rational amid chaos, using clemency as a tool of strategy rather than sentiment. This restraint won Massinissa's loyalty, making him a decisive factor at Zama. In the end, Scipio's ability to control himself—and shape the environment to his benefit—ultimately defined his success, (Photo: Courtesy of Alamy).

In this way, Scipio ensured that every decision, every action, and every battlefield victory moved him closer to his broader strategic goal. His ability to align short-term choices with long-term outcomes kept him focused, avoiding unnecessary battles—military or political. His synthesis of vision and action ensured his efforts delivered not only tactical victories but lasting strategic results.

Secondly, **Scipio accepted the inevitability of the Fog of War and Friction.** He readily acknowledged that uncertainty and obstacles are inherent in any endeavor. "I am aware of the power of fortune," he acknowledged, "and I know that everything we do is subject to a thousand mishaps."[37] Rather than protest and resist these essential elements of chaos, Scipio leveraged them for his benefit. It was his last-minute adjustment at Ilipa, for instance, that led to his greatest battlefield triumph.

Finally, **Scipio demonstrated exceptional skill in improvisation**. His ability to exploit fleeting opportunities was no accident—it stemmed from relentless preparation and disciplined training. He reduced the stress of improvisation by ensuring his men were ready to seize the initiative at a moment's notice, forcing the enemy to fight on his terms. That control over timing and direction gave Scipio a decisive edge. Even in the most unpredictable conditions, he stayed in command while others scrambled to react.

Mastering the Uncontrollable

Scipio's success wasn't just a product of tactics or timing—it was rooted in character. He embodied a set of core Roman virtues that directly influenced his leadership style and the success of his campaigns.

As Edith Hamilton illustrates in *The Roman Way*, these virtues were foundational to Roman identity and leadership. Scipio earned his reputation for courage (*virtus*) as a young man, rallying retreating troops after the disaster at Cannae. His clemency (*clementia*) toward conquered peoples turned enemies into allies and reinforced his sense of justice to his own men, even winning the loyalty of Masinissa. His industriousness (*industria*) was evident in his skillful use of deception and psychological warfare. Finally, his seriousness (*gravitas*) instilled unwavering focus and commitment to victory, even when the odds were repeatedly against him and his men.

Scipio knew his Productive Purpose. When criticized for not directly attacking Hannibal in Italy, he replied, "My mother gave birth to a general, not a warrior."[38] He clearly understood his natural talents and his professional value. Scipio saw himself as a man of destiny, driven by the utter conviction that his unique strengths would play a pivotal role in shaping Rome's future. Advancing the success of his army—and Rome's interests—was the surest way to advance himself.

His projection of self-confidence acted as a force multiplier, earning him the unwavering trust and respect of his men. Each success reinforced their belief that his vision was worth following, and that his victories were theirs too. Scipio's confidence also instilled a sense of invincibility within the ranks, fostering resilience and a readiness to tackle challenges head-on. Under his command, victory didn't just seem possible—it felt inevitable.

Scipio's embodiment of *pietas* (dutifulness) ensured Instrumentality. He saw himself and his army as instruments of Roman purpose—not agents of conquest for its own sake. His men were the hammers of Rome's will, but Scipio was wise enough not to treat every problem as a nail. By signaling to enemies that peace was an option, he avoided costly battles that could weaken Rome's ability to govern. Most importantly, Scipio understood that credibility and restraint could be just as powerful as swords and shields. By pairing force with purpose, he earned not only victories, but the authority to shape what came after.

The Road to Productive Purpose

Now that we've defined what success looks like in chaos, it's time to chart the path that leads there. In the chapters ahead, we'll break down the four levels of Constructive Chaos, showing how each one builds the foundation for Productive Power. Then we'll turn to the other side of the equation—Destructive Chaos—and expose the common traps that cause leaders and teams to unravel when the pressure mounts.

PART IV

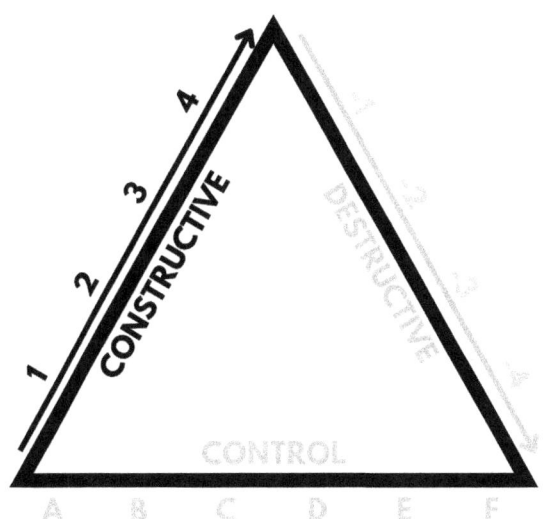

Chapter 8
Unity

In chaos, survival as a team isn't about individual strength or skill alone; it's about cohesion. When resistance strikes, unity is what makes teams resilient under stress. Without it, even the most professional team can unravel as individuals instinctively retreat into isolation and self-preservation under pressure.

Unity is a necessity in chaos. Unified teams withstand the disintegrating pressures of friction. Differences in behavior, values, and perspectives stop being liabilities and start becoming assets. They give the team the full range of capabilities needed to pivot, respond, and thrive when conditions shift unexpectedly.

Unity marks the first level of Constructive Chaos. It's the starting point for building a strong, professional team. It also serves as the team's first line of defense against the destructive forces of chaos. This chapter will guide you in establishing that essential foundation, enabling your team to perform as a cohesive, robust force.

We'll begin by defining and differentiating unity, moving beyond surface-level cooperation to understand its deeper significance. Next, we'll break it down into four core elements. Then we'll explore the legendary story of the Ten Thousand—a testament to unity's power against overwhelming odds. Finally, you'll find practical steps to foster unity within your own team, equipping them to face any challenge together.

The People Element of Chaos

Unity is first and foremost a mindset—a deliberate outlook on teamwork. Individuals agree to prioritize the needs of the mission and the team over their immediate wants, desires, or personal preferences. Each person sets aside bias and ego and commits to working together toward a common purpose, without hesitation or self-interest. When this commitment is freely made and consistently upheld under pressure, unity takes hold.

Achieving unity is the responsibility of every team member, not just the leader. It requires self-awareness, emotional maturity, and the discipline to balance feeling with reason. This effort can be mentally and physically exhausting—but it's necessary. It's the price of cohesion.

Cohesion is the product of unity. But don't be misled: simply seeing people work alongside each other doesn't mean unity is present. Many people merely co-exist—collaborating because it's required, not because they're truly aligned or inspired. If this sounds familiar, you may be working with a group, not a team.

Teams vs. Groups

Not all collaborations are created equal. The difference between a group and a team lies in their purpose and accountability. Unity isn't a necessity for groups. As Jon R. Katzenbach and Douglas K. Smith explain, "A working group's performance is a function of what its members do as individuals."[39] Groups are associations, like committees or councils, where members operate independently and aren't accountable to one another.

Teams, on the other hand, require unity because they are expected to achieve specific outcomes together. Team performance depends on the unique contributions of each member toward shared goals. As Katzenbach and Smith continue, "A team is a small number of people with complementary skills who are committed to a common purpose, set of performance goals, and approach for which they hold themselves mutually accountable."[40]

So ask yourself honestly: Is your team aligned in purpose and accountability—or are you leading a group of individuals wearing the same logo?

The Essence of Unity

What makes unity possible? There are four essential ingredients: seamless integration, a social contract, discipline, and identity. These elements should be your standard for unifying a team.

Unity as Seamless Integration

Seamless integration requires every team member to treat collaboration as just as essential as their individual contribution. Each person represents a role, and each role is one thread that completes the whole fabric of performance. Pull one loose, and the whole thing risks unraveling.

This principle is most visible in the relationship between the leader and the team. It creates the psychological safety needed for people to act without hesitation or second-guessing. Team members begin to anticipate the leader's intent before it's spoken. They start to see the mission through the same lens and complete critical tasks before they're even assigned.

But seamless integration doesn't stop at the team level. In high-functioning organizations, teams must align with each other. They must offer cross-functional support, shift priorities as needed, and contribute beyond their lane. When teams move in sync, unity becomes a force multiplier. And in chaos, that makes all the difference between resilience and fracture.

Based on a Social Contract

Unity may sound simple, but it never is. It raises the question of control: "Do I really have to follow this person? Why can't I just do what I think is best?"

These questions are resolved through an unspoken agreement—a social contract between leader and follower. The idea has roots in political history, from the Magna Carta to the U.S. Constitution. Civilization overtook barbarism. Societies, once ruled by force, learned to function through mutual consent, not coercion.

The same principle applies in leadership. The leader agrees to take responsibility for the mission and the team's well-being. In return, the team agrees to follow that leader's direction to the best of their ability.

There is no blind obedience in a social contract. Cooperation is voluntary. Each person, leader and follower, agrees to put the mission first—even if conditions are uncertain, or even when it is hard and uncomfortable.

Unity is built when people honor that contract—especially under stress. That's when the instinct to break off, question orders, or prioritize personal comfort is strongest. And that's when unity matters most.

Reinforced by Discipline

Discipline is a powerful tool for success, but it's hard to build. It demands stepping outside your comfort zone and doing what needs to be done—even when you're tired, frustrated, or tempted to cut corners. True discipline means letting willpower override emotional discomfort, physical fatigue, and the voice in your head that says, "not today."

In leadership, discipline is non-negotiable. The urge to skip steps or chase quick fixes is always there. The pressure of chaos only sharpens the temptation. But discipline—consciously developed and upheld by moral resolve—is what holds the line. It enforces order, preserves standards, and creates the consistency teams rely on to perform under pressure.

Professional teams prioritize self-discipline. Each member commits to shared principles that reinforce trust and predictability across the team. They show up ready—not just for themselves, but for each other.

For leaders, discipline requires holding themselves accountable to very high standards. They must consistently go the extra mile so the team sees what's expected of them. Whether it's submitting a report after a long, tedious day or upholding standards that seem trivial, discipline means following through when compromise would be easier. It's about modeling the truth that success demands constantly going above and beyond—especially when the body and mind say, "put it off until tomorrow."

Discipline doesn't just maintain order. In chaos, it's often the difference between a team you can count on and one that falls apart.

Exhibited by Identity

Unity is earned, and one of the most powerful ways to secure it is through a shared identity.

Teams, like individuals, develop overtime a distinct understanding of who they are, what they stand for, and what sets them apart. Identity forms through consistent behaviors, visible standards, and a proven track record. The more impressive the record, the greater the pride in being part of the team. That pride drives members to protect and uphold the reputation they've built.

Identity has practical benefits. First, it acts as a psychological force multiplier. It clarifies what's expected of members and defines what it takes to uphold the team's standards. The mindset becomes: "This is who we are. This is what we do. We take on the hard work others can't—or won't—because that's what makes us successful."

It also aligns individual motivation with collective purpose. When members see themselves as part of something larger, they're more likely to prioritize team success over personal gain. Instead of working at cross-purposes, they channel their effort toward shared goals.

Identity creates a sense of belonging that acts as protective armor. With trust in their teammates, individuals take risks more confidently, knowing they're part of something stable and strong. This internal commitment helps teams withstand pressures that would break less cohesive groups.

It fuels growth and competitiveness. To maintain their standing, members feel a responsibility not just to support one another, but to push themselves—to achieve more and strengthen the team's reputation.

Leaders reinforce identity by promoting camaraderie and healthy internal competition. They make identity visible. They create and protect symbols—names, traditions, and rituals—that reflect the team's uniqueness. These elements give unity form, making it tangible and unmistakable.

But the true test of unity doesn't appear in ceremonies or symbols—it emerges under pressure. One of history's most extraordinary examples of identity-driven unity came from an ancient army stranded deep in enemy territory: the Ten Thousand.

The Ultimate Test of Unity: The Ten Thousand

In 401 BCE, a Greek mercenary army found itself stranded deep in enemy territory—leaderless and vulnerable. Their royal employer, Cyrus the Younger, had been killed in battle. Days later, their senior officers were murdered in a trap. This army, known as the Ten Thousand, began a desperate retreat with no allies and no logistical support. For nine months, they marched nearly 1,500 miles through unfamiliar and hostile lands. They crossed barren deserts, forded turbulent rivers, and climbed snow-covered mountains, all while under constant attack from enemy states and local tribes.

Xenophon, an Athenian officer who rose to senior command during the retreat, recorded their extraordinary journey in *Anabasis* ("The March Up Country"), preserving the story for generations.

Xenophon's story is a powerful case study in leadership. In his 1954 landmark book *The Practice of Management*, Peter Drucker—the patriarch of executive management—called *Anabasis* "the first systematic book on leadership" and declared it "still the best book on the subject."[41] More than two millennia later, Xenophon's account remains a timeless testament to the power of unity in the face of chaos.

Winning the Battle but Losing the War

In 401 BCE, Xenophon was persuaded by a friend to join a military campaign funded by the Persian prince Cyrus the Younger. Officially, the mission was to clear Cyrus's provinces of local bandits. A Greek mercenary army of approximately ten thousand hoplites—heavily armed infantry—marched inland, easily sweeping aside hostile forces in their path.

Soon, rumors began to circulate: Cyrus's true aim was to overthrow his brother, King Artaxerxes II. Feeling betrayed, the Greeks nearly mutinied. Cyrus quickly responded by doubling their pay. The army accepted the new terms and marched straight into a Persian civil war.[42]

The campaign culminated in the Battle of Cunaxa. By then, the Greek contingent had grown to about 13,000, bolstered by Persian volunteers recruited along the way. They faced off against a Persian royal force of 40,000.[43] Renowned for their discipline and prowess, the Greek hoplites seemed nearly invincible in battle.[44]

At a critical moment, Cyrus ordered the Greeks to seize a decisive position. For reasons still debated, the Spartan commander failed to comply. Undeterred, Cyrus charged ahead without their support and was struck in the face by a javelin, killing him instantly.[45]

Despite the Greeks' overwhelming success—they suffered only one wounded man—their victory meant nothing when they found Cyrus dead on the battlefield.[46]

The Persians demanded the Greek army surrender. The proud Greeks refused. Knowing they faced a lethal foreign force deep inside their territory—and that their own army was no match—the Persian governor Tissaphernes offered a deal: supplies and safe passage, so long as they left immediately. Eager to return home, the Greeks agreed.

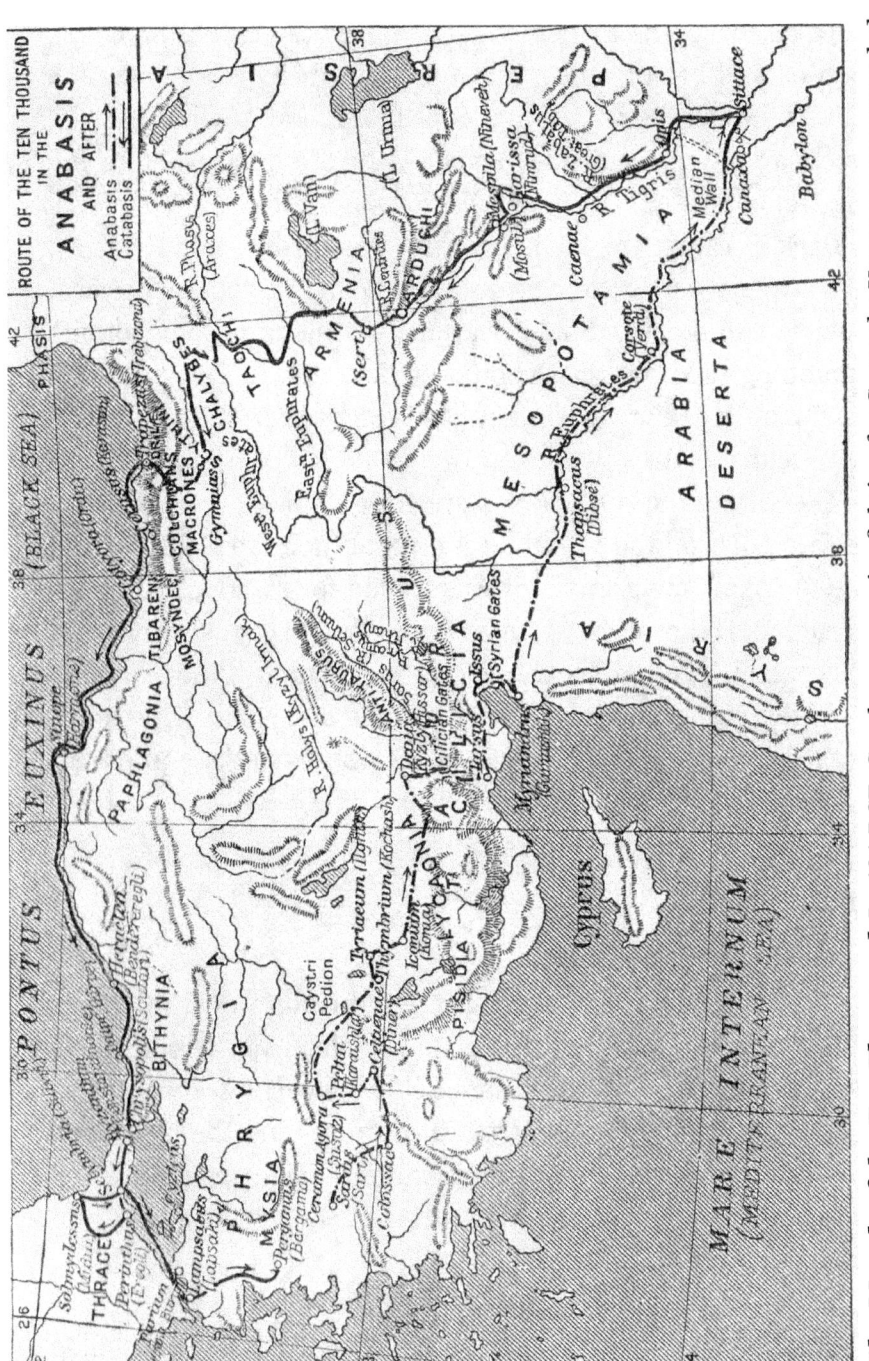

The March of the Ten Thousand. In 401 BCE, Greek mercenaries fighting for Cyrus the Younger were stranded a thousand miles inside Persia. Under Xenophon's leadership, they marched over 1,500 miles through hostile terrain and brutal conditions to return home. (Photo: Courtesy of Alamy.)

To celebrate the agreement, Tissaphernes invited the Greek generals and senior officers to a feast in their honor. It was a trap. As the Greeks raised their cups in celebration, the Persians struck, arresting them on the spot. All were hauled before the king and beheaded.[47]

Back at camp, the Hellenic army was thrown into disarray. Their leaders were gone, and with them, any clear path forward. Panic spread quickly. Soldiers argued—some in despair, others demanding to know what should be done. Plead for a pardon? Beg for mercy? For a moment, the army teetered on the edge of Anarchy.

Then, from the confusion, stepped Xenophon, the Athenian. He urged his comrades to take control of their fate. This was no time for panic, he argued—it was a time for reason, judgment, and action. If they were to survive, they had to choose their path deliberately, together, by voting on the army's next move.

In the end, after intense debate, the army voted to return home. That very night, they cast aside non-essential equipment and prepared for the long march back home.

The Sea! The Sea!

The hoplite army began its long retreat north toward the Black Sea. Relentlessly pursued by Persian cavalry—masters of horse and bow—the Greeks were harassed by swift, hit-and-run attacks. Arrows rained down from a distance, and the horsemen withdrew before the Greeks could counter. Each assault inflicted casualties and chipped away at morale, leaving the army frustrated and exposed.

To neutralize the Persians' range advantage, the Greeks adapted. They reorganized their formations and enlisted skilled slingers from Rhodes—skirmishers renowned for hurling stones with deadly precision over long distances. Their attacks disrupted the Persian cavalry before it could close in. These tactics bought the Greeks just enough time to widen the gap with their pursuers.

The Battle of Cunaxa. The Greek mercenaries won a decisive tactical victory against their Persian foes but suffered a devastating strategic loss: Cyrus the Younger, their political backer, was killed in battle. Overnight, the victorious army found itself stranded 1,000 miles deep in enemy territory. Shortly thereafter, the army's senior leadership was lured into a trap and executed. (Photo: Courtesy of Alamy)

The Persian cavalry adapted too, finding new ways to harass the retreating Greek infantry. Sensing the enemy's growing confidence, the Greeks responded again—repurposing small baggage horses to form a rudimentary cavalry unit. It was no match for the Persian force, but it gave the Greeks a way to contest their enemy's mobility.

Under Xenophon's leadership, the Greeks devised a bold plan to turn the tables. With patience and precision, they lured the Persian cavalry into a well-laid trap. At the decisive moment, Greek infantry struck, ambushing and scattering the enemy ranks. The reversal shifted the momentum of the retreat firmly in the Greeks' favor.[48]

The army exited Persia and entered what is now southeastern Turkey, then home to the fierce Carduchii tribe. Although enemies of the Persians, the Carduchii did not welcome a foreign army marching through their lands. The seven days spent fighting through their territory, according to Xenophon, were harder than anything they had endured under Persian pursuit. The Greeks were, he wrote, "continually fighting, and they suffered more evils than all which they had suffered taken together at the hands of the King and Tissaphernes."[49]

The Ten Thousand then entered the mountains of Armenia during a massive snowstorm. In addition to dodging rock-throwing tribes and navigating treacherous terrain, the Greeks now faced a new enemy: nature itself. Without winter clothing, many hoplites lost fingers and toes to frostbite. Some went snow blind. Exhaustion, injuries, and cold without a doubt sapped their energy, willpower, and focus.

Yet amid the misery, a glimmer of hope appeared. An Armenian governor offered provisions and clothing. But as the Greeks began to accept the gifts, their leaders noticed suspicious movements. It was a trap. Realizing they were being set up for an attack, the Greeks struck first, destroying their duplicitous hosts.

In the spring of 400 BCE, the army reached Mount Theches. A loud commotion erupted from the front of the column as they climbed upward. Xenophon, heart racing, sprinted toward the noise, bracing for yet another attack. But instead of battle cries, he heard something unexpected: "Thalatta! Thalatta!"—The sea! The sea![50]

Stretching out before them was the Black Sea, its waters glinting in the distance. Along its shores lay the promise of Greek towns. In that moment, the mercenaries—hardened by fifteen months of relentless trials—broke down in tears. Battle-worn veterans who had endured every imaginable hardship embraced each other, overcome by the realization that home was finally within reach.

But their relief was short-lived. Shortly after arriving at the coastal town of Trapezus, the Greeks encountered the Colchians, vassals of an enraged Persia. Wearied, and now very annoyed, the Greeks decisively crushed them.[51]

Though safe, their ordeal was far from over. The army turned west, navigating treacherous paths by foot and by sea. Of the original Ten Thousand, only about 6,000 remained. For many of them, this was not the end. Battle-scarred and restless, some joined new mercenary armies, still seeking purpose in the endless cycle of war.

What Saved the Ten Thousand?

In chaos, shifts in tasks, missions, or purpose happen regularly. But Xenophon's case was extraordinary because it wasn't merely a shift—it was a near-total reversal. His army's original mission was to dominate, to win a war. That collapsed in an instant. Suddenly, their objective was no longer to achieve victory, but to survive.

That kind of reversal is deeply destabilizing and a gateway to chaos.

Armies are built for dominance. Their structure, training, and mindset are all designed to advance, attack, and impose control. But when the mission flips 180 degrees, that same design works against them. Soldiers trained to strike are now expected to retreat. A winning mindset is replaced with the need to endure.

This reversal creates a deep psychological challenge. The soldier's training no longer fits the reality. Their instincts—fight, press forward, dominate—now get in the way. And worst of all, cooperating with those who aren't trying to win no longer feels logical. Every person has a rational excuse to stop acting like part of a team. This internal conflict—between what they were taught to do and what the situation now demands—generates hesitation, stress, and doubt. And that's exactly where unity begins to break down.

That was the central crisis facing the Ten Thousand. After the Battle of Cunaxa, their employer and commanders were dead. The route home stretched over a thousand miles through hostile territory. There were no reinforcements, no supplies, and no allies waiting for them.

Every man could have made a case for breaking ranks and acting on his own behalf. Self-preservation—fear, hunger, exhaustion—now competed directly with loyalty, discipline, and cooperation. Why follow the orders of strangers when you feel you know better? Why help a fellow soldier when he's slowing you down? Why maintain formation when you could slip away and fend for yourself?

This is how teams collapse under pressure. Not in one dramatic moment, but gradually, as individuals choose self over the unit. Teams devolve into groups: people might move in the same direction, but they are no longer accountable to one another. When that happens, they become easy to divide, demoralize, and ultimately defeat.

Unity, then, wasn't a luxury for the Ten Thousand. It was the only thing that could keep them alive. If they lost it, even briefly, the army would dissolve.

That's what makes Xenophon's leadership so remarkable. He didn't just keep the army together—he forged a new kind of unity under the worst possible conditions. His leadership didn't rely on obedience or over-controlling authority. No, it relied on conviction, clarity, and influence. He gave the men a reason to follow when every instinct told them to scatter.

For students of chaos, this case is foundational. It answers one of the hardest questions in leadership: *When everything falls apart—structure, mission, direction—how do you hold a team together?*

Let's examine how Xenophon did it.

Xenophon's Background

Xenophon was a writer, soldier, and philosopher—one of the most unusual minds to ever lead an army. Born around 430 BCE into a moderately wealthy Athenian family, he came of age during the Peloponnesian War, a 27-year superpower conflict between Athens, Sparta, and their proxies. The war left Greece fractured, and flooded with unemployed soldiers who turned to mercenary work just to survive.

Xenophon of Athens.
Philosopher. Historian. Athenian. He built unity through reason and example, not fear or obedience. (Photo: Courtesy of Alamy)

Xenophon's intellectual roots ran deep. He was a student and personal friend of Socrates, the father of Western ethics and the teacher of Plato. From Socrates, he learned how to think—how to question, probe, and reason. He also absorbed a deep reverence for Hellenic ideals: democracy, law, and individual responsibility. These values didn't just shape his writing—they shaped his style of leadership.

But make no mistake: Xenophon was also a warrior. His belief in order and discipline came from the Greek way of war, centered on the phalanx—a tightly packed formation of hoplites who moved as one. The phalanx only worked if everyone did their part. That made unity not just a virtue, but a battlefield necessity.

So what kind of man was Xenophon, really?

He was unusually well-rounded. He traveled more, fought more, and wrote more than almost any other Greek of his time. He studied politics, ethics, strategy, and everyday life—and he practiced what he learned. His philosophical mind gave him an edge most soldiers lacked: he understood that people aren't driven by force alone, but by belief. His leadership reflected that insight. He didn't just command, he convinced.

And that's what made him effective.

So when the Ten Thousand teetered on collapse, Xenophon did something remarkable: He unified the army by reorienting their minds.

Let's look at how he did it.

Reinforced the Common Goal

Despite their dire situation, the Greeks had one crucial advantage: they had no other choice. No one needed to be persuaded that sticking together was their only shot at survival.

The goal of staying unified was unmistakably clear. The greatest threat wasn't the enemy—it was desertion. If soldiers abandoned their roles without warning, the army couldn't function as intended, and the entire force would be exposed.

During the Greek conference prior to marching out of Persia, it was unanimously agreed that "the desertion of any considerable number would make it extremely difficult for the rest to secure even safe return."[52] In other words, desertion was a death sentence.

That shared understanding became a powerful motivator. Every man, regardless of rank, had a personal stake in holding the line. Unity didn't have to be imposed from the top; it was reinforced from within.

Seamless Integration

The Ten Thousand represented the most formidable force of their time. Each man fulfilled his role within this disciplined, highly skilled unit. Though mercenaries—bound by purchased loyalty—the situation ironically compelled them to act as loyal countrymen, united by a shared goal of survival. Besides, the Persians made it clear what fate awaited any Greek if the team failed to support one another.

Xenophon took no chances. He kept the army moving, ensuring every ounce of energy and focus was directed toward progress. With each mile, they widened the gap between themselves and Persian influence, reducing the enemy's ability to stir dissent or bribe allies through backdoor deals.

But even professional teams are vulnerable to incompatible leadership. While Spartans were raised under the harshest discipline in Greece and forged into fearsome warriors, their generals led everyone as if the entire army had been trained the same way. That severity nearly led to disaster. "Klearchos nearly caused a riot on more than one occasion due to his (mis)use of his baton, while Cheirisiophos, after beating an Armenian guide in the remote highlands of eastern Anatolia, caused the man to flee during the night, leaving the army lost."[53]

Xenophon led differently. He embodied broader Greek values of reason, persuasion, and respect. The Athenian "preferred to use words instead of a baton to achieve his ends." That distinction mattered. His leadership fostered loyalty, trust, and cohesion across a wildly diverse group of men, temperaments, and nationalities.[54]

Discipline

"For discipline, it seems, keeps men in safety," Xenophon observes, "while the lack of it has brought many ere now to destruction."[55]

Xenophon's ability to instill discipline did not rely on commands or coercion, but on the power of his own example. During a brutal blizzard that buried the troops in snow, they were reluctant to rise from their warm, makeshift shelters. Xenophon recognized the peril of inaction—it is how people needlessly die.

"The Sea! The Sea!" the Greek mercenaries cried out as they reached the Black Sea. They were exhausted, wounded, but never broken. Nearly half of them died along the march, but the survivors never fractured as a team. What saved them in chaos was neither luck nor force: it was unity, tested by relentless pressure. (Photo: Courtesy of Alamy)

As the text recounts, "But once Xenophon had mustered the courage to get up without his cloak and set about splitting wood, another man also speedily got up, took the axe away from him, and went on with the splitting. Thereupon still others got up and proceeded to build fires and anoint themselves."[56] By rising first and modeling the necessary actions, Xenophon inspired his men to follow suit—indirectly shaming them—into doing what needed to be done despite the discomfort and inconvenience.

Discipline was also about restraint. Some soldiers, lured by quick gain, snuck off at night to loot nearby villages. Many were killed in ambushes, exposing the army to unnecessary risk. The lesson was clear: survival required professionalism. That meant resisting short-term temptations and maintaining high standards of conduct at all times.

Shared Identity

Mutual values, customs, and backgrounds played a pivotal role in keeping the Greeks unified despite historic and ethnic rivalries. Their common Hellenic heritage—respect for reason over blind faith, righteous law over arbitrary edict, and self-rule over authoritarian control—helped them draw strength from one another and remain focused on the mission, even amidst the constant friction.

No matter their differences and historical animosities, the Ten Thousand proudly recognized that "in the presence of barbarians they were all Greeks."[57] This shared identity fostered a deep sense of moral superiority—and matching confidence—reinforced by their past victories. They had defeated the Persians before and were convinced they could do it again if necessary.

This shared identity became a source of empowerment. During the conference where the army prepared to vote on whether to stay and fight or leave, Xenophon wrote that every man had the freedom to express his opinion. The ability to voice concerns openly and take part in the decision gave the soldiers a sense of control over their fate and strengthened their resolve to continue as a unified, fighting force.

As a professional team of Greek warriors, leader and follower were bound by an unspoken social contract. Xenophon's leadership earned the soldiers' trust—and their consent to be governed. This dynamic fostered mutual respect and predictability, forming the foundation of the unity that enabled their survival against all odds.

Achieving Unity in Your Team

How can you satisfy this first level of Constructive Chaos? Here are five steps:

1 – Reorient Yourself to the Task

- **Think in terms of outputs, not inputs.** Unity is not something you declare; it's something you achieve. For example, internal harmony in a team is the result of resolving conflict and engaging in honest, difficult discussions. It's not a state that can be imposed on demand.

- **Accept the human factor.** Not everyone thinks like you, and not everyone behaves like you, either. Learn to work with others as they are, not as you wish them to be.

- **Unity is a work in progress.** Don't expect it to happen overnight. It takes time, deliberate effort, and the moral strength to resist detaching from others under stress.

- **Lead by example.** Hold yourself accountable. Show your commitment to working together by openly collaborating with other leaders and teams. Reinforce the fact that unity is a non-negotiable for the team's success.

- **Guard membership.** Being part of the team is a privilege, not a right. Aggressively uphold the high standards that define it. Take pride in the honor of belonging to a professional team.

2 – Complete a Behavioral Inventory

You must truly understand the people you work with and yourself. A behavioral inventory is a powerful tool for increasing self-awareness and improving team dynamics. It helps ensure the team stays aligned and focused, rather than being derailed by misunderstandings that arise because of conflicting working styles.

Have each team member complete a behavioral survey, as outlined in *The Driver of Chaos*. Detailed tool requirements are provided in *Your Turn*. Bring the team together to review and discuss the survey results. Focus on two things: fostering collaboration and identifying potential points of friction. The insights gained from a scientifically validated tool will highlight:

- **Natural strengths** of each individual, along with their areas of discomfort, such as speaking up or handling sudden change. Understanding these differences fosters empathy and encourages more supportive interactions.

- **Unique motivators** that clarify why each person comes to work and engages with the team. These insights provide common ground for mutual appreciation and a shared commitment to success.

- **Energy distribution** that shows where each person is most effective across a project lifecycle. This insight helps the team assign individuals more strategically.

- **Motivating conditions** that enhance cooperation and

engagement by fostering an environment where each person can thrive.

- **Demotivating conditions** that disrupt and diminish performance. Recognizing these allows the team to anticipate challenges and implement specific actions to help each member stay focused and engaged.

Beyond individual insights, the inventory reveals broader team dynamics. For example, does your team have a balanced mix of skills and traits, or does it rely too heavily on one or two areas? Recognizing these patterns allows you to make targeted adjustments that improve cohesion and performance. Here are a few examples:

- **If impatience dominates the team**—Adding a patient member can slow the tempo just enough to prevent rash decisions and promote more thoughtful execution.

- **If the team is heavy on technical experts**—Adding a generalist can help bridge the gap between tactical excellence and achieving big strategic goals.

- **If the team is mostly quiet and reserved**—Bringing in a natural extrovert can lift team energy and open new communication channels, creating an overall more open and engaged environment.

- **If the team lacks control-oriented individuals**—Hiring a take-charge individual can bring clarity and decisiveness, helping the team focus and drive the mission under pressure.

3 – Define What Success Looks Like

It's your team, so you have the final say in how it should operate and how people should behave. But the team needs a voice too.

What does unity look like to them? Use this opportunity to make them feel like true stakeholders. The more ownership they have in shaping the team's definition of success, the more willing they'll be to endure chaos to achieve it. When people are personally invested, they self-correct, stay accountable, and take initiative—without needing constant oversight.

Engage the team further. Ask, "What is the value of unity?" Encourage them to visualize it: What does effective teamwork *look* like in practice? How should we act when things get tough? Most importantly, what should we avoid doing when stress becomes overwhelming to us personally?

Once everyone has shared their thoughts, press for more detail. Ask, "What does your insight mean for _____?" and fill in the blank with categories like:

1. Communication

2. Mutual respect

3. Mutual support

4. Collaboration

5. Conflict resolution

Leverage the inventory! Use the behavioral insights to help team members understand how to best support each other. Identify likely friction points. Which behaviors are likely to cause frustration, and why? More importantly, how can those reactions be managed constructively?

4 – Implement Practices

Use insights from earlier discussions to develop custom practices, rituals, and standards that foster mutual support.

Have the team create a list of three to four habits they believe will strengthen teamwork. Prompt them with questions like:

- "Which practices are essential for keeping us aligned during difficult times?"

- "How do we ensure everyone is actively supporting one another?"

- "What habits can we adopt that reinforce unity in the team?"

Once the team agrees on these practices, invite them to suggest additional ones they feel are essential and ask them to explain why. This exercise not only tests how well the team collaborates but also reinforces behavioral insights, particularly around control-oriented behaviors.

Next, secure individual commitments. Yes, each person must pledge to follow through. Consider creating a team charter where everyone—including yourself—signs their name. This act symbolizes a collective commitment to uphold the practices and stay accountable to one another. It also makes clear they'll be held responsible for their support, or lack of it. Unity, after all, is non-negotiable.

5 – Maintain Unity

Always assess progress. Are team members following through on their commitments? If not, find out why.

Gauge cohesion. Ask: Is the team's unity weak, average, or strong? Are members proud to be part of this group? How do they perceive trust levels? Seek honest feedback on areas for improvement and use it to drive meaningful change.

Hold people accountable. Are subordinates delivering on their promises? If they are, ask what support they need to perform even better. If they're not, address it immediately. Identify and resolve anything that threatens cohesion. Success is on the line, along with your reputation.

Learn to manage personalities under stress. For mission-oriented leaders, avoid shutting people down or coming across as punitive when interpersonal clashes arise. How you communicate is just as important as what you say. For people-oriented leaders, get comfortable with discomfort. Do not let fear of upsetting others prevent you from enforcing the standards the team has agreed upon.

From Unity to Purpose

Unity is the first step to gaining strength in chaos. The Ten Thousand didn't survive their ordeal simply because they were elite or well-equipped—they made it out because they stuck together as a team when everything else fell apart around them. That unity was no accident; it was deliberately forged through strong leadership and reinforced by the team through every mile, decision, and hardship they faced.

Unity doesn't happen on its own. It takes deliberate effort, consistent communication, and a deep understanding of each person's strengths and motivations. As the leader, your job is to build it, reinforce it, and protect it. That requires discipline, patience, and constant vigilance.

Still, unity alone isn't enough. A unified team needs to know where it's going and how to work together as it moves forward. The next chapter introduces Forward Integration—a high-level capability that connects strategy, organization, systems, and culture into a single force, enabling teams to stay aligned and effective under pressure.

Chapter 9
Forward Integration

The second level of Constructive Chaos is called **Forward Integration (FINT)**. This level satisfies the unique Impact Area known as Direction + Order. Just as that pairing combines distinct but essential aspects of leadership, FINT operates at a higher level of complexity. It aligns four powerful domains—**strategy, organization, systems,** and **culture**—into one integrated, functional whole. When that happens, adaptability and resilience become hardwired into the team's ability to operate under pressure.

FINT is the most complex level in the Constructive Chaos model. Each domain is its own multi-million-dollar industry, with specialized experts and competing methodologies. And yet, all four must be broadly understood to be effectively implemented. The goal of this chapter is to help you do exactly that. You'll gain a practical understanding of each domain, then learn how to connect and apply them to build stronger, more coherent performance under chaos.

Next, we'll examine FINT in action. Andrew Grove, former CEO of Intel, is an outstanding case study. He embodied the power of Forward Integration, equipping his team to execute one of the most successful strategic pivots in modern business history.

Successfully implementing Forward Integration is no small feat. Leaders must overcome real friction to make these elements work together rather than pull apart. That friction reveals three key challenges—each one critical to building a team that can thrive in chaos.

The Challenges of Forward Integration

The first challenge is recognizing that Forward Integration is an interconnected system, not a collection of independent elements. People often treat strategy and culture, for instance, as entirely separate domains. Yet neither operates in isolation; in fact, they depend on one another. This is true of all four elements of FINT if a team is to function effectively in chaos: **strategy *directs*, organization *connects*, systems *enable*, and culture *animates*.** Without integration, teams become unbalanced. The result is misalignment, inefficiency, stagnation, and missed opportunities.

The second challenge is building and sustaining a culture that bridges the human side of chaos with the conceptual infrastructure needed to adapt to it. Too many organizations rely on boilerplate values and trendy slogans that sound good in a slide deck but do nothing in real life. Forward Integration demands more. It requires values with teeth—like accountability, adaptability, and reliability—because these drive the behaviors needed to thrive in chaos. But values alone aren't enough. They must be woven into the other domains: strategy must reward initiative and risk-taking; organization must support and enforce shared expectations; systems must reinforce and scale consistent behavior. Without this alignment, culture becomes theater.

The third, arguably greatest challenge for you is recognizing your limited role in developing FINT. Senior leadership is customarily responsible for establishing it. Does this mean you are powerless? No. Influence up. Lead by example. Apply the FINT lessons to your team the best way you can. Good leaders will notice and want to understand more. Help them succeed, and in doing so, establish yourself as someone who understands how to lead in chaos.

The Essentials of Forward Integration

The four elements of FINT are arranged in their logical sequence, each one building on the last to create a cohesive, high-performing team. Everything begins with strategy, the framework that establishes the team's direction and goals. Next is organization, the structure and roles aligned to meet the strategy's demands. Then comes systems, the practices and procedures that enable the team to work together efficiently. Finally, we focus on culture: the mindset and values that foster the resilience needed to adapt and succeed in chaos.

The Strategy Element

Strategy is the process of defining what we want to achieve in the future and determining how to achieve it using our capabilities and available resources.

Too often, strategy is misunderstood and mistaken for a plan. To be clear: plans are snapshots, detailed sequences of tasks given current conditions. Strategy is the broader framework that guides our planning.

Consider the origin of the word. *Strategos* was the title of an Ancient Greek military general responsible for winning a war, not just a battle. Battlefield victories, for example, depended on recruitment, leader selection, training, organizational structures, communication systems, campaign planning, political coordination, supply logistics, and a host of other interconnected elements. They functioned like the veins and nerves linking our organs to the brain. A failure in one could spell disaster for the body, just as it could lead to defeat for the *strategos*.

Strategy is the foundation of planning. It anchors our focus to a single, overarching aim. From there, we define what success looks like. We break the aim down into strategic goals, which are then translated into specific metrics for success. In effect, this broad framework sets the borders of the mission, defining the arena we are operating in. Only then do we develop plans, based on the current situation, capabilities, and resources, to achieve those goals and actualize the strategy.

Unlike planning, strategy also accounts for execution. Situations evolve and circumstances change, often in unpredictable ways. Strategy must be broad enough to allow flexibility in planning, enabling course corrections without losing sight of the ultimate objective.

Strategy is essential for navigating chaos:

- It narrows our focus to what truly matters, reducing the overwhelming possibilities into a manageable set of priorities.

- It provides clarity that allows us to pivot from our intended path with confidence, remaining focused on the ultimate objective.

- It integrates people, processes, and resources to deliver the maximum effect of our efforts.

- It forces us to define our unique strengths, and limitations, guiding us in deciding when, where, and how to best apply them.

- A well-conceived strategy becomes a self-correcting

system, encouraging the adoption of effective tactics and discarding those that no longer serve our goals.

Strategy and Planning at the Individual Level

Strategy is just as important for individuals and small teams as it is for massive armies and large corporations.

Let's imagine you are a college freshman fascinated by medicine; your aim in life is to become a brain surgeon. Your strategy is to do everything you need to graduate a prestigious medical school while staying close to your family. To achieve this, you must earn a very high GPA, demonstrate your dedication to medicine through extracurricular science activities, and focus on the best school in your state.

Execution becomes key. You adjust your schedule to prioritize academic performance. You trade weekends, social events, and parties for late-night study sessions, science clubs, and workshops. The greater the reputation of the medical school, the greater the effort, energy, and focus required to get in.

Now, let's say that in your senior year, you recognize a new, but unrealized passion: animals. In fact, your love for them rivals your fascination with medicine. After some deep reflection, you decide to become a veterinarian surgeon.

This is how strategy and planning work at the individual level. Your vision of success evolves with experience. But your aim—to build a fulfilling medical career—remains largely intact. Only the form has changed.

Your planning changes too. You shift your tactics and maybe loosen your schedule some. In the end, you will see patients; only they will have four legs instead of two.

Strategy is just as valuable in both large organizations and at a personal level. It is not a rigid, step-by-step plan, but instead the broader framework that guides decisions, effort, and resource use toward a meaningful goal.

A good strategy allows for adjustments to new insights and evolving circumstances. This flexibility allows us to reevaluate our visions and missions as necessary, ensuring they align with current realities. When circumstances shift, plans adapt. Strategy endures, unless the aim itself becomes obsolete.

How Do You Develop a Strategy?

In the corporate world, strategy is often reduced to a vague vision or mission statement. By itself, that's not enough. Yet this remains the all-too-common product of "strategy work" among executive teams.

There are several key elements I learned in the Army that many private-sector companies routinely overlook. The following approach will help you clarify what you're trying to accomplish, while maintaining flexibility in how you achieve it.

Remember: even if you're not setting the overarching corporate strategy, you can still create one for your team and link it directly to headquarters. When you do that—and make sure senior leaders take notice—you demonstrate a rare and valuable skill: the ability to connect your team's work and tactics to the bigger picture. It's the kind of strategic alignment many executives struggle with, no matter their pedigree or position.

The Intent Statement

Also known as the Commander's Intent in the military, this brief section has profound implications for how your strategy is conceived, developed, and ultimately executed.

In just a few paragraphs, a senior leader describes what

success looks like. From this, essential goals, tasks, and metrics are derived. What's not described is how to make it all happen—that's left to the team to determine. Once they've done so, they report back with a plan for approval.

When writing an Intent Statement, ask yourself: "What does success look like—exactly—in the end?"

Paint a mental picture using key dimensions:
"In terms of mission completion, we will _____."
"In terms of team collaboration, we will _____."
"In terms of quality, we will _____."
"Our customers will _____."

The answers to these questions give your team a concrete picture of what matters most to the boss. They clarify expectations across multiple dimensions, so that when your team builds a plan, they know exactly what they're working toward. Every decision, action, and adjustment should be traceable to these expectations. If it doesn't support them, it's off track.

Dimensions, or "Lanes"

A good strategy begins by identifying all the essential dimensions of success. These can then be translated into broad, strategic lanes that guide decision-making, cross-functional work, and frontline alignment.

Think back to the surgeon-veterinarian example. Although academic success was the top priority, other parts of life—family, relationships, financial well-being, physical health, and spiritual health—were just as important and still had to be accounted for. It was only a question of prioritization. But ignoring any of them creates an imbalance that affects performance. If not addressed early, those gaps become costly distractions that can ultimately undermine the overall mission.

Strategy in teams and organizations work the same way. It requires breaking down the mission into broad areas—or lanes—that collectively form the whole. Doing this naturally invites cross-functional engagement and alignment across teams.

For example, instead of thinking only in terms of "sales," one specific function, consider the broader lane of "revenue generation," which includes contributions from other teams as well. This kind of thinking encourages collaboration and uncovers opportunities that siloed teams may miss—for instance, marketing may have ideas about how to sell that sales hasn't considered, and vice versa.

Ask: "If you had to break down this mission into major categories, what are the big buckets that other tasks fall into?"

These become your strategic lanes—priorities like revenue generation, organizational development, or product development. When communicating them to the team, keep it simple. Use visuals if needed. If you can explain them on one hand, they're probably clear enough to stick. The goal is for everyone to walk away knowing exactly what the priorities are and how their work supports them.

Contingencies

We all expect our plans to work as intended—to drive directly toward our main goal with minimal disruption. But what happens when we're forced to change course? Under what circumstances would you or your team need to take a detour and still achieve the original objective?

Contingency planning is often overlooked because it starts from an uncomfortable premise: your plan might not work. The exercise can feel defeatist in spirit, causing people to avoid the topic altogether. But nothing could be farther from the truth.

Contingency planning maps out the major lanes inside your

strategic highway forward. If Route A becomes blocked, Route B is already on the table. Even Route C is available, if necessary. At a minimum, the exercise uncovers hidden capabilities or gaps—we can't take this approach because we're missing a key tool, a decision-maker, or internal alignment. It also helps expose potential obstacles early, giving you the opportunity to address them before they become real problems.

I once worked with the VP of Corporate Communications at a company under scrutiny from federal regulators. We wargamed several scenarios that could derail the organization during an upcoming product launch. Within a week, one of those exact issues arose. It could have cost the company $2 million in government fines. But the team didn't flinch—they had already built a contingency for it. Within hours, they executed the plan and neutralized the issue before it escalated. The penalty was avoided entirely.

When developing contingency plans, ask: "What's the worst thing that could happen to us?" Then follow with: "What must we do to stay on course if it does?"

The answers to those two questions will help you identify the critical tasks that must be built into the larger plan—ensuring your team is ready to adapt, not just react, when chaos hits.

An Emphasis on Execution

The most important principle in strategy isn't building the perfect plan—it's building a solid one your team can execute under pressure. Success doesn't come from elegance or sophistication on paper. It comes from a team prepared to adapt under real, changing conditions. Your team's ability to adjust during execution—while staying focused on what truly matters—*is* the margin of victory.

Flexibility is key in both strategy and chaos. Execution must be prioritized from the start. One of the most important lessons I learned in the Army was the 1/3–2/3 rule: spend one-third of your time planning, and the remaining two-thirds preparing to execute. That means rehearsing the plan, testing assumptions, identifying gaps, and making sure the team is ready to adapt under real conditions. Preparation is what turns a solid plan into successful execution.

Teams must be willing and able to change course or bypass steps to maintain momentum and reach the final objective. It's on the leader to get comfortable with this kind of volatility and to develop their subordinates to do the same.

Preparation and execution go hand in hand. That means investing in the kind of training and education that teaches people to strategize, plan, and operate in chaos. A strategy only works if the people carrying it out can think, adjust, and deliver in real time, under pressure.

The Organization Element

As the second element of FINT, organization naturally follows strategy: *what* needs to be accomplished determines *who* is responsible for accomplishing it, based on both talent and the value they bring to the mission.

Organization consists of two key components: the **roles** within a team and the **structure** that connects them. Together, they ensure you have the right people in place, and that they're arranged in a way that supports effective decision-making, the seamless flow of information, and, of course, adaptability. Let's break each down.

Roles

Roles are clearly defined responsibilities essential for team performance. In chaos, they become even more critical to success because they remove ambiguity and establish exactly who is accountable for what. Without that clarity, execution slows, decisions stall, and turf-battles spread.

Here are three considerations to consider when filling roles:

- **Clear and Focused Descriptions**: A role isn't a job title—it's a contract for performance. When defining a role, don't list everything the person might do. Instead, specify exactly what they must do to move the mission forward, based on their unique talents. Strip the role down to its mission-critical outcomes. Over-defining—especially by including non-essential tasks—creates confusion, dilutes focus, and discourages discretionary effort. If everything matters, nothing does.

- **Necessary Behaviors**: Identify the key behaviors the role demands. Does it require analytical thinking to process information, precision to ensure quality, or urgency to drive fast-paced execution? Choose three or four action verbs—like evaluate, ensure, drive, or implement—that reflect what success actually looks like in the role. These verbs become the behavioral anchors that guide hiring, coaching, and performance.

- **Motivator Compatibility**: Motivators are the core values that drive behavior and decision-making, typically identified through a behavioral tool. Matching a person's motivators to their role is essential for predicting their drive, focus, and intensity in a project. Motivators act like governors on an engine, regulating the energy and enthusiasm someone brings to their work. When a role aligns with an individual's motivators, their engagement and effectiveness aren't just enhanced—they're amplified, driving greater performance and satisfaction.

Structure

Once roles are defined, the next critical step is organizing the team for optimal performance. Structure connects those roles in a way that enables seamless information flow and continuous feedback loops for rapid decision-making.

A strong organizational structure reflects the unique needs required to execute the team's specific strategy. The two are interdependent. As Alfred Chandler observed in his seminal work *Strategy and Structure,* "Unless structure follows strategy, inefficiency results."

For example, a small software company focused on rapid growth may benefit from a flat structure with decentralized authority to speed up decisions. In contrast, a large, heavily regulated organization sensitive to government oversight might require a tall structure with multiple layers of approval to ensure compliance.

Even if you're not in a position to change the broader organization's structure directly, understanding how roles connect is key to unlocking better performance. A clear view of these interactions exposes bottlenecks and misalignments that quietly undermine progress. Are technical leaders stuck managing people instead of applying their expertise? Are vague reporting lines muddying communication and slowing down decisions?

Structural flaws aren't surface-level nuisances or temporary setbacks—they're anchors that drag performance down over time. Identifying and correcting them—by reallocating responsibilities, tightening workflows, or clarifying authority—often triggers immediate impact. Small, targeted changes shift momentum and help the team move faster, with greater confidence and control.

The Systems Element

Systems define how things get done in a team. They include the processes, procedures, and routines a team consistently uses to operate with efficiency and control. If structure is the skeleton and organs of the body, then systems are the nervous and circulatory systems that bring the body to life and keeping it running.

When systems are thoughtfully chosen, standardized, and applied consistently, they create predictability. They allow both simple and complex tasks to be executed with minimal friction and maximum return. A team with strong, reliable systems signals capability and confidence. They operate like professionals—disciplined, prepared, and in control—not like amateurs scrambling to figure things out.

Developing Your Systems

Systems answer the recurring questions every team faces:

- How do we operate together?

- How do we communicate?

- When do we escalate?

- What do we do to improve?

Here are five essential components:

- **Common Lexicon**: Action depends on thought, and thought relies on the use of words. When unfamiliar terms or jargon creep in our work, miscommunication occurs—and that directly impacts performance. To avoid this, teams need a shared set of terms and definitions that everyone agrees to use the same way.

  For example, one team might say "launch" to mean when a project is handed off to stakeholders. Another might think "launch" means when the final product goes live. That gap can wreck timing and expectations. Identify words like these with multiple interpretations, define them precisely, and publish those definitions so the team stays aligned when it counts.

- **Uniform Planning Template**: A standardized planning template ensures consistency in how tasks and decisions are structured. A common framework for setting goals, organizing efforts, and executing plans removes guesswork, streamlines decision-making, and ensures alignment across the team. The template doesn't need to be complex, but it must be consistent in its application. Standardized planning fosters predictability, which in turn speeds up execution. With a uniform approach, anyone on the team can create a plan that others can immediately understand and act on.

- **Prioritized Information Requirements**: In an age of information overload, clarity is power. It's essential to determine who needs to know what and when. Just as important, they must decide what doesn't need to be shared. Excessive information creates cognitive drag, slows decisions, and dilutes focus. Prioritizing information flow ensures the right people receive the right message at the right time. It eliminates clutter and enables the team to move faster, cleaner, and with more precision.

- **Solutions-Oriented Culture**: High-performing teams don't just report problems—they solve them. Build a culture where people are expected to propose alternatives, coordinate with others to test viability, and take full ownership of outcomes. A solutions-oriented team lifts the burden of decision-making from leadership, enabling faster response times and allowing senior leaders to stay focused on the bigger picture.

- **Growth Integrated into Systems**: Every mission is a chance to get better—but only if growth is built into the system. Many leaders skip this step, thinking they don't have time or that people will just learn as they go. That's a mistake. People need support in processing what just happened, especially when they're overloaded.

    Strong leaders make time for growth. They don't just mandate growth practices—they lead them. They facilitate after-action reviews or post-mortems. They ask the right reflective questions and ensure the process fits the team's learning styles and experience levels. They guide the discussion so the lessons stick and the trajectory toward becoming a professional team never loses momentum.

The "Forward" in Forward Integration

There's something admirable about the person who looks into an uncertain future and says, "Bring it on." It's the kind of boldness we admire in our favorite movie characters. And it's the kind of courage chaos demands.

"Forward" represents the cultural element of FINT. It's a

mindset rooted in inevitable growth and progress, no matter what stands in the way. This outlook fuels a willingness, even a fearlessness, to face chaos head-on. Challenges become more than obstacles; they become tests of will—proving grounds for strength and resolve.

The confidence that comes with a forward mindset becomes contagious. One bold example inspires another. As it spreads, this mindset reinforces itself—through repetition, shared struggle, and results.

The "Forward" mindset powers the other elements of Forward Integration:

- **In Strategy**, this mindset is what makes flexibility possible—both in planning and execution. It emotionally steels people to anticipate uncertainty and respond to it without panic when things go off-script. Teams stay grounded, adapt quickly, and execute contingencies with confidence. Improvisation doesn't feel like failure—it feels like part of the plan.

- **In Organization**, roles are filled based on capability, not seniority or politics. Structures are designed for action, not appearances. The best-positioned people are empowered to lead from wherever they stand. The focus is on outcomes, not adhering to rigid hierarchy.

- **In Systems**, processes are built to support execution, not to enable top-down micromanagement. Systems must enable adaptability, efficiency, and speed, equipping frontline performers with the tools and autonomy to act without hesitation or unnecessary delay. When designed right, they support clear decisions, consistent standards, and rapid learning—even when leadership isn't in the room.

What does "forward" look like in practice?

A forward-leaning culture doesn't happen by chance. It's built on three internal drivers that fuel consistency in chaos:

- **Conviction:** The deep belief that the mission is achievable—and that your team can do what others won't or can't. It's not blind optimism; it's earned confidence, grounded in experience, effort, and reflection.

- **Determination:** The resolute drive to act boldly and push forward, even when conditions are harsh, unclear, or exhausting. Determination keeps the team moving—without complaint, without pause—focused on accomplishing the task at hand.

- **Pride:** The deep personal fulfillment that comes from achieving hard-earned victories under pressure. Pride strengthens commitment to victory because one *must* succeed. It pushes individuals and teams to pursue excellence and exceed their own expectations.

These aren't just feelings—they're spiritual fuel that keeps a team advancing forward, regardless of the challenges that lay in front of them. But internal drivers aren't enough. To truly take root, they must be reflected in the values your team lives by.

Selecting Your Values

Values must reinforce the behaviors your strategy demands. Whether your mission depends on speed, flexibility, precision, or something else, your values should strengthen the team's ability to deliver under all conditions.

Here are some examples worth considering:

- **Courageous Initiative:** We value the courage to act when others hesitate.

- **Calculated Responses:** The team avoids knee-jerk reactions and considers the outcomes before acting.

- **Accountability:** Team members own their decisions, including failure. No excuses, no deflection.

- **Calculated Risk-Taking:** We seize opportunities based on a clear understanding of risk and reward.

- **Transparency:** We communicate directly and honestly, so issues—no matter how uncomfortable—are faced head-on.

- **Mutual Respect:** Trust and collaboration thrive when every team member is treated as a valued contributor.

- **Discipline:** We follow process and systems because we believe in being reliable.

A team driven by conviction, determination, and pride—and grounded in values that support bold execution—becomes unstoppable. That's what Forward Integration looks like in practice: strategy, structure, systems, and culture working in sync.

Few leaders embodied this more completely than Andy Grove.

The Virtue of Paranoia

In the midst of chaos, there lies opportunity.
— Andy Grove

In the mid-1980s, Intel faced a Strategic Inflection Point: a critical moment when a major shift in the competitive environment demands a fundamental change in business strategy to ensure survival.[58] Intel's core business of manufacturing memory chips had become highly competitive and increasingly unprofitable. Worse, memory chips were being commoditized, eroding the competitive advantage they held since the late 1960s.

Faced with this existential threat, Intel had two choices: continue business as usual and risk obsolescence, or pivot to a new and untested product. Intel eventually chose the latter, shifting its business to manufacturing microprocessors.

The decision was anything but easy. Grove had to persuade Intel's leaders and engineers—people comfortably sitting at the top of their industry—to abandon the core of their business and venture into uncharted territory. Resistance was predictably formidable. One middle manager noted: "It was kind of like Ford deciding to get out of cars."[59] Reflecting on the ordeal, Grove described it as walking through their own "valley of death." Every step forward felt like a fight for survival.[60]

Despite the initial resistance, Intel pivoted successfully. Over time, this decision proved not only timely and smart, but transformative. The company emerged as the world's leading microprocessor manufacturer, with revenues soaring from $1.9 billion to over $26 billion in the decades that followed.[61]

Andrew Grove. Intel's survival wasn't guaranteed, even at the top. Facing a brutal choice—fight a losing war or pivot in a radical new direction—Grove didn't just make the call; he had to convince his people to follow. Intel reoriented, reset, restructured, and decentralized for adaptability. The result? They reclaimed their dominance. (Photo: Courtesy of Alamy)

Grove recounts this grueling experience in *Only the Paranoid Survive*—an incredible book packed with invaluable lessons on leadership and crisis management. His story is essential for understanding how teams can adapt to evolving circumstances without breaking under the pressure of internal and external friction.

Let's examine Intel's pivot through the lens of the four elements of Forward Integration: forward mindset, strategy, organization, and systems.

Forward Mindset

Grove fully embodied the "forward" outlook, recognizing that uncertainty is a natural part of life. Instead of resisting it or wishing it away, he embraced it and adapted.

Consider the title of his book. Paranoia, in its everyday sense, implies a psychological flaw—an irrational suspicion of one's surroundings. But for Grove, paranoia was a virtue. It was a heightened vigilance absolutely essential for survival. In a hyper-competitive world, paranoia wasn't optional—it was a life-saver. After all, in the wild, it's not the confident gazelle sipping water that survives; it's the one constantly scanning for lions and crocodiles.

Consider Grove's management philosophy. Known as "constructive confrontation," it emphasized addressing problems head-on. "We encourage our people to deal with problems without flinching," he explains.[62] This abrasive approach fosters a culture where blunt, honest communication is the norm. The goal is to generate the strongest solutions, not to protect egos or entertain wishful thinking. One former Intel executive noted, "If you went into a meeting, you'd better have your data; you'd better have your opinion; and if you can't defend your opinion, you have no right to be there."[63]

Grove understood the crippling effect of fearing the unknown. While natural, that fear must never block the honest exchange of information. The truth will always surface. That's why bad news must be shared immediately, without fear of punishment. Suppressing it doesn't protect the team—it sabotages it.

Another critical aspect of the forward mindset is the confidence required to navigate uncertainty. For Grove, intuition—gut feeling—was indispensable in the fog of war. Intel's situation was unprecedented. With no historical data to rely on, Grove faced a major challenge: persuading Intel's engineers and scientists—professionals conditioned to rely on data, precedent, and methodical thinking—to radically change course at the company's peak, based only on a fraction of the information that might justify the move.

Their hesitation was understandable. To them, acting without complete data felt reckless. Some even used the lack of information as an excuse to delay or resist. Grove called out this behavior directly: "You can always hide behind the data. Until you stop dealing with this, you will not get anywhere."[64]

He reminded his team that progress requires the courage to move without perfect answers. It demands the confidence to act decisively with the limited information you have.

Influence, not obedience, was the only method of leading. Companies don't turn on a dime, and people won't follow just because they're ordered to. People have to want to change course. That's why Grove spent countless hours debating with his leaders, knowing Intel's success depended on people willingly participating and contributing because they believed in the mission—not because they were pressured into it.

Strategy

"Clarity of direction is exceedingly important during a company's transformation," Grove wrote in *Only the Paranoid Survive*.[65] He stressed that in turbulent times, leaders must create and communicate a clear vision of what the company should become. And it must be one that *everyone in the company* can understand.

Pivoting Intel's core business required a complete overhaul, mentally and structurally. "We adopted a whole different attitude to our product, including cost improvements," Grove said.[66]

Intel adopted a strategy of segmentation rather than chasing a single, broad market. Each business unit focused on a distinct customer segment—such as personal computers or enterprise solutions—while still operating under the unified goal of making Intel the world leader in microprocessor technology. This structure empowered teams to innovate and respond quickly to their market's demands, without being slowed by bottlenecks from over-centralized control. At the same time, Grove retained strategic oversight, ensuring every unit remained aligned with the company's broader vision.

This new direction was only as strong as the commitment of those executing it. Without buy-in, a strategy is nothing more than a wish list. Thus, Grove emphasized the importance of leading by example. Implementing changes first—and then demonstrating their value—was far more effective than making optimistic promises and hoping people would follow through. In essence, people need to see first in order to believe.

Organization

The new strategy of segmentation required a compartmentalized organizational structure. Business units were expected to operate with autonomy, each focused on specific objectives yet firmly aligned with Intel's strategic vision. This decentralized model fostered targeted innovation to their unique customer base as well as rapid responsiveness to market shifts, directly supporting the company's broader goals.

This bottom-up approach proved critical during Intel's pivot to microprocessors. Grove noted, "While Intel's business changed and management was looking for clever memory strategies and arguing among themselves, men and women lower in the organization, unbeknownst to us, got us ready to execute the strategic turn that saved our necks and gave us a great future."[67]

Middle managers, equipped with local authority, played an unexpectedly critical role. They had the discretion to reallocate resources toward emerging, profitable opportunities—one of which turned out to be microprocessors. When headquarters finally made the formal pivot, they discovered the groundwork had already been laid. Execution was smoother, faster, and far less painful than expected. This wasn't the result of top-down orders to change, but the product of an organization empowered to respond to a shifting world—and already moving before anyone had to tell it to.

Systems

Intel needed to be smart about how it advanced through the fog of war. That meant implementing systems that accelerated adaptability and reduced friction during times of transition.

One such system was continuous intelligence gathering. Intel's ability to recognize its precarious position early on stemmed from this emphasis on scanning the external environment. Grove institutionalized this practice by encouraging routine inquiry: Who is our greatest competitor? What do our customers need? What is the market demanding? These questions weren't reserved for the C-suite. Grove believed the best insights came from the front lines: "People in the trenches are usually in touch with impending changes early."[68] Intel's system relied on middle managers to funnel real-world intelligence back into strategic decision-making.

Innovation, too, was systematized. Grove created space for experimentation, empowering managers and engineers to test ideas aligned with market needs. His directive to "let chaos reign in order to explore your alternatives" wasn't just a philosophy; it was a process.[69] What looked chaotic from the outside was, in reality, structured innovation.

Finally, Grove made open communication a non-negotiable system. He hardwired the expectation that information must move quickly and candidly up the chain—even when the news was bad. "It is extremely important to be able to listen to the people who bring you bad news," he said.[70] This norm wasn't cultural theater; it was an operational discipline designed to surface issues early and avoid strategic blindness.

Together, these systems—intelligence gathering, structured innovation, and open communication—made Intel faster, sharper, and more resilient. They didn't just help the company survive its pivot. They helped it outpace the competition.

From Purpose to Execution

The journey through Forward Integration is far from simple. It demands the seamless alignment of strategy, organization, systems, and a forward-focused culture—each working together to give teams the clarity and structure needed to succeed, even in chaos.

As Andy Grove's experience at Intel shows, adaptability isn't just a strategic advantage. It's a requirement for survival. His virtue of paranoia highlights the power of vigilance, open communication, and the willingness to embrace discomfort as a catalyst for innovation and growth.

Having FINT is one thing. Leading with it is another. That means guiding your team with competence, confidence, and the ability to maneuver in real time.

That's where Mission Command begins.

Chapter 10
Mission Command

The third level of Constructive Chaos focuses squarely on the Impact Area: Leadership + Management—a unique pairing of two disciplines that cannot exist without each other. This level is about producing results *through others*, under pressure, in real time. Most of all, it's about learning how to relinquish control over people and systems when chaos comes, empowering them to execute without your direct intervention.

That's no easy task. It requires preparing your people to respond to disruption without waiting on you. It also means sustaining the Unity and Forward Integration you've already built.

The multi-billion-dollar leadership industry has tried—and largely failed—to solve this challenge. But a powerful solution exists, and it comes from an unexpected source: an 18th-century Prussian military philosophy called **Mission Command**. (Yes, you read that right.) Stripped of its battlefield origins, Mission Command becomes a powerful system of decentralized leadership for the private sector—exactly what modern executives are searching for, without realizing it already exists.

Mission Command isn't a list of tactics. It's a leadership philosophy—a system of interconnected principles built around decentralization. It guides leaders and teams to operate effectively in volatile, chaotic environments by pushing decisions down to the level where information is freshest and action is fastest.

For Mission Command to work, it must first be internalized, then adapted to your organization's own processes and protocols. But once embraced, the results are unmistakable: teams become highly adaptive, resilient, and capable of achieving exceptional outcomes—just like Lord Horatio Nelson's fleet at the Battle of the Nile.

Nelson and The Nile

Lord Horatio Nelson is one of history's great case studies in applied Mission Command. The British admiral is widely regarded as one of history's Great Captains. His decisive naval victory over Napoleon's fleet at the Battle of Trafalgar (1805) secured British dominance of the seas for more than a century. His legacy is literally carved in stone—immortalized at Trafalgar Square in central London.

Although the philosophy of Mission Command wasn't formally articulated until after Nelson's era, his leadership exemplified its core principles. Nowhere is this more evident than in the events surrounding the Battle of the Nile (1798).

"Victory is not a name strong enough for such a scene."

Admiral Nelson spoke these words as he gazed upon the carnage in Aboukir Bay, 20 miles outside Alexandria, Egypt.[71] It was the early morning of August 2, 1798. Shattered planks, charred clothing, and the lifeless bodies of sailors—mostly French—floated among the charred remains of colossal "ships of the line," the dominant warship that defined the Age of Sail. This devastation marked the aftermath of the Battle of the Nile, a triumph that stands as one of the most decisive naval victories of the 18th century.[72]

The Battle of the Nile was the dramatic culmination of a three-month chase across the Mediterranean. General Napoleon Bonaparte, the future emperor of France, sought to deliver a crippling blow to Britain by seizing Egypt. Controlling this key territory would disrupt Britain's vital trade routes to India and Asia, delivering a strategic masterstroke against their empire.[73]

To achieve this, Napoleon launched a full-scale expedition: his navy escorted a sizable land force across the sea with the aim of conquering Egypt and securing a foothold in the region.

The British, aware of the French fleet's departure but unaware of its destination, recognized the threat. Admiral Nelson was given command of the Mediterranean squadron and tasked with tracking and intercepting Napoleon's forces. What was he planning? Where were his ships headed? For three months, Nelson's squadron pursued its elusive target, piecing together clues from ports across southern France and Sicily.

Despite relentless effort, the French remained just out of reach until August 1, 1798.

Late that afternoon, Nelson's fleet spotted the enemy anchored in Aboukir Bay near Alexandria. The anchored French ships had formed a strong defensive line: their port side shielded by the coast, their starboard exposed to open water. It was a commanding position. Any ship entering the bay would come under immediate fire.

The French spotted the British squadron as well. The timing couldn't have been worse. Roughly a third of their crews were ashore resupplying.[74] Confident in the strength of their position, the late hour of the day, and the madness of fighting at nightfall—conditions no typical commander would willingly choose—the French admiral didn't panic as he assumed the battle would wait until morning.[75]

He was wrong.

Nelson and his officers didn't hesitate. Without a planning session or time to rally, he signaled his column to attack immediately. The squadron charged forward as French crews scrambled to their battle stations and the seamen ashore raced desperately back to their ships. But it was too late—the battle had begun. The British seized the upper hand—both positionally and psychologically—and relentlessly exploited these critical advantages in the hours to come.

The Battle of the Nile was not just a decisive British victory, but one of the most daring and lopsided engagements in naval history.[76] Overnight, Nelson shattered Napoleon's navy, leaving his army stranded in Egypt. While French armies might dominate continental Europe for now, the seas—and everything around them—belonged unequivocally to Britain.

The Decisive Point

What makes the Battle of the Nile so compelling to students of Mission Command is not just its dramatic outcome, but how that outcome came to be.

Nelson's plan of attack, developed through countless discussions in his cabin, was unmistakable. The British would strike the French fleet on their seaward side, with Nelson's lead ships targeting the vanguard of the enemy fleet while the rest of the squadron surged forward to hammer the center. In other words, the entire British squadron would concentrate all their power on one-half to two-thirds of the French fleet, using speed, surprise, and overwhelming force to divide and defeat them before the rest could react.[77]

Of course, the plan did not go according to plan.

Captain Thomas Foley, commanding the lead ship *Goliath*,

spotted a critical weakness in the French formation as he approached. A noticeable gap separated the lead French ship from the shallow shoreline waters—a sloppy oversight. Foley reasoned that if the French considered their shoreward sides safe, their guns on that side were likely unprepared for combat. If *Goliath* could slip through the gap—and the rest of the squadron followed—the British could catch the French completely off guard and gain overwhelming tactical superiority.

Without waiting for Nelson's approval aboard the flagship *Vanguard*—stationed mid-column to preserve command and control—Foley ordered *Goliath* into the gap. The ships behind him followed.

Foley's gamble paid off: the French cannons were completely unprepared. Shocked French sailors, ready to fight on the bayside, scrambled to ready their shoreward guns, all while absorbing withering British fire. Meanwhile, crew members returning from shore were forced to run a gauntlet of deadly blasts, dodging shrapnel and fire as they raced back to battle stations already under attack.

How did Nelson react to Foley's improvisation? Did he panic and halt the attack to reassert control? Not at all. He immediately understood Foley's intent and went along. Seeing the opportunity created by the confusion, Nelson signaled the second half of the fleet to follow him down the bayside of the French column— the original intended path.

It was a devastating one-two punch. Foley forced the French into a panicked rush to defend their exposed side, while Nelson struck their prepared flank. Overwhelmed and trapped between simultaneous threats, the French crews struggled to recover.

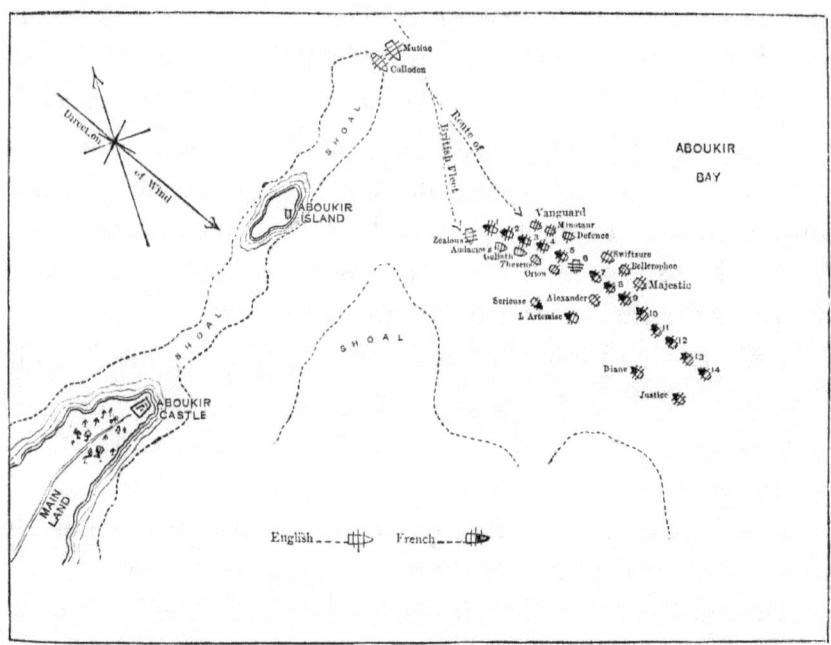

The Battle of the Nile. Nelson's squadron charged straight into battle without a formal planning session. Risking night combat, Nelson instinctively put the enemy on the ropes. Captain Foley exploited a gap in the French line, catching them completely unprepared. Over the next several hours, Nelson's men escalated the chaos, overwhelming the French and delivering the most decisive naval victory of the 18th century. (Photo: Courtesy of Alamy)

The battle devolved into a brutal slugfest, typical of the time, but the British held the advantage. Around 11:00 p.m., after hours of relentless fighting, the French flagship *L'Orient* erupted in a massive explosion when British cannon fire ignited its gunpowder magazine.[78] The blast lit up the night sky, shaking the bay and delivering a catastrophic blow to French morale.

By dawn, the battle was over. All but two French ships lay on the bottom of the bay. Nelson's squadron sustained serious damage—but lost no ships. For the first time in 18th-century naval warfare, an entire fleet had been utterly annihilated.

The Origin of Victory

The Battle of the Nile stands as one of the most remarkable victories in military history. Its success, however, was not solely the result of the "Great Man." Nelson did not single-handedly secure the day through genius, tactical brilliance, or uncanny strategic foresight. As Nelson himself conceded, the victory belonged to his captains.[79] And yet, they were his captains—trained, trusted, and empowered—so the triumph still reflects Nelson's leadership in preparing and developing them.

Nelson's willingness to relinquish control was the key to his success. Any leader knows how difficult this is. Still, Nelson did it by adapting to the requirements of his role, his profession, and the nature of chaos itself.

Consider Nelson the man. Seemingly born for the sea, he began his naval career at the age of thirteen. Nelson was whip-smart, ambitious, and arrogant—a wunderkind who achieved remarkable success early in life.[80] His daring victory at the Battle of Cape St. Vincent in 1797—where he defied orders, broke from his squadron, and boldly attacked an escaping Spanish fleet to turn the tide of battle—cemented his reputation as a maverick.

He carried with him an unshakable sense of self and a certainty in his destiny. Even after losing an arm, nearly dying in battle, and going blind in one eye, he remained as ambitious and sharp as ever. Over time, experience tempered his approach to leadership without dulling his drive. No longer just the star performer, he had become the captain of a star crew.

Behaviorally, Nelson was intensely vision- and relationship-oriented, likely in that order. He was ruthless, single-mindedly focused on achieving decisive results. He was both a strategist and a master tactician. In respect to people, he was described as kind, charismatic, and deeply committed to supporting his colleagues.[81] His control over the team was rooted in informality, open dialogue, and frank, candid discussion.[82]

His competitiveness and impatience were legendary, shaping his decisions at every turn. He likely leaned heavily on intuition, making confident, split-second calls with limited information. For Nelson, changes in a plan weren't setbacks or threats—they were opportunities to seize the initiative and drive his enemies into reactive, error-prone positions he could exploit.

Nelson matured into his role as a commander, evolving from a maverick driven by individual brilliance into a leader who empowered his team to achieve collective success.

As a commander, Nelson led by delegation, granting others the same independence he exercised. But initiative and discretion came with a price: excellence in judgment and execution. Leaders with this behavioral profile surround themselves with A-players—real and potential—because only those individuals can operate reliably at the high standards they hold for themselves.

Most remarkable about the man was his embrace of chaos. His era was defined by scientific and cultural advancement.[83] Civilization thrives on order, and order depends on rules, stability, and above all, predictability. Nelson exploited this deep-seated psychological need against his opponents. His signature approach to warfare, the "Nelson Touch," became synonymous with bold, direct, in-your-face aggression rooted in do-or-die defiance that completely upended the standard, linear-thinking approaches to war at the time. Battle then was treated like a gentlemanly, if lethal, chess match, not like a barroom brawl.

So how did Nelson get his captains to embrace chaos the way he did and deliver unprecedented outcomes?

The answer lies in three indispensable elements that made relinquishing control not only possible, but effective: preparation, mastery, and the human element.

Preparation

Preparation is how we keep everything from falling apart the moment chaos hits us.

Nelson prepared his captains because he had to: the nature of his profession demanded it. When the chaos of battle commenced, he wouldn't be there to guide his captains. Success as a team was possible only if there was deep alignment in thought, intention, and action among all his captains. Each one had to anticipate the others' decisions the moment combat began or they wouldn't fight as a team.

His personal wiring matched the professional need. No doubt shaped by his own craving for independence, Nelson reinforced the need for captains to act on their own judgment and initiative too. Preparation was his way of ensuring they did so according to his standards.

Horatio Nelson. On the left: the rising prodigy—ambitious, arrogant, but brilliant in battle. On the right: the legendary admiral—scarred, seasoned, and still just as determined. Now, a commander of men just like himself. Over time, he learned to relinquish control and forge a team that turned chaos into both sword and shield. (Photos: Courtesy of Alamy)

Then there's the matter of opportunity. Impatient leaders—like Nelson—often skip preparation in favor of immediate action. But the long lulls of the Nile campaign turned out to be a gift. Nelson used the time to regularly hold conferences with his captains. These weren't just planning sessions; they were exercises in shared thinking. His captains didn't just learn what to do in specific situations; they understood why. Most importantly, they internalized his expectations. That clarity of intention enabled each captain to act independently in the moment. It also enabled them to support one another with minimal communication—a significant edge for any team fighting in the smoke, noise, and mayhem of sea combat.

Preparation was just as technical as it was cultural. These conferences forged unity and close bonds. The team declared themselves, "Band of Brothers," borrowed from Shakespeare's *Henry V*.[84]

Through constant rehearsal, discussion, and scenario planning, Nelson and his team built a shared mental playbook for the chaos they would soon provoke and endure. His captains didn't have to improvise blindly—they had already gamed out the possibilities and understood their roles in bringing his intent to life.

Most of all, preparation helped mitigate the psychological strain of chaos. The mental frameworks they built reduced hesitation and eased the pressure of operating in isolation. This was especially valuable for those less comfortable with Nelson's aggressive style. Under pressure, they could be counted on to deliver.

Preparation isn't optional. Take control of your environment. Make time to build your people. It's the price of admission for exceptional results.

Mastery

Mastery ensures the team performs with confidence and precision, even when the pressure is high and you're not there.

British sea crews were renowned for their technical skill and discipline. While the French boasted larger ships and more firepower, the English consistently outperformed them by maximizing their tools with lethal precision and speed.[85]

This edge was clearest in their ability to execute complex maneuvers, rapid-fire sequences, and intricate anchoring tactics—even in the bedlam of battle. Nelson's leaders, equally bold and skilled, exploited these advantages. Foley's risk-taking, for example, paid off in spades when he was able to suddenly position his ship at the point of greatest advantage.

Technical mastery reinforces psychological readiness. Mastering your craft—especially under pressure—builds confidence not only in your own abilities, but in the belief that those around you can perform just as well, or better. That shared self-assurance conditions a team to take bold, calculated risks, even amid the uncertainty of conflict.

The ultimate test came during the battle. Nelson was wounded and temporarily incapacitated, bleeding so badly he believed he was dying. Yet his captains fought on, unshaken. Mastery enabled them to act independently without losing sight of what victory looked like.

Mastery, supported by preparation, provides the certainty, confidence, and consistency required to exceed expectations without supervision. Nelson didn't just prepare his captains for chaos—he ensured they could dominate within it.

The Human Element

Finally, relinquished control requires convincing others to take risks because they want the win as badly as you do. That means influencing people, treating them as humans and not as expendable cogs in a wheel.

For Nelson, leadership wasn't just about treating his captains with dignity and respect. It was about empowering them to realize their ambitions while advancing the mission. Like him, they were professionals, just as hungry for opportunities to prove themselves.

At the Nile, they rose to the occasion. The more traditional, top-down Lord Howe remarked in astonishment. Not only was the victory unparalleled, he wrote, but the most remarkable aspect of it was that every one of Nelson's captains not only had the opportunity to distinguish himself, but did.[86]

The heart of Nelson's success was the understanding that people—especially seasoned professionals—cannot be controlled. He famously noted, "The best way to control veteran subordinates was not to try."[87] It is equally an astute observation as a personal confession.

Nelson embodied the balance between influence and autonomy by deliberately involving his captains in planning and decision-making. He didn't dictate. He guided. Through open dialogue, he often framed his ideas in ways that allowed others to claim them as their own. This people-centric approach fostered trust, alignment, and an ownership mentality among the very individuals expected to deliver victory.

Nelson's human approach wasn't altruistic. He did it because it supported his philosophy of warfare. His style demanded personal initiative and boldness—even the courage to disobey orders if the situation called for it. To achieve that, Nelson prepared his captains so thoroughly in his vision and intent that they could adapt seamlessly to changing conditions.

By engaging his captains as individuals with something to prove, empowering their autonomy, and aligning them to a shared vision, Nelson transformed relinquished control into a force multiplier. It wasn't about letting go. It was about building trust strong enough to make chaos work for them rather than force them to react to it.

The French flagship L'Orient explodes mid-battle. Once Nelson gave the order to attack, his captains adapted in real time, supporting one another while steadily gaining the upper hand. When Nelson was wounded, they still pressed on. Their preparation, mastery, and mutual trust gave them the edge they needed to break the French fleet. (Image: Courtesy of Alamy)

A Sword and A Shield

Nelson's ability to relinquish control allowed his team to weaponize chaos as well as weather its effects. They exploited the progressive disorder they unleashed, forcing his opponents into a purely reactive state. That disruption shattered not just their plans—if they had any—but their psychological footing, leaving them vulnerable to every unexpected turn.

Nelson and his team deliberately kept the pressure on. With each strike, his captains compounded the confusion, seizing the upper hand while triggering a cascade of panic among the French. They didn't allow the chaos to distract them. Mentally and emotionally aligned, they stayed locked in on the mission. They supported one another inside the very storm they had unleashed and kept pressing the attack.

How can modern leaders achieve this kind of dual mastery of chaos? How can they confound their competitors with their results? How can they remain intact and focused amid chaotic environments?

Nelson's success wasn't just about letting go; it was rooted in a deeper philosophy of leadership and management. That philosophy, embodied in the principles of Mission Command, offers a timeless framework for thriving in uncertainty and leading with precision through chaos.

A Philosophy of Decentralized Leadership

Mission Command isn't tied to a specific era, industry, or team size. Whether you're an 18th-century admiral, a modern-day CEO, or the leader of a ten-person unit, the principle remains: empower those closest to the action to make decisions that support the broader objective.

To understand its power, we have to look at the conditions that demanded it.

In the late 18th and early 19th centuries, science and technology were transforming how nations fought. Improved logistics—especially roads and supply systems—enabled armies to move farther, operate longer, and strike faster. Forces could now divide across miles of terrain and still converge on an enemy with precision and surprise. These new capabilities made deception possible at scale, disorienting enemies and dismantling their ability to respond.

No one used this more effectively than Napoleon. In 1806, at Jena-Auerstedt, he humiliated the highly regarded Prussian military. The loss wasn't just tactical—it exposed the rigidity of traditional command. In response, Prussian thinkers led a revolution in military philosophy.[88]

Their answer was **Auftragstaktik**—what English-speaking militaries today call **Mission Command**.

It was a radical shift in an industry characterized by obedience. Commanders would still set the overall vision, but they would delegate authority to junior and mid-level leaders to decide how best to achieve it. The people on the ground were now responsible for turning intent into action.[89]

Mission Command rejected the top-down model. Instead of waiting for orders, leaders were expected to act based on local conditions, even if that meant overriding outdated directives. Initiative wasn't punished; it was expected.

Done well, this approach turns volatility into opportunity. It prevents delays, avoids bottlenecks, and keeps momentum alive—even when conditions shift.

The Art of Relinquishing Control

Mission Command offers a powerful competitive advantage to its practitioners. But adopting it requires a counterintuitive approach to leadership and management.

First, leaders must think in essentials. Not everything is important in the moment. The art of relinquishing lies in stripping away complexity so that everyone—especially front-line personnel—can retain what matters most amid the noise and pressure.

Second, leaders must communicate clearly about what needs to be achieved, while resisting the temptation to dictate how it should be done. That's for their people to determine through experience, initiative, and judgment.

Third, planning must be flexible. Something will always go off script, and the fault will rarely lie with the person executing. The system must be built with that reality in mind.

Above all, leaders must invest in developing their people— through coaching, mentoring, and real-time guidance. Mission Command is for professionals only. It cannot survive in organizations where development is delayed because leaders are "too busy," or in cultures that claim to empower while enforcing excessive control.

A Deeper Level of Engagement

Mission Command isn't about giving orders and stepping back. It's demanding—physically, mentally, and emotionally. It means building a team, connecting them to the strategy, and ensuring they're prepared to navigate chaos.

That requires constant engagement. Leaders must move fluidly between people and mission, between oversight and support. They must ensure alignment, clarify intent, and anticipate obstacles—internal and external—so they can be removed before the team ever hits them. Their job is to make the team the stars, not themselves.

Paradoxically, decentralized execution requires centralized standards. There must be consistency in thought, language, and action across the organization. From the front line to the executive suite, everyone must speak the same operational language for planning, tasking, and decision-making.

Just as critically, Mission Command requires a forward-focused culture. Teams that are expected to take initiative must operate in a system that promotes judgment, boldness, and responsibility. If those values aren't cultivated and rewarded, initiative dies.

Most of all, Mission Command demands presence. Leaders can't lead from behind a desk. They must be out front, setting the tone, upholding standards, and embodying the tempo they expect from others.

Of course, leaders can't be everywhere at once. So they position themselves at key points in the project—not to micromanage, but to ensure decisive moments aren't missed and to accelerate support when needed.

Teams must step up, too. They must seek clarity when direction is lacking, own their performance, and hold each other accountable. They also must be ready, willing, and able to take the reins when the situation demands it.

The Benefits of Mission Command

Why adopt this philosophy of relinquished control? Consider the strategic return:

- **It Unlocks Productive Power.** Teams don't just do their jobs—they drive big outcomes. They solve problems without burdening leadership, exceed expectations under pressure, and influence strategy from the ground up. These teams become internal benchmarks.

- **It Builds Durable Teams.** Unity is easy in calm waters. Mission Command sustains it under pressure. Involving the team in execution strengthens commitment—to each other, the mission, and the leader. The result is shared ownership, not passive compliance.

- **It Increases Engagement**. Mission Command gives people ownership of outcomes. That autonomy, combined with clarity and trust, creates high-performing teams where individuals are more satisfied, more committed, and more likely to take smart risks. Discretionary effort goes up along with performance and retention.

- **It Drives Continuous Learning.** After-action reflection is built into Mission Command. Teams learn quickly from failure, recalibrate, and adapt. This habit of deliberate improvement strengthens organizational learning and positions the team to handle larger, more complex challenges over time.

- **It Builds Bench-Strength.** Mission Command creates

future leaders, not just better followers. As team members learn to think, decide, and act independently, they develop the judgment and confidence leaders need. That doesn't just ease the load on senior leadership. It builds a deep bench of proven talent ready to step up when it counts.

- **It Delivers a Competitive Advantage.** In high-pressure environments, speed and execution win. Mission Command creates teams that don't freeze when conditions change. They act fast, solve problems without waiting, and keep momentum when others stall. That agility compounds—and becomes the edge that separates winners from everyone else.

Then there are the personal benefits to you.

- **It Makes Your Life Easier.** Letting go of control over something you're responsible for isn't easy: it takes time, patience, and discipline. But once you learn to do it wisely, the benefits are clear. You'll guide your team forward without getting dragged into every minor issue. The bonus? Your people will thank you for trusting them instead of stepping in to do it for them.

- **It Leads to a More Satisfying Professional Experience.** A high-performing team creates momentum. Momentum makes work meaningful. When people are trusted to think, solve, and deliver, they show up stronger. And when your team thrives, so do you. The job stops being a grind and starts becoming something fun and fulfilling.

- **It Prepares You for Executive Trials.** Building and leading a professional team is the best preparation for greater responsibility. Success builds confidence, and the skills you develop now will serve you across teams and industries. As your reputation grows, so does your ability to win trust, secure resources, and unlock bigger opportunities. Leading well now sets the stage for leading better in the future.

Overcoming Obstacles

If Mission Command is so great, why doesn't everyone use it? Here are the most common reasons why some leaders avoid it:

"Command": Strip away the image of an authoritarian. The real meaning of command is simple: to exert purposeful influence over people and events. That's the job. As leaders, we aim to command attention, respect, and action. No other word captures the blend of leadership and management as precisely.

Business is not war: Some dismiss Mission Command as irrelevant to the private sector. It's a common objection—and it's dead wrong. Ignoring this approach means overlooking a critical part of human experience, particularly one centered on leading and managing in chaos.

The key to overcoming this misconception is thinking conceptually. Focus on the similarities, not the differences. Generals (C-Suite), their staffs (VPs), and subordinate leaders (directors, managers, supervisors) all guide front-line teams against enemy forces (competitors). Both must navigate friction—whether internal politics or external challenges—and neutral factors like weather or geopolitical events. In business, these challenges might take the form of recessions, pandemics, or supply chain disruptions. While the contexts differ, the principles remain the same.

Fear of relinquishing control: The greatest obstacle to

Mission Command is you. Your natural behaviors and professional experiences shape your preference for control, directly influencing your ability to delegate effectively. This struggle is particularly acute for entrepreneurs and small business owners. With so much at stake, the fear of losing control feels justified. As a result, they instinctively tighten their grip on people and processes, attempting to manage every detail. Ironically, this approach often backfires, leaving them consumed by their businesses instead of leading them.

Cultural misalignment: Excessively mission-oriented cultures often equate independence and freedom with a loss of quality control, leading to rigidity that stifles initiative and disregards the human element. On the flip side, overly people-oriented cultures celebrate autonomy but fail to enforce accountability, enabling subpar performance that ultimately demotivates the team. Both extremes create obstacles to embracing Mission Command, which relies on balancing autonomy with alignment and accountability.

Accepting Mission Command

Mission Command only works if you reframe your role. You're not here to control chaos. You're here to build a team that can fight through it.

Reorient Yourself to Your Role

Your job is to build a team that can deliver—under pressure, without you in the room. That requires development, preparation, and coaching. It's not a bonus. It's the job.

Accept that chaos is inevitable. Plans will change, and people may react unpredictably under pressure. Acknowledging this reality allows you to approach surprises and setbacks with composure and self-control. Rather than chasing a perfect plan, focus on minimizing the impact of mistakes or mishaps and capitalizing on the opportunities they often create.

Acknowledge the Control Factor

You must come to grips with the fact that chaos affects everyone differently. Some people withdraw from it. Others lean in. Control-oriented individuals often step forward, trying to assert direction or bypass what they see as unnecessary procedures. That instinct can be a liability—or an asset—depending on how you lead. Recognize initiative for what it is: energy that wants to be useful. Your job is to guide it, not squash it. But if someone becomes disruptive or undermines cohesion, you must be ready to correct and coach them—or, in the worst case, remove them.

Understanding the Control Factor means knowing both yourself and your team. Who thrives under pressure? Who hides? Who needs a firmer hand? Establish yourself as a leader who is in control: fair, firm, and decisive.

Acknowledge the Nonlinear Path to Success

Success is rarely a straight line. The fog of war and friction will obscure the way forward and slow your progress. Mistakes are inevitable, but harsh punishment—whether directed at yourself or your team—does more harm than good. Instead, focus on completing the mission to the best of your ability. Celebrate your team's initiative, and treat mistakes as chances to sharpen judgment and avoid repeat errors.

People Perform Best When They Feel Valued

The team—not you—is the most valuable asset. They are the ones executing your vision, so recognizing and rewarding their efforts is crucial. Acknowledging their contributions fosters loyalty, trust, and a sense of shared purpose, all of which strengthen the team's cohesion and durability.

Those in the trenches are best positioned to identify opportunities for improvement. Don't become the aloof manager, cut off from the reality they live every day. Stay connected. Use their insights to refine strategy and support senior leadership. This not only sharpens decisions—it proves the value you and your team bring to the mission.

Real success comes from alignment at every level. On the ground, team members must support each other to accomplish their tasks. But that same coordination must exist at the operational level, ensuring the entire operation moves as one, not as disconnected parts.

Adopting Mission Command

Beyond preparation, technical mastery, and the human element of leadership—as demonstrated by the Nelson example—here are concrete steps to help you relinquish control effectively.

Assume you will lose control. That's right—prepare as if all contact with your team will be cut off once the assignment begins. The fog of war will separate you from them, yet they will still need to execute the mission without your direct input. And yes, you'll still be held accountable for their results. With that reality in mind, focus on preparing both yourself and your team to operate independently while staying aligned with the organization's broader goals.

Learn to balance mission and people priorities. Neither pillar should dominate the other, yet achieving this balance can be incredibly challenging. Imbalance risks disincentivizing your people from taking personal initiative. If you're intensely mission-focused, make sure you don't come across as indifferent or dismissive when their input matters most. Take time to understand them, show genuine concern for their well-being, and build trust.

If you lean heavily toward people, don't lose sight of the mission. Your team exists to deliver results. Keep them focused, encourage calculated risks, and enforce accountability. Don't avoid hard conversations out of fear of upsetting feelings. Address non-performers quickly to prevent distractions or a breakdown in team culture.

Think in terms of outcomes. Your job isn't to assign every task—that's impossible in a changing landscape. Instead, your job is to define what success looks like. That means clearly articulating the desired end-state: what exactly must be achieved, why it matters, and which elements of success are non-negotiable. By defining the "what," you give your team the freedom and responsibility to determine the "how." This sharpens decision-making, encourages ownership, and builds the autonomy required to thrive in chaos.

Sharpen your delegation skills. Mission Command thrives on delegated authority, but people respond to it in diverse ways. Overly specific guidance limits flexibility and stifles your team's ability to exercise judgment. On the other hand, instructions that are too broad can lead to confusion, faulty assumptions, or allow more dominant personalities to take control. To delegate effectively, tailor your communication to each team member's need for structure and the level of detail they require to operate independently within the mission's parameters.

Focus on developing and protecting trust. Assume

your life depends on it. In many ways, it does. Trust is the foundation of reliability, creating the psychological safety your team needs to take risks and deliver results. Your people must believe you have their back if you expect them to take bold actions on your behalf. Because trust is so nuanced and critical, the next chapter explores it as the final step to gaining strength in chaos.

From Execution to Sustained Success

Mission Command isn't just a historical artifact—it's a modern leadership framework for navigating uncertainty and seizing hidden opportunities. When applied with intention, it unlocks a team's ability to adapt, innovate, and perform under pressure. Like Nelson's captains, today's teams can turn it into both a sword and a shield in competitive environments.

But Mission Command can't stand alone. In the next chapter, we explore trust, the lifeblood of leadership in chaos. It's what holds teams together when pressure mounts and what sustains them over time, making them reliable in the eyes of teammates, leaders, and the organization they serve. Master trust, and you unlock the final key to reaching your team's Productive Power.

Chapter 11
Trust

A team that achieves the first three levels of Constructive Chaos has accomplished something significant. The next challenge is sustaining that achievement over time. Trust—the final level in gaining strength through chaos—makes that possible.

Trust is verified reliability. In chaos, it's the conviction, born of experience and observation, that someone will willingly absorb the kind of stress that causes others to freeze, falter, or retreat. It means they can be counted on to make the hard, uncomfortable, but necessary decisions to achieve the mission. That's why trust isn't built on blind faith or good intentions; it's built on pattern recognition and proven performance.

We trust people to do what they're supposed to do because we've seen them do it—again and again, when it mattered. Trust is confidence grounded in past behavior, giving you reasonable certainty about how someone will perform under pressure.

It isn't instant. Trust is earned. That's why it's priceless—and why it stands as the final level of Constructive Chaos. It comes only through repetition, trial and error, and the hard-won clarity of watching who refines, adapts, and improves, even when growth demands extra effort.

For leaders and teams striving to become strong, Trust closes the loop on Constructive Chaos. It sustains Unity through friction, ensures focus and efficiency through Forward Integration, and upholds Mission Command when pressure tempts leaders to overcontrol. Without Trust, each level can rapidly unravel.

In this chapter, we'll break down how trust is built and maintained. Specifically, we'll examine:

- **The Cognitive Factor** in Trust—what's within your control to develop

- **Unreliable Indicators** of Trust—external signals that distort judgment and create false confidence or misplaced doubt

- **The Behavioral Factor** in Trust—how unconscious patterns shape our perception of who is (and isn't) trustworthy.

To drive this home, we'll study one of the most important, effective, and trustworthy leaders in modern history: George C. Marshall. His ability to build and sustain trust under extraordinary pressure was a decisive factor in the Allies securing victory in World War II. But first, let's examine why trust matters beyond any moral or ethical appeal.

The Practical Value of Trust

Just as chaos is more than a vague emotional response to disorder, trust isn't just an abstract virtue or feel-good ideal. No, it's a concrete asset with real, measurable value in teams. Understanding its impact isn't optional if you want to take your team to its Productive Power.

First, trust leads to original or creative solutions. It encourages team members to speak up, challenge assumptions, and actively contribute to success without fear of retribution or unfair judgment.

Second, trust accelerates sound decision-making. A leader who trusts their team receives real-time insights and actionable solutions grounded in reality—not just filtered reports designed to avoid upsetting leadership. Teams that provide reliable updates and well-considered options free their leader to make fast, high-quality decisions—without getting bogged down in unnecessary details or endless evaluations.

Third, trust unlocks individual potential. When people trust their leader and teammates, they focus on doing great work instead of managing appearances. A team built on trust wastes no energy on pretense, second-guessing, or hidden agendas. Instead, teammates lean on each other's expertise, ensuring that the best ideas—not the loudest voices—drive action.

Fourth, trust accelerates integration. In high-trust environments, new people and new ideas are absorbed faster. Teams don't waste time vetting motives or protecting turf—they adapt, apply, and move forward without agendas. Trust reduces the internal friction that comes with change.

Finally, trust empowers improvisation. When trust is strong, teams take calculated risks, self-correct without waiting for orders, and improve processes before problems fully surface. They don't just react to chaos—they stay ahead of it.

A trustworthy team *is* a competitive advantage. And it has real dollar value. What would a serious, competitive company pay for a team that solves problems fast, adapts under pressure, and executes without politics or drama? Millions. Because that kind of rare team can be counted on to consistently deliver outcomes far beyond their cost.

As you can see, trust isn't just an ethical benchmark. It's also a state of being that allows high-functioning teams to reliably deliver extraordinary results in high-risk environments. Few understood this better than George C. Marshall.

The Archetype of Trust

George C. Marshall is often considered the most important American leader since George Washington. His achievements as a soldier and statesman are nearly unparalleled in American history.

A glance at Marshall's accolades reveals a leader of extraordinary caliber. He is the only soldier to receive the Nobel Peace Prize, for the Marshall Plan, which saved Europe from starvation and communist expansion. He served as Army Chief of Staff, Secretary of Defense, Secretary of State, and even led the Red Cross. Winston Churchill called him the "Architect of Victory" for Allied victory in World War II.[90] President Franklin D. Roosevelt considered him absolutely indispensable, while Harry Truman called him "the greatest living American."[91] Even Stalin acknowledged his integrity, declaring, "I would trust General Marshall with my life.[92]

Marshall's influence extended far beyond government and the military. Peter Drucker, the patriarch of executive management, hailed him as one of the 20th century's greatest leaders and industrial managers, featuring his leadership model in *The Effective Executive*. Fred W. Smith, founder and CEO of Federal Express, shared Drucker's admiration: "As I grew up, I searched for role models in all the history I read. And I've tried to model my life on Marshall's leadership."[93]

What set Marshall apart from his contemporaries was his ability to impose order on chaos at the highest levels. Nowhere was this more evident than in his service during World War II. Time and again, he reinforced Unity, drove Forward Integration, and cultivated Mission Command across the entire Allied war effort. The result was Trust—earned from the Army, the president, and the nation.

Marshall became Army Chief of Staff on September 1, 1939—the same day Germany invaded Poland. World War II officially began. The obstacles he faced on the first day on the job were staggering:

- **Convincing a war-weary nation**—still reeling from World War I and the Great Depression—to prepare for another global conflict.

- **Fighting fierce political resistance** from those who were determined to keep America out of another European war.

- **Overcoming skepticism from allies** who viewed American military leadership as inferior—particularly the British high command, which dismissed U.S. military leadership as inexperienced or naïve.

- **Navigating uneasy partnerships**, most notably with the Soviet Union, which had initially allied with Hitler before being invaded and turning to the Allies for help.

- **Coordinating a global war effort** that required supplying England, China, and later the Soviet Union with critical resources needed for home.

Yet one problem overshadowed all others: the US Army was unfit for modern war. By 1939, it had only 197,000 active-duty soldiers, ranking 19th in the world in size, right beyond Portugal. Plus, its tactics and equipment were outdated.[94] Its tactics and equipment were grossly outdated. Fixing it required more than just new recruits and new rifles—it demanded a complete overhaul of its structure, equipment, tactics, and leadership.

Dire Times Require Drastic Changes

The Army needed soldiers, fast. Getting them meant a ferocious fight in the political arena. Marshall went to Congress and played a pivotal role in securing the Selective Training and Service Act of 1940—one of the most controversial measures in American history: the first peacetime draft. It was his reputation as a consummate professional, with no perceived political agenda, that helped convince a skeptical and largely non-interventionist civilian government to conscript its young men for a war—a European one, thousands of miles away. It was no small task. Yet, Marshall's relentless drive helped overcome the resistance, ensuring the Army had its ranks filled when the country was swept into the deadliest conflict in human history.[95]

Then there was the issue of performance. The U.S. Army simply wasn't ready for modern war. This was the age of Blitzkrieg, or *lightning warfare.*

In World War I, Germany spent four years trying—and failing—to take France, losing nearly a million soldiers in the process. But in 1940, using coordinated tank assaults, fighter aircraft, and highly mobile ground forces—practicing Mission Command—the Wehrmacht conquered the country in less than five weeks, and at a fraction of the cost in lives and resources.[96]

The U.S. Army of 1939 couldn't compete. It was still structured for the trenches and its slow, rigid, and methodical pace. If it didn't evolve, it too would be decisively outmaneuvered and annihilated like so many other superior European armies.

But fixing equipment and tactics wasn't enough. The most urgent transformation had to happen in the Army's mindset. The old military culture, Marshall observed, "achieved obedience at the expense of initiative. It excluded 'thought' of any kind."[97] That wasn't just outdated—it was a death sentence in a modern war where chaos was intentionally weaponized.

General George C. Marshall. The gold standard of leadership and executive management. America's first Five-Star General, Marshall rebuilt the U.S. Army from a third-rate force into the most powerful military on Earth. He cut through politics, cleared out the "deadwood" in senior officer ranks, and promoted purely on merit. There has been no modern equivalent since. (Photo: Courtesy of the George C. Marshall Foundation in Lexington, Virginia.)

Battlefield success depended on rapid adaptability. Soldiers couldn't afford to wait for orders: they had to show initiative and exploit opportunities as they arose. But that required discipline—not the blind obedience of the past, but one rooted in judgment and sound risk-taking. As Marshall emphasized, discipline had to be "based on respect rather than fear; on the effect of good example given by officers; on the intelligent comprehension by all ranks of why an order has to be and why it must be carried out."[98] Marshall's vision demanded soldiers who didn't just follow orders—they had to understand them, adapt, and think on their feet. Anything less meant failure.

Changes in leadership were essential. So, Marshall famously began clearing out the "deadwood"—the old, inflexible officers who couldn't keep up with the demands of blitzkrieg warfare. In a bold and controversial move, he fired more than 600 senior officers, including generals with powerful political connections.[99] Reflecting on the decision, Marshall later said, "I was accused of getting rid of all the brains in the Army, but I was eliminating considerable arteriosclerosis."[100]

Marshall then overhauled the Army's promotion system, prioritizing merit over seniority. One of the clearest examples was his protégé, Dwight D. Eisenhower. In 1941, he held the rank of lieutenant colonel—the military equivalent of a mid-level director in a Fortune 500 company. Just three years later, Eisenhower rose to five-star general—akin to becoming the CEO or a senior board member of that same company.

One of Marshall's most critical contributions was unifying the Western Allies by shaping the Combined Chiefs of Staff (CCS)—the senior American and British military leadership coordinating the war effort. Established in 1942, the CCS kept Allied operations strategically aligned across multiple theaters, avoiding duplication, inefficiency, and internal conflict. Without coordination, the Allies could have easily sabotaged their own war effort—just as the Axis ultimately did.

The CCS became the central platform through which Marshall advanced and maintained one of his most consequential strategic achievements—the "Europe First" policy. While Pearl Harbor triggered an emotional push for immediate retaliation against Japan, Marshall recognized that Nazi Germany posed the greater threat. With Great Britain and the Soviet Union nearing collapse, he secured a unified Allied strategy focused on defeating Germany first before turning full attention to Japan.

Marshall's efforts decisively contributed to the Allied victory. Within four years, the Third Reich and Imperial Japan were utterly destroyed. The United States emerged as a superpower, and its army—peaking at 8.3 million strong—became the world's premier modern military force.[101]

Marshall's Leadership

Marshall's success wasn't luck. It came from a precise balance between executing the mission and taking care of his people.

When asked what makes a good leader in war, his answer was equally relevant to leaders in chaos: *common sense, physical strength, energy, cheerfulness*, and *optimism*. But leadership wasn't just about personal traits. He also emphasized *mastery of the profession, unwavering loyalty*, and *relentless determination* in adversity.[102]

The Joint Chiefs of Staff. Army. Navy. Air Corps. Four leaders, three institutions, one war. At Marshall's insistence, they met for lunch every week—no aides, no politics. Ego and interservice rivalry were replaced with collaboration, coordination, and mutual accountability. These meetings became the living embodiment of Unity and Forward Integration at the highest level. (Photo: Courtesy of the George C. Marshall Foundation in Lexington, Virginia.)

Marshall's leadership embodied the very essence of strength in chaos. The following lessons show how he applied its principles in real time.

Know who you work for. Marshall never lost sight of his responsibility to the American people. Their country was built on democracy and individual freedom, and that meant his army would not treat soldiers as cannon fodder.

Extreme accountability. Marshall had no patience for mediocrity. Just as American soldiers received the best training, resources, and equipment, they also deserved the best leadership.

His generals didn't need to be tactical geniuses—but they had to be competent, adaptable, and cooperative. Most of all, they had to deliver. As author Tom Ricks put it, Marshall's expectations of them were simple: "Succeed, die, or be replaced."[103]

Success is all business. Marshall's firings weren't punitive or career-ending moves. Being relieved simply meant someone wasn't the right fit for that role—nothing more. In fact, some generals he relieved were later promoted to roles that better matched their strengths.[104]

Adopt the *Forward* mindset. Marshall had no patience for excuses. Great leaders don't complain about what they lack— they overcome. "The truly great leader overcomes all difficulties," Marshall told a class of officer candidates in 1940, "The lack of equipment, the lack of food, the lack of this or that are only excuses. The real leader displays his quality in his triumphs over adversity, however great it may be."[105]

Get things done. Marshall was a man of action and outcomes. He demanded the same from his subordinates. Meetings existed to make decisions, not to host endless debates. Every participant was expected to come prepared, armed with both an informed opinion and a recommended course of action. If you couldn't do that, you didn't belong in the room.[106]

Simplify everything. Reduce complexity to its bare essentials, then communicate those essentials clearly and succinctly—so that everyone, regardless of rank or position, can understand. Memos, for example, were expected to be no longer than one page. Marshall believed that if you couldn't distill an issue to its core, you didn't truly understand what you are trying to communicate.[107]

General George C. Marshall at Fort Benning, 1940. He never forgot the American soldier—the one asked to risk everything for victory. He went to extraordinary lengths to take care of them, making sure they had everything needed to succeed, including competent leaders. Behind his icy, no-nonsense reputation was a deep loyalty to everyone who served—from the front lines to the supply lines. (Photo: Courtesy of the George C. Marshall Foundation in Lexington, Virginia.)

Truth to Power. Marshall never withheld objective facts to protect himself. During World War I and as a mid-level officer, he directly challenged General Pershing, the commander of all American forces in France. Years later, he openly refused to go along with President Roosevelt's opinion on how to man the services. In both moments, the consensus of other officers was that Marshall had ended his career. Instead, they cemented his reputation as the man who told the truth, no matter the stakes. And in both cases, he was elevated to the most trusted positions.

Embrace and protect teamwork. For Marshall, teamwork was non-negotiable. He had no tolerance for leaders who operated in silos or put personal agendas ahead of the mission. A failure to cooperate was, by itself, grounds for removal. For example, he seriously considered firing Brigadier General Simon Buckner, Jr. for openly reading a poem mocking the Navy—a rival service, but still a teammate.[108]

The Mission Side of Marshall

Marshall's leadership wasn't just about setting high standards. It was about making hard decisions in real time—and doing so without hesitation. The following moments illustrate why he became the ultimate archetype of Trust.

Deferring to Admiral King

By all rights, Marshall could have fought for the top spot in the Combined Chiefs of Staff. But he didn't. Admiral Ernest King wanted it.

King's reputation was legendary. He was notoriously irritable, aggressive, and difficult to work with. His abrasive nature often clashed with both British high command and his own American counterparts. Even his own daughter once remarked, "He is the most even-tempered man in the Navy. He is always in a rage."[109]

Rather than waste energy on an internal power struggle, Marshall let King take the top role. This wasn't selflessness—it was strategic. Putting an intensely control-oriented King into a subordinate role would only create unnecessary friction between the Army and Navy—at a time when absolute coordination was critical to winning the war.

By stepping aside, Marshall didn't lose power—he prevented potential chaos from becoming a distraction. He preserved Unity, reinforced trust between services, and kept the military focused on defeating the enemy rather than fighting itself.

Churchill & Rhodes

Winston Churchill, Prime Minister of the United Kingdom and counterpart to the President of the United States, was one of the most forceful personalities of World War II. Charismatic and bold, he was also prone to grand ideas and emotional decision-making.

Eager to recover British control in the Mediterranean, he pushed for an operation to seize the island of Rhodes off the coast of Turkey. "His Majesty's Government can't have troops standing idle. Muskets must flame."

To Churchill, inaction meant further delaying Britain's ability to reclaim lost imperial power. Marshall saw through it immediately. It was a distraction, one that risked diluting the focus of the entire Allied effort.

In a rare moment of visible irritation, he snapped: "Not one American soldier is going to die on [that] goddamned beach."[110] That ended the discussion. American forces would stay focused on what mattered most: defeating the Axis as swiftly as possible, and the road to victory led directly to Berlin.

D-Day & Marshall's Hardest Decision

By 1944, Marshall had served for nearly 45 years in the US Army. He had trained, studied, and mastered the art of war. And like every infantry officer, he wanted one thing—a combat command, the opportunity to lead troops into battle.

He was the most qualified man to lead the D-Day invasion. But Franklin D. Roosevelt saw things differently. "I feel I could not sleep at night with you out of the country," the president confessed to his top general.[111]

At the defining moment of his career, Marshall didn't argue or lobby for the role. He told the president that he "would cheerfully go whatever way he wanted me to go."[112]

Roosevelt made the call: Marshall would stay in Washington. His protégé, Eisenhower, would lead the long-awaited invasion into Fortress Europa.

Marshall didn't complain, didn't show resentment, and didn't look back. For him, success was never about his personal ambition—it was about accomplishing the mission as a team, and he was doing his part.

The People Side of Marshall

Despite his reputation as an icy, cold-blooded executive, Marshall never lost sight of who the Army existed to serve. Every day, he carved out at least 20 minutes to read letters from soldiers and their families. When complaints came in, he either responded himself or made sure they were handled immediately.[113]

One of the most fascinating observations on Marshall's leadership came from an unlikely source: Hollywood.

On July 27, 1970, Orson Welles, the legendary director of *Citizen Kane*, appeared on *The Dick Cavett Show*. During the interview, Welles reflected on his encounters with world leaders, including Churchill, Roosevelt, and even Adolf Hitler. When asked who impressed him the most, Welles responded without hesitation: George Marshall. He described Marshall as "the greatest man I ever met" and "the greatest human being who was also a great man."

Welles recounted a story. At a party celebrating Roosevelt's re-election, a young soldier entered the ballroom and recognized Marshall. He nervously approached him. Surrounded by high-ranking officials and the grandeur of the evening, Marshall stepped away, sat down with the young man, and made him feel welcome.

Welles stressed that Marshall didn't know he was being watched. He simply took the soldier aside and spoke with him for half an hour, ensuring he felt at ease. This quiet act of kindness—by the man leading the Allied war effort—was done without audience or expectation. It showed that beneath the uniform was a leader who never forgot the citizens he served, or the sons and daughters they had entrusted to him.

Reflecting on Marshall's legacy, Welles emphasized that his willingness to engage with anyone—regardless of status—set him apart from other leaders. Welles concluded by calling him "a tremendous gentleman, an old-fashioned institution which isn't with us anymore."

Developing Trust

How do you gain the trust needed to master this final level of Constructive Chaos? In my experience, three key aspects are critical: the **cognitive factor**, which is fully within your control; **unreliable indicators**, which can mislead you; and the **behavioral factor**, which often creates blind spots through a lack of self-awareness. Mastering trust requires understanding all three.

The Cognitive Factor in Trust

There are four factors you must consciously develop to earn trust as a leader: Intellectual Honesty, Competency, Adaptability, and Productive Purpose. These are non-negotiable if you and your team are going to succeed in chaos.

Intellectual Honesty

Trust begins with a leader's ability to see reality as it is, not as they wish it to be. Intellectual honesty means confronting hard truths—about yourself, your team, and your situation—no matter how uncomfortable that might be.

Consider a marketing executive who founds a software company. While brilliant at branding, he is out of his depth as CEO, struggling with decision-making and focusing only on marketing while neglecting the rest of the organization. Instead of recognizing this blind spot and seeking help, he clings to his title, convinced it proves his capability. His team sees the cracks, but he refuses to. Over time, they lose trust in his leadership. Worse, they stop bringing him problems, knowing he won't face them.

When you practice intellectual honesty, you show your team that truth is safe, clarity matters, and reality—not ego—will drive action. That's how you create a culture of accountability and trust, even in chaos. Without it, you don't just lose trust; you invite dysfunction, silence, and failure.

Competency

In stability, you can bluff. In chaos, you're exposed. Competency isn't a nice-to-have—it's mandatory for trust.

Nothing destroys trust faster than pretending knowledge you don't have. Your title won't save you when pressure hits; only your proven capability will. People don't follow leaders who are faking it, especially when stakes are high. Your team must see that you deserve your role, that you possess the judgment, knowledge, and skills required—or that you're relentlessly working to gain them.

Competency involves more than technical skills. It's equally about navigating people and personalities. You might be brilliant at strategy, but if you fail to handle difficult individuals or interpersonal conflicts, trust quickly evaporates. Conversely, you may be charismatic and inspiring, but without strategic understanding, you'll eventually betray your team's confidence.

Your team isn't expecting perfection. They're expecting growth. Trust comes when they see you continually sharpening your skills, improving your judgment, and committing to be better every day. That's how you earn the right to lead when the chaos hits.

Self-Control

Chaos invokes frustration, stress, and fear. In those moments, trust isn't built by fake confidence or naïve positivity—it's built by self-control.

Self-control enables adaptability. Without it, leaders swing between emotional extremes. Rigid leaders refuse to change course when the situation demands it. That stubbornness signals insecurity or delusion. Impulsive leaders, by contrast, overcorrect. They bounce from one reaction to the next, forcing the team to adapt not to the chaos, but to their boss's volatility. Both destroy trust.

Self-control reinforces resilience. A leader who holds steady when the environment turns volatile becomes a psychological anchor for the team. They create stability just by how they carry themselves. That's extraordinarily powerful. By setting the example, others learn to regulate themselves and stay focused on the mission.

A leader's emotional state sets the tone for the rest of the team. If they see you pause, read the moment, and act deliberately—even when it's hard—they'll follow you. Not just because they have to. Because they trust you.

Respect

People shouldn't follow you out of duty. They follow because they believe they can win through your leadership—and because they believe their contributions matter.

When leaders respect their people's time, effort, and commitment, they lay the foundation for trust. People give their best when they know leadership has their back and values their contribution.

The fastest way to break trust? Waste their time. Treat them like expendable cogs. Ignore their strengths or their input. Even the perception that you're taking advantage of them can unravel everything.

To build trust, recognize their work. Show them how it matters. Emphasize that they're needed.

And protect them—aggressively. Don't let dysfunction, double standards, or outside interference erode the trust they've invested in the mission. Stand up for them now, and they'll stand with you when the chaos hits.

Unreliable Indicators of Trust

It's easy to mistake certain qualities or credentials as proof of trustworthiness. This is flawed thinking. These assumptions often create a false sense of security, leading leaders to trust the wrong people, for the wrong reasons. Here are some of the most common traps that sabotage leaders and their people:

Association

The fallacy of association is the belief that a shared background—same hometown, same school, same military unit, same company—automatically signals trustworthiness. It doesn't. Trust is built on choices, not common history.

People are complex, and we all process our experiences differently. Familiarity is not the same as reliability. Leaders must judge others by what they do—not by how close they feel, or what they assume others know or believe. Confusing the two creates blind spots that quietly erode judgment and weaken team performance.

Personality

Trust is built on performance and results—not surface-level traits.

For example, eccentricity doesn't make someone untrustworthy. Leaders must judge people by their consistency and effectiveness, not by how well they conform to social norms or polite expectations. That said, quirks should never be so distracting or off-putting that they disrupt team cohesion.

Consider General Stonewall Jackson, one of the most

accomplished—and oddest—military commanders in U.S. history. As a professor at VMI, his cadets called him "Tom Fool" for his bizarre habits: raising one arm while riding horseback to "balance his circulation," refusing to eat pepper because it made his left leg ache, and even falling asleep mid-meal with food still in his mouth.[114]

But when it counted, Jackson delivered extraordinary results—tactical victories with strategic consequences. His peers were left envious, his enemies in awe. Ultimately, Jackson became the most trusted lieutenant of the Confederacy's top general, Robert E. Lee.

Education

Trust is earned through performance, not credentials. Yet degrees are often mistaken for intelligence, sound judgment, or even competence. This is a serious mistake. A college diploma—especially in today's academic climate—guarantees neither critical thinking nor sanity.

In some disciplines, particularly the liberal arts, rigorous inquiry has been replaced by political activism. Academic environments that once promoted critical thinking and open debate now often reward grievance, conformity, and approved narratives. The result? Graduates who elevate personal ideology above organizational purpose.

When praised for the number of his advanced degrees, an intensely competitive senior executive correctly replied: "Degrees mean nothing without results. You know what else has degrees? Thermometers—and you know where you can stick those."

Character

Many assume that if someone seems honest, hardworking, or well-intentioned, they'll also be reliable under pressure. That is not always true. But while moral character is valuable, it doesn't guarantee trust in chaos.

Moral values matter, but so does value alignment with the team and mission. The demands of Disciplined Initiative require more than good intentions; they demand resilience, clarity, and action under stress. A preference for autonomy, a need for recognition, or a desire for harmony can either strengthen or weaken a team's performance in volatile conditions. Someone may keep their word—but will they still do so when the pressure hits?

Work Experience

Past experience is about habits. It shows how people solve problems, how much direction they need, and how they respond to structure or ambiguity. More importantly, it reveals the specific conditions, constraints, culture, and resources they're used to.

The longer someone works within a particular system, the more they become shaped by its norms—how much control they had, what pace they worked at, and what support they relied on. If your team operates differently, those habits may not transfer. They may even clash.

Trust isn't about what someone did elsewhere. It's about how well they'll function here and now.

Professional Record

Past achievements don't guarantee future ones. Awards and accolades reflect who someone was—not necessarily who they are now.

Many people live off their résumé. Their success was earned through hard work and dedication. That's commendable. But it happened under different conditions—with different people, systems, and expectations.

In my executive coaching work, I've told many experienced, confident candidates: "Great track record. Now tell me, what can you deliver today?"

That changes the conversation—big time.

Trust is earned by what someone can do now—not by what they did ten years ago.

Past success might open the door. Present performance keeps them in the room.

The Behavioral Factor in Trust

The final—and often most critical—factor in trust-building is natural behavior.

As covered in Chapter 4: *The Driver of Chaos*, natural behaviors are hardwired early. They shape how we instinctively lead, communicate, and respond under pressure. This reveals whether we lean toward mission-first or people-first leadership, and how intensely we express that orientation.

Despite the flood of personality assessments, few leaders truly understand how behavior shapes trust. What feels natural to us isn't always right or effective. There is no one-size-fits-all approach to earning trust in chaos.

Without that understanding, people naturally assume

their style is the correct one. They judge others against it. Miscommunication follows, along with unfair personal judgments that extend beyond style or personality into deeper assumptions—about mindset, values, even motive. The result is a rapid and sometimes irreparable breakdown of trust.

But when behaviors are recognized, understood, and respected for their strengths, trust deepens quickly. Teams become more adaptable, more resilient, and far more prepared for chaos.

A Matter of Impression

Mission-oriented behaviors focus on achieving the objective. People-oriented behaviors focus on creating the conditions that make mission success possible. Leaders must grasp this distinction because trust is built through behavior, and behavior always leaves an impression.

The **Vision Trait (V)** demands victory. These take-charge individuals operate at the macro level, focusing on big-picture goals and long-term impact. Gaining their trust requires proving you can deliver results. That means being able to take control of a situation wherever you are. They expect you to handle challenges independently and accomplish the objective without hesitation.

At times, they may seem overbearing or dictatorial, especially as pressure mounts. But beneath their intensity is a deep fear of losing.

How to Gain Their Trust:
- Be direct. Get to the point quickly and clearly.

- Push back when it matters. They trust people who challenge ideas, not those who protect feelings.

- Focus on solutions and momentum—not problems and excuses.

- Speak in terms of forward progress, not process.

- Show confidence and decisiveness in words, body language, and actions.

How to Lose Their Trust:
- Get bogged down in tactics or irrelevant detail.

- Fail to speak up when your voice is needed.

- Dwell on setbacks instead of driving forward.

- Display hesitation, insecurity, or passivity.

- Miss deadlines, underdeliver, or fail to follow through.

The **Task Trait (T)** expects perfect outcomes. These mission-oriented individuals are obsessed with delivering precision and quality at the micro level. For them, trust is built through consistent adherence to the highest standards and established systems.

These perfectionists are driven by the deep-seated need to ensure excellence in everything they do. Under pressure, they may come across as overbearing or rigid, demanding that everything meet exacting standards. Beneath that intensity is a fear of imperfection, because even small errors can feel catastrophic.

How to Gain Their Trust:
- Demonstrate a real drive for excellence and high standards.

- Be precise. Present details in a logical, structured order.

- Adhere to proven systems, policies, and best practices.

- Show real appreciation for their precision and discipline.

- Communicate with clarity and professionalism in both words and tone.

How to Lose Their Trust:

- Dismiss their expertise or unfairly second-guess their work.

- Display incompetence, disorganization, or carelessness.

- Push untested or overly risky ideas without clear justification.

- Communicate vaguely, imprecisely, or without sufficient detail.

- Fail to follow through on quality commitments or deadlines.

The **Relationship Trait (R)** expects a warm, safe, and ideally enjoyable workplace. These individuals build trust through connection, empathy, and collaboration. Their priority is fostering positive relationships, which makes them natural team builders and conflict diffusers.

At times, they may seem overly focused on keeping interactions pleasant. They often avoid hard conversations, especially the uncomfortable but necessary task of holding others accountable. Mission-oriented leaders may see them as prioritizing emotions over results. This trait avoids anything that might hurt feelings or damage relationships.

How to Gain Their Trust:

- Be optimistic, approachable, and most of all, friendly.

- Encourage input from everyone—especially quieter voices.

- Acknowledge accomplishments in a way that feels personal and sincere.

- Show real interest in their feedback, ideas, and personal well-being.

- Foster a collaborative space that feels welcoming and inclusive.

How to Lose Their Trust:
- Act insensitively or show indifference toward others.

- Fail to recognize contributions or dismiss their input.

- Exclude them or others from meaningful discussions.

- Downplay relationship concerns, signaling you don't value team dynamics.

- Create a work environment that feels cold, rigid, or emotionally draining.

The **Team Trait (TM)** expects harmony and undivided loyalty. These individuals thrive on ensuring team success through preparation, organization, and structure. They trust those who respect the effort *to do things right, the first time around.* Every member is expected to uphold the systems that keep the team functioning and honor the plans that keep everyone focused on success.

This trait values steady process. They may come off as rigid—or even harsh—toward those who ignore preparation or fail to honor their commitments. Beneath that intensity is a deep fear of disharmony. To them, a chaotic, unstructured team means they've failed.

How to Gain Their Trust
- Promote order and structure in everything the team does.

- Respect preparation and follow established processes.

- Show patience and persistence in pursuing team goals.

- Involve them in setting goals, building agendas, and establishing schedules.

- Give them time to reflect and process.

How to Lose Their Trust:
- Regularly rush them.

- Act impulsively in ways that undo or disrupt their work.

- Be inconsistent in communicating direction and priorities.

- Introduce unnecessary conflict into the team dynamic.

- Push them into avoidable confrontations.

The Fourth and Final Level of Constructive Chaos

Trust is not simply one aspect of Constructive Chaos—it is the final element that ties everything together and enables the team not only to withstand the forces of chaos but to exceed expectations as they reach their Productive Power.

Marshall's example teaches us that trust is built not just on competence and discipline but also on character and human connection. His ability to navigate extreme pressure, inspire confidence in his vision, and care deeply for those under his command offers a timeless model for leaders. His legacy reminds us that trust is earned through an unwavering commitment to both the mission and the people responsible for carrying it out.

As a leader, your role in building trust cannot be overstated. It is your responsibility to cultivate an environment where intellectual honesty, competence, adaptability, and a shared sense of purpose are the norm. Just as important is staying vigilant against false indicators of trust—signals that can create unrealistic expectations and lead to disappointment or resentment. These misleading signs often conceal deeper issues and, if left unaddressed, can quietly erode the very foundation you're working to build.

Trust is not a one-time achievement. It is a continuous process that demands reflection, self-awareness, and a deep understanding of the behaviors that drive your team. When you recognize each person's natural tendencies—whether mission- or people-oriented—and align them with the team's goals, you build a resilient, cohesive unit capable of adapting to anything chaos throws at you.

In the end, trust is the counterbalance to unpredictability and the key to unlocking your team's Productive Power. By building and sustaining it, you enable your team not just to survive chaos but to emerge stronger, more innovative, and ready to lead in a changing world.

PART V

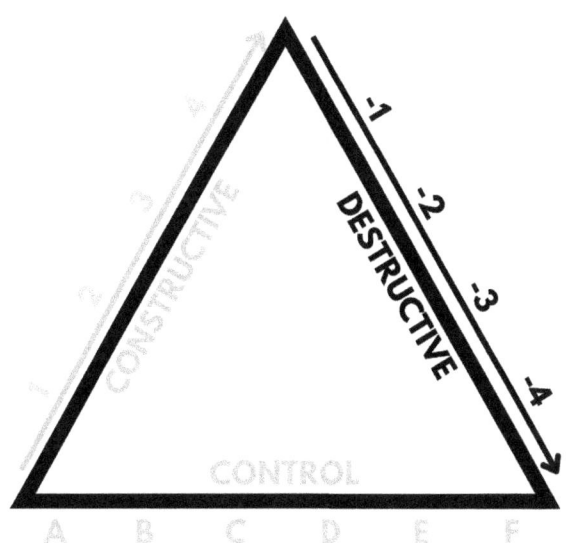

Chapter 12
Disunity

The descent into Destructive Chaos begins here.

Disunity is the first level of Destructive Chaos. It is the most pervasive level because it involves people and their willingness to work together. As long as a team remains in Destructive Chaos, Disunity will always be present.

Disunity is dangerous because it strikes directly at relationships, the glue that holds a team together. At its root, it is an escalating pattern of emotional conflict that breeds skepticism, antagonism, resentment, and eventually anger, even among well-intentioned people. It often begins with something small: a perceived slight, a tone taken the wrong way, a disagreement over priorities. But if left unaddressed, it calcifies into bickering, passive resistance, and ultimately, outright refusal to cooperate.

This breakdown in unity is what separates teams that withstand chaos from those that collapse under it. Unified teams absorb chaos' blows. They take the hit, realign, and drive forward. Disunified teams don't adapt—they fracture. They also don't rally or resolve their issues. And because they lack strong leadership to pull them together as one team, tensions are left to fester and spread. Like a ship with a cracked hull plowing through a storm, they take on water with every wave. At first, it seems manageable. Under sustained pressure, however, the structure fails and the entire vessel comes apart.

The same happens to teams. When cracks in relationships are left unresolved, they spread and calcify. People retreat into silos and stay there—because it's safer, and less exhausting than trying to fix what's broken. And when the storm hits, the team doesn't bend, it breaks.

Disunity is dangerous because it drains the precious energy to adjust in chaos and win. Time gets burned dodging teammates, managing tension, and avoiding hard truths. And here's the irony: the very conflicts people fear are often the ones that, when faced head-on, build real strength and durability. But instead of leaning in, people hold back. Critical ideas go unspoken. Potential breakthroughs never surface. Over time, meaningful conversations fade into surface-level exchanges—and teams devolve into groups.

Disunity destroys teams from the inside out. Worse, it's often invisible. From the outside, a team might appear functional. No one's yelling, and desks aren't flying across the room. In fact, conversations happen. People look busy.

But quiet isn't unity.

Beneath the surface, the team is devolving into a group. The team's collective power erodes—not because people aren't working, but because they aren't working *together*.

What Disunity Looks Like and Why

Disunity takes many forms. Some are personal, others professional.

Personal disunity stems from beliefs and values: religion, politics, lifestyle, or other deeply held convictions. As a leader, your job isn't to change personal belief systems. Rather, it's to ensure full cooperation.

This section focuses on professional disunity, which is more appropriate and frankly, more manageable. Unlike personal conflict, professional disagreements can often be resolved—if people are open to learning and adapting.

In chaos, professional disunity tends to show up in four distinct forms. Each has its own behavioral trigger. As a leader, your job is to recognize these patterns, identify the root cause, and apply pressure or accountability where needed.

Table 8. The four types of professional disunity

Type of Disunity	Drivers	Accountability
People-to-People (PP)	Subjective standards Low adaptability Pop-psychologizing	Everyone in the team and organization, including leadership
Team-to-Leader (TL)	Exclusion Unclear expectations Breaching the social contract	Team members and leader
Team-to-Team (TT)	Non-cooperation Lack of oversight	Leader and senior leadership
Team-to-Organization (TO)	Lack of alignment	Senior leadership

Person-to-Person

This is the most common form of Disunity, stemming from damaged interpersonal relationships. It affects everyone, from frontline employees to senior leaders. Common signs include:

- A tense atmosphere resulting in disengagement.

- Communication breakdowns that lead to delays and mistakes.

- Gossip and behind-the-back disparagement of teammates.

- Finger-pointing and scapegoating.

- Unresolved conflicts that drag on and undermine performance.

Three key drivers fuel this behavior:

Driver #1: Subjective standards

We naturally judge others through the lens of our own talents, values, and life experiences. The challenge comes when we hold people accountable to *our* ideals and preferred leadership traits as opposed to using an unambiguous, objective set of standards. For example, we may emphasize "decisiveness" or prize "prudence"—but what do those traits actually look like in practice? And who defines them?

Consider a newly promoted sales manager who built her career on aggressive networking and bold deal-making. She values extroversion, quick decisions, and risk-taking because that's what led to her success. Now in a leadership role, she evaluates her team by those same traits. She rewards those who push hard and act fast while subtly dismissing those who take a more analytical, methodical approach. Without realizing it, she creates an invisible divide, favoring those who match her style and over-looking the contributions of those who don't. Half of her team feels underappreciated and disrespected. Engagement drops, collaboration suffers, and disunity takes hold.

There's nothing inherently wrong with evaluating others through personal standards—it's human nature. But self-aware-ness is essential if you are going to unite a diverse collection of individuals, all with personalities and very different work expe-riences, and make them a team.

Take a step back to reflect on how your experiences shape your expectations. Make sure your criteria are fair and relevant to your mission, current team, and environment. This perspec-tive allows you to judge more objectively and foster stronger collaboration.

Driver #2: Low adaptability

Interpersonal conflict often stems from a lack of understanding—and appreciation—for how others respond to chaos. We expect others to react the way *we* would—and when they don't, friction starts. The less adaptable someone is, the more likely they'll mis-judge or mishandle others who behave differently under stress. That rigid mindset becomes a source of persistent tension.

Instead of cooperating, people retreat into their preconceived notions. Frustration builds. Relationships deteriorate. The team stops functioning as one unit.

Different behaviors seek different forms of control in chaos:

- **Taking Charge:** Some people immediately try to seize control when they feel off track. Their behavior may come across as dictatorial or disrespectful, easily interpreted as a challenge to your authority. In reality, they're acting out of fear and instinct, operating in survival mode. They're doing what feels right to them, even if it isn't the most appropriate response.

- **Re-Planning:** Some people will automatically want to hit the pause button in chaos. If planning is your default mode, this makes sense. But if you lean toward execution, the pause might feel like a waste of time. Worse, it can be interpreted as a way to avoid hard decisions in tough moments. In reality, planners like these are trying to prevent disaster by resetting priorities and regaining clarity in what feels like an out-of-control situation.

- **Rallying the Team:** Some will drop everything to re-motivate the group when they sense confusion creeping in. To many, this can feel like empty pep talk when what's really needed is a clear decision. But for highly extroverted people, rallying the team is how they regain control. After all, a demotivated team can't be expected to survive chaos—let alone thrive in it.

Driver #3: Pop-psychologizing

Pop-psychologizing is a lazy, self-sabotaging way to explain other people's behavior. It's the practice of diagnosing others—their mentality, stability, or competence—by casually throwing around clinical terms or pop culture labels without understanding what they really mean.

This behavior harms both sides. The target of the critique is no longer seen as being simply different or difficult, but is instead branded as defective, potentially beyond help. Their perceived value to the team is damaged.

The offender looks worse, though. In my experience,

pop-psychologizing not only reflects a failure to think critically, but it is a sign of poor emotional regulation. People who willingly and openly announce sloppy diagnoses aren't making careful, reasoned assessments; they're reacting impulsively, often out of frustration or misunderstanding. Instead of recognizing valuable differences in how others operate and contribute, they reduce complexity to convenient, even popular, but grossly inaccurate and damaging labels. In a serious team environment, this makes them a liability.

Heather and John

To John, Heather is "crazy."

John is a perfectionist. He built his career in IT by mastering his craft, meticulously staying up to date on the latest procedures and practices. He prides himself on being the professional everyone turns to when things need to be done right. Precision, order, and predictability define his work, and he expects the same from those around him.

Heather is also in IT, but she couldn't be more different. She's full of ideas—too many, in John's view. Most seem like off-the-cuff, impractical suggestions. To the untrained ear, they might sound exciting, but John knows better. "No one's ever done that before!" he thinks. To him, Heather is well-meaning but not a professional. Her ideas, which he sees as reckless, represent too many unnecessary risks.

What John fails to see is Heather's value. Her ideas, while some are unconventional, are grounded in reality and offer the innovative solutions the company desperately needs. Like John, Heather has an advanced degree, but unlike him, she's willing to explore uncharted territory. Heather thinks years ahead, searching for ways to make the business more efficient and competitive. In fact, she's the only one pushing boundaries in an otherwise rigid environment.

Unfortunately, John—and others like him—shut her down before her ideas even have a chance. They stifle her creativity, which only discourages her from speaking up and contributing. Heather could be a transformative asset, but the question remains: how long will she stay on a team that constantly ignores or dismisses her?

Team-to-Leader

This type of disunity arises when the relationship between the leader and team members breaks down.

It often stems from an imbalance of power or trust. Some team members perceive a weak leader and become insubordinate. They undermine their decisions, forcing others to take sides and putting the leader in a humiliating position. More often, the root problem is a domineering or absentee leader—someone who imposes controls that kill collaboration and discourage the team from fully engaging.

Signs of Team-to-Leader Disunity:

- Open hostility toward leadership and their decisions.

- A team culture marked by apathy or bitterness.

- Certain stakeholders feel unwelcome or excluded.

- Quiet team members don't speak up—and aren't encouraged to.

- The unspoken rule: success depends on compliance and avoiding conflict, not genuine contribution.

There are three major drivers of Team-to-Leader disunity:

Driver #1: Exclusion

Exclusion sacrifices the team's power by sidelining individuals for personal or group biases. It manifests as withholding opportunities for certain team members to speak up, participate, or contribute meaningfully. These individuals become outcasts, excluded from key decisions and activities that build team cohesion. Exclusion results in siloes, alliances, and cliques on one side, and disengagement and dissatisfaction on the other.

Favoritism is another form of exclusion. When a leader shows preferential treatment to a select few—allowing them to avoid accountability or to dominate decision-making—the team becomes fractured. The favored few comply because it benefits them personally, while others follow reluctantly, without enthusiasm or investment.

When people are made to feel unwelcome, it's not just an injustice to them; it's a loss for the entire team. The unspoken message is clear: "We don't need your input. Just do your job, and let us handle the important work." These individuals are rendered voiceless and powerless, even though their roles remain essential for the team's success. When they can't contribute, someone else carries the weight. Is it going to be you?

Driver #2: Unclear Expectations

Disputes arise when there is ambiguity about how team members should work together, what cooperation looks like, and which behaviors are acceptable and unacceptable. Without clarity, team members are left guessing at the leader's intentions. Worst of all, they don't know how their performance will be evaluated.

This uncertainty breeds hesitation and distrust. People stop taking initiative—not because they're incapable, but because they fear making the wrong move. Worse, consequences become inconsistent: one person gets reprimanded, another gets a pass. Over time, frustration builds: "Why am I being held to this standard when others aren't?" "What does success even look like here?" The result: resentment, disengagement, and a breakdown in team cohesion.

Where Expectations Matter Most

Some expectations seem so obvious that leaders leave them unstated: Don't be rude. Don't waste people's time. Don't tell offensive jokes. The result? People assume what is fine and what isn't. Everyone begins operating from a different playbook. That's when chaos creeps in.

Leaders must eliminate ambiguity about what's acceptable and what's not. They must take charge of the team and officially declare the basic expectations of behavior.

Use the following categories to expose assumptions and prevent the misalignment that fuels Disunity. Pay close attention to how your team responds—what they say (and don't say) will reveal where they're strong and where they're vulnerable to Disunity.

1. Respect and Professionalism

- How do we disagree constructively without personal attacks?

- What's considered acceptable vs. toxic behavior in discussions?

- How do we give and receive feedback, especially criticism?

2. Communication and Engagement

- Should all team members have a voice in discussions?

- How should venting, frustration, or complaints be handled?

3. Trust and Collaboration

- What does "having each other's backs" actually mean in practice?

- When mistakes happen, is our culture blame-oriented or solution-focused?

4. Conflict and Accountability

- How do we handle conflicts? When do we escalate?

- Are people held to the same standard or does favoritism exist?

Driver #3: Breaching the Social Contract

Leaders have obligations to their people: protect them, respect them, and lead them with purpose. When they break that promise—or allow others to—any reason to faithfully follow the leader evaporates. Treating subordinates like tools or pawns sends a clear message: *You don't matter.* And once people feel expendable, they don't just get angry—they check out.

The first response to a broken social contract isn't open rebellion. It's worse: apathy. People disengage. They follow orders, but only mechanically. They stop caring, stop striving, and stop rising to meet the demands of chaos. The fight is gone, and so is the priceless resilience that makes recovery possible.

But this contract cuts both ways. Team members who put their ego, comfort, or pride ahead of the group do just as much damage. They strain the team. They generate resentment. They detach from the team and refuse to adapt. And when things go sideways, no one rushes to their aid. Not because the team is cruel, but because that person made themselves impossible to support.

Team-to-Team

Team-to-Team Disunity occurs when one team isolates itself from others within the organization. The leader—intentionally or not—allows them to "stay in their lane" and avoid collaboration with adjacent teams, even when they're working toward the same mission. This isolation comes at a cost: delays, inefficiencies, duplicated efforts, and wasted resources.

Common signs of Team-to-Team Disunity include:

- Delayed information flow that undermines decision-making.

- Compartmentalization that becomes an excuse for withholding support.

- Rivalries that turn toxic and undermine collaboration.

- A fragmented culture: some teams report high morale while others feel frustrated, confused, or ignored.

- Resistance to adapting, even when the competitive landscape demands speed and alignment.

There is no better example of Team-to-Team Disunity than the breakdown between the Federal Bureau of Investigation (FBI) and the Central Intelligence Agency (CIA) prior to 9/11. Their refusal to fully cooperate didn't just hinder their joint mission; it directly contributed to one of the most catastrophic failures in modern U.S. history.

The FBI-CIA Rivalry and the 9/11 Security Gap

The CIA is America's foreign intelligence service, tasked with collecting and analyzing threats abroad. The FBI spies too—even on U.S. citizens. Although it is the nation's premier law enforcement agency, it is also responsible for domestic surveillance and intelligence gathering. Together, these two organizations were supposed to safeguard the United States from threats at home and overseas. Yet by September 11, 2001, their bitter rivalry had become so toxic that it allowed nineteen terrorists to orchestrate the deadliest attack on American soil in history.

The consequences of their disunity were catastrophic. The failure of two key agencies to cooperate had ripple effects that reshaped the nation for the worse. It became the convenient justification for endless military interventions around the globe—including two decades of failure in Afghanistan and Iraq. At home, the federal government ballooned, with new layers of bureaucracy stacked on the old, compounding inefficiency and corruption. The Patriot Act—a set of surveillance laws ripped from the pages of *1984*—eroded individual liberties in the name of security. The freest nation on Earth became one of the most surveilled, even to this day. Why? Because senior political leaders failed to unify a divided system around a common mission.

The Roots of Disunity

In the 1990s, the FBI and CIA were at odds over how to confront the growing threat of Islamic terrorism against the United States. The FBI treated it as a criminal matter, focused on arrests and legal prosecutions. The CIA, by contrast, saw it as an act of war. They focused on disrupting overseas funding networks, enhanced interrogations, and targeted killings.

Not surprisingly, each agency viewed its approach as the only viable one. This belief justified their refusal to cooperate. Each could claim, according to their own logic and perception of their unique mission, that the other's approach would undermine their efforts and lead to failure.

Left: CIA Headquarters, Langley, Virginia. Right: FBI Headquarters, Washington, D.C. These headquarters aren't just buildings—they're fortresses. Like individuals, these institutions have identities: distinct worldviews, agendas, and buried secrets. Their territorial grip on mission and domain makes alignment nearly impossible without strong leadership. (Photos: Courtesy of Alamy)

This institutional dysfunction was magnified by two clashing personalities: John O'Neill, head of the FBI's Counterterrorism Division, and Michael Scheuer, the founding chief of the CIA's Alec Station (the Bin Laden unit). Their rivalry epitomized the agencies' broader dysfunction, a dynamic captured in Lawrence Wright's *The Looming Tower: Al-Qaeda and the Road to 9/11*, winner of the Pulitzer Prize.

O'Neill was a larger-than-life figure—charismatic, ambitious, and relentless in his pursuit of Osama bin Laden. However, his abrasive demeanor and persistent focus on elevating the FBI's profile often alienated colleagues and partners. Scheuer, by contrast, was blunt, extremely intelligent, and uncompromising, viewing Islamic terrorism as a serious threat to the United States that needed to be ruthlessly eliminated.

To call their conflict toxic is an understatement. Both men viewed the other as an obstacle to success. Scheuer didn't hold back in his assessment of O'Neill, calling him "duplicitous" and asserting, "He had no concerns outside of making the Bureau look good."[115] Likewise, O'Neill had little patience for the CIA's reluctance to share intelligence, reportedly believing that Scheuer's approach was reckless and shortsighted.

O'Neill's story took a tragic turn. In 2001, he was forced out of the FBI and took a job as head of security at the World Trade Center. On the morning of September 11, he was in the North Tower and died during the attack—a bitter irony that he was killed by the very man and terrorist group he had been pursuing for years. Years later, Scheuer's bitterness remained when he remarked in a congressional hearing, "The only good thing that happened to America on 11 September was that the building fell on him."[116]

Interestingly, in 2004, Scheuer, writing under the pseudonym *Anonymous*, published the New York Times bestseller *Imperial Hubris*. He argued that the U.S. was losing the War on Terror precisely because it was treating it as terrorism—an episodic, law enforcement problem—rather than as a global insurgency requiring a war-fighting strategy. His book was a scathing indictment of American foreign policy, echoing the very divide that had defined his battle with O'Neill and Washington's political leadership.

Reasons for Disunity

If two of the most powerful institutions in the U.S. government—with tens of thousands of employees and billion-dollar budgets—could fail to work together, what makes you think your organization is immune?

The dysfunction between the FBI and CIA wasn't just about personal rivalries. It was systemic. Years of institutional barriers, conflicting priorities, and weak leadership made meaningful cooperation nearly impossible. Instead of uniting around a shared national security mission, the two agencies remained in a bureaucratic Cold War.

Several key factors explain their failure to collaborate:

- **External barriers:** *The Wall* was a legal restriction separating domestic law enforcement (FBI) from foreign intelligence (CIA), designed to protect civil liberties.[117] But instead of finding ways to collaborate on a common mission, many used it as an excuse to avoid cooperation altogether.

- **Opposing ethos:** The FBI catches bank robbers; the CIA robs banks. These fundamentally different philosophies didn't just shape how they approached threats—they also shaped how they viewed each other.

- **Conflicting priorities:** The FBI wanted to prosecute terrorists, including at the lowest levels. The CIA wanted to capture or kill decision-makers, especially senior leadership.

- **Jurisdictional fights:** The FBI oversaw domestic threats, while the CIA was legally barred from operating inside the U.S. Yet terrorists operated both in and outside the country.

- **Technological failures:** The two agencies couldn't even email each other—literally. Their computer systems were incompatible, making real-time intelligence-sharing practically impossible.

- **Institutional self-interest:** Each agency feared that too much collaboration would make them look less valuable, thus threatening their funding and influence from Congress. Cooperation became a liability instead of a necessity.

Leadership Failures That Allowed Disunity to Fester

The FBI-CIA rivalry before 9/11 was shaped by bureaucratic inertia, legal restrictions, and deeply ingrained institutional cultures. In government, these obstacles are often immovable. But in the private sector, you have far more control over your environment.

Here are some lessons worth considering:

- **Take control before dysfunction sets in.** Unlike government agencies bound by legal and jurisdictional barriers, you have the power to define how teams work together and enforce unity of effort.

- **Don't let competition turn into rivalry.** Healthy competition can drive performance, but when teams see each other as adversaries instead of allies, cooperation breaks down—and the mission suffers.

- **Ensure teams align with the company mission, not just their department's goals.** The FBI and CIA fiercely protected their autonomy, budgets, and turf. You don't have to tolerate that kind of institutional self-interest. Success should be measured by how well teams serve the company's strategic objectives, not just their own performance metrics.

- **Make tough decisions, even if they're unpopular.** Government and institutional leaders often avoid politically costly moves; you don't have that excuse. If cross-team dysfunction is hurting performance, step in and fix it.

- **Eliminate technical and process barriers before they become excuses.** The FBI and CIA couldn't even email each other. That wasn't just a failure of infrastructure; it was a failure of leadership. In your business, outdated systems aren't inevitable. They're a choice.

The lesson of the FBI-CIA rivalry is clear: If your organization is experiencing the same kinds of silos, turf wars, and misaligned priorities, the problem isn't bureaucracy—it's leadership.

Team-to-Organization

This kind of disunity occurs when a team disconnects from the larger organization and its strategy. It's as if the team has gone rogue, prioritizing its own agenda over the mission.

This kind of disunity often presents itself in two ways:

- **Confusion**, due to a lack of clarity about how the team should support other teams and parts of the organization.

- **Defiance**, or the deliberate choice by a leader to disconnect and focus only on their own lane.

Team-to-Organization disunity doesn't happen in a vacuum. It's a shared failure of both the team and senior leadership.

Sometimes, team leaders isolate themselves. They operate independently, misaligned with the broader strategy. That can stem from confusion, neglect, or ambition. Other times, senior leaders create the conditions for disunity. They fail to demand cross-functional support, don't set clear expectations, or tolerate siloed behavior because it serves their own power.

Senior leadership as the driver of Team-to-Organization disunity. Here are the most common reasons why:

- **Lack of perspective:** Some executives don't understand what unity of effort means or what it looks like across a whole, integrated organization. And if they don't understand it, chances are their bosses don't either.

- **Unclear expectations:** Without a shared definition of team success, team leaders run their own race—forgetting they're part of a team sport.

- **Leadership avoidance:** Senior executives assume their subordinates already know how to lead effectively. It's also a convenient way to dodge the hard, people-oriented obligations of leadership that involve developing, coaching, and mentoring the next tier of leaders.

Team-to-Organization disunity isn't just a problem for the team involved—it's a strategic risk. It threatens the success of any organization operating in a highly competitive environment. Resolving it requires both team leaders and senior executives to take ownership, communicate effectively, and address the underlying misalignments head-on.

The Multi-Million-Dollar Dilemma

Gregory was a rockstar in the world of marketing. Ivy League-educated and a veteran of a top management consulting firm, he had built a reputation as one of the best. When he joined a fast-growing startup backed by top-tier venture capital, the fit seemed perfect. As the new head of marketing, Gregory led a team of nearly 20 professionals and managed a multimillion-dollar budget. It was his moment to shine.

The board and executive leadership were thrilled with their hire—until Gregory's decisions cost them $30 million in a single quarter. He poured millions into an ambitious but poorly conceived campaign that recovered barely half of what was spent. How did this happen? Had he gone rogue?

The company had a "strategy," but it was vague, and the expectations of marketing were unclear. Worse, oversight was nonexistent. The CEO didn't bother to monitor or challenge his decisions—he was the expert, right? Gregory interpreted the lack of supervision as a green light to prove his brilliance. So, he launched a campaign he believed would make his mark in marketing history. The result? One of the company's largest financial missteps—and a major embarrassment for leadership.

The chaos snowballed. The CEO was blindsided and humiliated. He had to go back to his venture capital partners and grovel for more funding. Not surprisingly, the board began questioning whether he was the right person for the job. A power-hungry rival saw blood in the water and began maneuvering for the top spot, forcing the CEO into survival mode.

Gregory, however, survived the fallout. The company refused to fire him. That was out of fear that his talent—though not his judgment—was still too valuable to hand over to a competitor despite the damage done.

The damage extended far beyond finances. The board

tightened control, and the CEO found himself on a short leash. What had once been a bold, risk-embracing company became cautious, seemingly hesitant.

The company continued to grow, nonetheless. But the damage had been done: it lost its appetite for risk, its edge, and its willingness to embrace chaos. It stopped chasing decisive victories and started managing to avoid failure.

What You Can Do to Prevent Disunity

Disunity doesn't happen overnight. It grows in the gaps left by unclear leadership, unresolved conflict, and unchecked behavior. As the leader, it's your job to ensure those gaps don't widen. It's your responsibility to create the conditions where cooperation is expected, and divisions are dealt with before they fracture the team.

1. Accept That Unity Depends on You

Team cohesion starts and ends with leadership. That means honing your people-oriented leadership skills and being willing to use them.

If you don't ensure alignment, it won't happen. You must be ready to confront personal conflicts, set clear expectations for behavior, and hold everyone—including yourself—accountable for cooperation and team support.

What This Means in Practice:

- **Confront tensions early.** Don't let disunity fester out of fear of conflict. Address issues directly and professionally.

- **Set non-negotiable expectations.** Make it clear: everyone is expected to collaborate respectfully—even when they don't personally get along.

- **Lead by example.** Model the collaboration and unity you expect from your team. Show that differences can be worked through productively.

Unity isn't about forcing harmony. It's about making sure surface-level differences don't become lasting divisions.

2. Clarify Roles, Expectations, and Accountability

Disunity thrives in the gaps between awareness and understanding of responsibilities within the team.

Most confusion isn't caused by a lack of direction or rules. Instead, it's caused by competing interpretations of what they mean and what they look like in practice. Think about it: titles don't designate all responsibilities, and job descriptions don't define current priorities. Even performance reviews reflect reality through the lens of the evaluator's personality.

People filter responsibilities through their own experience and behavioral profile. That's where misalignment takes root. Your job isn't to create clarity from scratch—it's to extract it from what already exists. That means:

- **Clarifying roles** by asking: "What are your top three responsibilities right now?"

- **Clarifying expectations** by asking: "What does a successful outcome on this project look like?" Follow that with, "What does that mean for you in your role?"

- **Clarifying accountability** by asking: "When something goes wrong, who owns the fix?"

When answers differ, don't rush to correct. Compare them. Every mismatch is a signal. The wider the gap, the more vulnerable your team is to breakdown. Close the gap before disunity spreads.

3. Balance the Team's Natural Strengths

You can't always choose your team, but you can learn to work with them. Instead of forcing everyone into a one-size-fits-all standard—which only aggravates differences—learn to balance their individual talents and natural behavioral styles.

Disunity often stems from behavioral imbalance. When one style dominates, friction rises. Planners get stuck in analysis. Executors bulldoze their way to the finish line. Innovators are dismissed for demanding too much change.

But when each strength is recognized—and people understand how their contribution supports the mission—alignment takes hold. The team becomes more resilient to dysfunction, especially the kind triggered by clashing styles and unchecked preferences.

What can you do? Assess your team's behavioral strengths and gaps, then plan accordingly.

- **Do you have a healthy mix of planners, executors, and innovators?** Or is the team behaviorally lopsided? Are risk-averse planners slowing execution? Are fast-paced doers creating too much disruption?

- **Who are your control-oriented personalities?** How strong is their need for control? How does it affect others? How does it affect your leadership?

- **Where do you need balance in the team?**
  Specifically, what type of new hires are needed and why?
  Will they reinforce what's working or introduce friction?
  What's the long-term effect of onboarding them?

4. Use Productive Purpose for Alignment

Disunity takes root when people stop seeing the point to work—when their daily efforts feel disconnected from what actually matters to them as individuals, with personal ambitions and desires.

As a leader, it's not enough to understand how people behave. You need to understand *why* they engage. What motivates them to show up? What gives their work meaning? How does it support their larger life goals?

Productive Purpose is the solution. It connects personal contribution with the efforts of the team. When people can't see how their work connects to it, they disengage. But when leaders uncover it and align it with the team's mission, people invest more, contribute better, and stick together when it counts.

For how to uncover and apply Productive Purpose, see Chapter 5: *Leadership in Chaos.*

The Opportunity of Disunity

Disunity may feel overwhelming, but it's also your opportunity to turn things around. The damage is still containable, and most team members still want to succeed. They will want to recover to back to Constructive Chaos. But, they need leadership to show the way. Use this moment to seal the cracks, before they become permanent fractures that lead to something worse.

Here's how to seize the opportunity:

- **Act immediately.** Tackle the issues head-on while people are still open to change.

- **Clear the air.** Use this moment to surface the underlying tension. Difficult conversations now prevent greater pain later.

- **Show you care.** People engage more during chaos when they see leadership invested in both their success and their future. The opposite is just as true.

Ignoring disunity will not make your life easier. Without intervention, expect two predictable outcomes:

- **Harmful practices persist.** Poor communication, ineffective behaviors, and misaligned priorities become standard. Friction builds. Performance falls.

- **Silos form.** Teams retreat into their own methods, language, and priorities—disconnecting from the mission and each other.

Your Role in Disunity

The slide into Destructive Chaos isn't inevitable, but preventing it demands strong leadership. You must get comfortable intervening directly in team dynamics and managing personalities without suppressing contribution. Align them. Lead them. If you don't, expect to slide into the next stage of Destructive Chaos: Disorientation.

Chapter 13
Disorientation

D isorientation is the second level of Destructive Chaos. Where Disunity disrupts relationships, Disorientation dismantles the clarity and alignment of purpose. Teams no longer know where to go or how to work together.

If Forward Integration (FINT) aligns strategy, organization, systems, and culture into a cohesive whole, then Disorientation is its collapse. The Direction + Order a professional team needs breaks down, and the negative consequences pile up fast. The people expected to deliver are left stranded without clarity, structure, or support. Confusion turns into frustration, and frustration calcifies into apathy and resentment.

This chapter breaks down how failure in each FINT element—strategy, organization, systems, and culture—leads to Disorientation and erodes a team's ability to perform. To bring it to life, we'll examine one of the least-known yet most pivotal examples of Destructive Chaos: Lord Germain and British strategy in 1777. It's one of history's most infamous—and avoidable—strategic failures, with consequences that reshaped the war and the world.

How Disorientation Unfolds

At a glance, a team in Disorientation may appear functional: deliverables arrive, emails get answered, and tasks get checked off. But beneath the surface, Destructive Chaos brews.

The team lacks clear direction. They work—but for what? So they disengage. After all, how can anyone stay focused when there's no clear path forward and no shared vision of where it leads?

Order—the underlying consistency that keeps teams centered, predictable, and efficient—begins to crumble. Meetings multiply and drag on, yielding little clarity or progress. Roles blur, and personalities clash as team members encroach on each other's domains. Decisions stall in a swamp of second-guessing.

Leaders quickly become overwhelmed. The crisis of the moment consumes their full attention. Narrowed by tunnel vision, leaders lose touch with the big picture, and team members retreat into silos, clinging to familiar tasks. Initiative fades, collaboration falters, and frustration gives way to resignation.

Under mounting pressure, low-adaptive leaders tighten their grip, isolating themselves with a trusted few. Feeling increasingly powerless, they resort to micromanagement—dictating tasks, demanding constant updates, and controlling every decision. This reactive approach deepens the dysfunction.

An instinct of self-preservation takes over. Team members focus solely on immediate tasks, the four walls of their office, and their trusted peers. Silos develop. Over time they harden into tribes, each chasing its own agenda, aligning with whoever holds the most power. This exclusionary dynamic drains morale, accelerates disengagement, and creates lasting fractures within the team.

Left unchecked, Disorientation breeds a toxic culture. Mechanical Compliance—doing only what's minimally required—can escalate into Malicious Compliance, where actions subtly but deliberately undermine leadership.

The Disorientation Test: Spotting Symptoms

Is your team caught in Disorientation? Look for these common symptoms:

- **Minimal effort:** Team members do only what's explicitly required.

- **Short-term thinking:** Focus narrows exclusively to day-to-day tasks.

- **Leadership dependence:** Individuals wait passively to be told what to do.

- **Declining collaboration:** Genuine listening and contributions fade.

- **Stagnation:** Growth halts as task overload consumes available resources.

- **Information hoarding:** Critical insights remain hidden unless explicitly demanded.

- **Factionalism:** Personal agendas clearly dominate decision-making and choices.

Next, ask your team these four basic questions. Everyone should be able to answer them clearly and consistently:

1. **Why are we here, and what are we supposed to be doing?**

2. **Who is responsible for what, and why?**

3. **How should we be working together?**

4. **How would you describe our culture?**

If your team struggles to answer these questions—or worse, gives conflicting answers—then Disorientation has already taken root.

The real question becomes: Why?

Breaking Disorientation Down

To fully understand Disorientation, we need to break it down across the four elements of FINT: strategy, organization, systems, and culture.

Strategy, the Heart of Disorientation

Disorientation almost always begins with a lack of strategy. Clear direction is missing. People can't answer, "Where are we going, and why?" Without this clarity, organizational structure feels arbitrary, haphazardly put together in the moment. That prompts cynicism about people and roles: "Why exactly is so-and-so in that position?" Systems meant to support teamwork instead become obstacles: "Why are we forced to go through three levels of approval when speed is constantly preached as a priority?"

To be clear, strategy doesn't have to be overly complicated. At a minimum, it should answer these foundational questions:

- What does this organization do?

- What do we do better than everyone else?

- How does the organization define success?

- What are the big goals that will make success a reality?

These deceptively simple questions help explain the "why" behind the organization. They inform us about what really matters and what doesn't. That in turn helps us make informed decisions and act with purpose.

What are the consequences of not being able to answer those basic questions?

It compounds disunity. Ambiguity breeds division. Those "in the know" exploit their access to information for personal gain, leaving others in the dark. Leaders under pressure may avoid tough calls, trading clarity for loyalty—and deepening team fractures.

Initiative is disincentivized. Uncertainty and confusion make risk-taking feel dangerous. Team members hesitate to act, fearing mistakes will be punished rather than rewarded. Instead of stepping up with bold ideas, they retreat into safe, routine tasks.

Myopia takes over. Without a clear strategy to anchor long-term focus, attention collapses into the now. Crises take center stage, adaptability weakens, and the broader mission disappears. Survival replaces success.

It stifles contribution. Complexity intimidates. Frontline employees withhold insight, fearing they'll look naïve or overstep. This silence kills innovation, halts progress, and robs the team of valuable thinking.

It wastes energy and resources. In the absence of strategic clarity, effort becomes misaligned. People stay busy—meetings, emails, projects—but little of it drives meaningful progress. High performers burn out. Precious resources are consumed by low-value work. Activity masquerades as progress.

How to Spot a Missing Strategy

Look for these warning signs:

- **No one knows what it is:** Team members openly admit they don't know what the team is working toward or where it's heading.

- **Priorities shift constantly:** What was essential last week isn't important today and will be forgotten tomorrow. This inconsistency kills momentum and breeds cynicism.

- **The strategy is just a mission and vision statement:** These basic elements describe purpose and ideals, but they don't tell the team how to win in a dynamic, competitive environment.

- **The focus is always on the short-term:** Pressure for immediate wins dominates. Long-term goals fade, and strategic thinking disappears.

- **Little connection between effort and progress:** Teams work hard but see no link between their output and the organization's goals. Work seems pointless other than collecting a paycheck.

- **Strategy is developed in a vacuum:** Senior leaders create it in isolation, excluding the middle managers and frontline operators who actually carry it out.

Inadequate *Organization*

Every strategy demands a team built to match. Roles and structure must reflect the mission's unique demands. When teams are shaped by personal preferences or generic templates, friction and inefficiency take hold. The strategy might still succeed—but often at too high a cost. Execution becomes so frustrating that great talent leaves, and mediocrity stays.

The fallout doesn't stop at internal dissatisfaction. Poor organizational design ripples across the business in other costly ways:

- Employee engagement drops when the wrong people are in the wrong role.

- Dissatisfied employees create dissatisfied customers.

- Operating costs rise due to poor structure, rework, and wasted effort.

- Trust in leadership erodes as decisions appear arbitrary or worse, self-serving.

- Fixing a broken structure feels like opening Pandora's box—so leaders avoid it. When this avoidance becomes habit, dysfunction becomes permanent.

Diagnosing an Inadequate Organization:

Start by asking a few basic questions:

- "Who is responsible for which task—and why?"

- "Do our reporting structures make sense?"

- "Are tasks assigned in a way that maximizes the team's strengths and potential?"

If the answers are unclear—or worse, dismissed with "That's how we've always done it"—you're likely facing deeper issues in design and alignment. These responses often expose structural flaws that quietly undermine performance.

Watch for these red flags:

Faulty design

- **Bottlenecked Approvals.** Are routine decisions sent up the chain for unnecessary signoff? When approvals pile up at the top, middle managers become messengers instead of leaders. If this is your reality, document the delays and push for clear decision boundaries—what your team can own without higher-level interference.

- **Preferential Appointments.** Do certain individuals seem "pre-selected" for key roles despite lacking the experience or fit? This creates resentment and undermines trust. Be prepared to call out mismatches in role-performance—privately. Make sure your recommend changes are based on performance data, not emotion.

- **Unclear Roles.** Do job responsibilities shift constantly, or feel too vague to act on? If your team's struggling to understand "who does what," stop and clarify roles in concrete terms. Even if HR doesn't fix it, you can define expectations locally and protect your team's focus.

Structural Breakdowns

- **Iron silos.** Do other teams act like collaboration is optional—or worse, a threat? If you have to escalate just to coordinate across functions, you're in a siloed environment. Start by building personal alliances across teams and showing your own openness. Model cooperation before demanding it. Document the impact of isolation so leadership sees the cost.

- **Workload Imbalance.** Is your team burning out while others coast? This isn't just unfair—it breeds resentment, erodes trust, and creates hidden strategic risk. Track the imbalance. Use data to escalate if needed—but be precise. Make sure the issue stems from poor planning or bias, not the reality that your team delivers where others can't. If that's the case, defend your team's contribution and advocate for stronger support.

- **Border Disputes.** Are people from other teams jumping into your lane, or is your own team unclear what their lane looks like? When roles are fuzzy, conflicts needlessly arise. Clarify boundaries. Articulate who owns what and why. Communicate clearly: write it, draw it, document it for all to see. This isn't about turf; it's about efficiency and trust.

Inefficient *Systems*

Work becomes sloppy and unpredictable. It's as if every team is speaking a different language or following their own rules. Messages reach some but not others. Critical tasks go unnoticed. Decisions rely on flawed or irrelevant inputs. At the root: a lack of the standardized systems that make effective collaboration possible.

Neglecting standardized systems carries a steep cost. These aren't just tools—they're stabilizing assets in chaos. Systems create predictability and order, giving teams clarity even when the environment isn't. You can't control volatility, but you can control how your team responds. Well-built systems keep people grounded, aligned, and ready to adapt.

Signs of Inadequate Systems:

- Repeated communication or planning mistakes that delay or derail project completion

- A pattern of missed deadlines

- Frequent miscommunications across the team

- Slow response times to critical needs

- Distribution of inaccurate or incomplete information

- Escalating customer complaints

- Internal disputes over how team members should perform

Reasons for Inefficient Systems

There are no standardized systems in place. Shared processes, tools, and practices ensure everyone knows how to communicate, plan, and execute tasks as expected. Without them, team members rely on individual preferences or experiences, resulting in:

- **Disjointed methods.** Each person operates differently, and their respective approaches, no matter how different, lead to confusion and internal conflict.

- **Inefficient collaboration.** Without a shared framework that everyone agrees to use, team members will always struggle to coordinate effectively.

- **Unpredictable outcomes.** Inconsistent methods

increase errors and reduce the team's reliability to operate as a unified team.

There is a lack of ownership. Some leaders inherit flawed systems—reporting, communication, feedback—and assume those problems aren't theirs to fix. But ignoring broken tools doesn't make them go away. No, it lets dysfunction spread. Worse, it signals to the team that the leader is either unwilling, or unable, to do what's needed to make them successful.

Current systems are unsuitable. Systems built for yesterday's priorities rarely meet today's demands. Instead of fixing what's broken or fighting for something better, leaders here continue as usual. "Get used to it," is the mindset. This is complacency, not leadership. It also signals cultural rigidity, not the adaptability needed to take on chaos.

Systems are not enforced. When leaders don't hold teams accountable to the systems they agreed to follow, certainty, predictability, and efficiency become optional. An unintended message is received by all: consistency doesn't matter. And that erodes the very order needed to manage chaos.

Systems as used to control: Leaders who impose tools or practices based solely on personal preference send a clear signal: "This is about me, not the mission." When control takes precedence over productivity, teams grow demoralized. Effectiveness is sacrificed—not because it's necessary, but because the leader's fear of chaos is driving their decisions.

Internal Complaints to Monitor

Below are common signs that your systems are inefficient. Use these to confirm issues or to surface the real problem hiding beneath the noise:

- **Overload, Not Clarity.** Too much information is just as bad as too little. If you're hearing, "I don't know what to focus on," it's a sign the system lacks filters. Help your team avoid analysis paralysis by clarifying what matters now.

- **Gatekeeping.** When access to key information depends on who you know—not what you need—trust erodes and delays multiply. If team members are missing updates, redoing work, or confused about next steps, your information flow is broken. Don't tolerate it. Clarify what must be shared, who needs it, and how it's delivered.

- **Slow Decisions.** Delays often reflect upstream confusion. If priorities are vague or tradeoffs unclear, people stall. Your job is to push for clarity. Don't let uncertainty cascade into your team.

- **Silo Complaints.** If you're hearing "They never loop us in" from other teams, you've got a systems issue. Build the bridge. Set clear points of contact and agreed ways of working across teams.

- **Empty Reviews.** Generic feedback kills learning and motivation to improve. Skip the fluff like, "You were decisive," or "You worked hard." Ask what led to a decision. Ask what they'd do differently and why. Make the review about thinking, not just feelings. That's how real improvement happens.

A "Backward" Culture

Disorientation carries deep psychological and cultural costs.

The emotional toll of repeated setbacks is fatiguing, and it weakens the drive to push forward, not just as a team but as an individual. It makes people feel lost and helpless, victims of forces outside their control. Psychologically, self-doubt sets in. Am I truly capable? Spiritually, it strips away the willpower—layer by layer—so essential for navigating chaos, let alone pursuing anything meaningful beyond mere survival.

If not addressed, this stress manifests as a "backward" mindset and culture: a regressive outlook fixated on past failures and setbacks.

This mentality isn't just a consequence of Disorientation; it can also be its root cause. When teams or individuals default to survival—to doing what feels safe instead of striving for progress—they undermine their own ability to adapt and stay resilient in chaos.

Whether cause or effect, a backward mindset fosters fear and paralysis. It discourages personal initiative and disincentivizes risk-taking in a group setting. But not everyone succumbs. Some stay strong—and that's when silos harden. The ambitious and driven distance themselves from those holding them back. It's a law of human nature: A-players associate with A-players, not B or C ones.

Indicators of a Backward Mentality:

- Aggressively clinging to outdated processes or tools.

- Constantly passing up challenging projects or assignments.

- Never proposing innovative ideas or solutions.

- Mocking ambitious goals as unrealistic or naïve.

- Exaggerating minor setbacks into major problems.

- Regularly blaming external factors to justify internal delay or inaction.

- Fishing for reassurance instead of asking how to get better.

- Echoing other's doubts and fears, spreading passive negativity and defeatism.

An Overriding Fear of Struggle and Conflict

Backward mentalities treat harmony as the ideal state. Struggle, conflict, and friction are viewed as threats rather than as the natural costs of progress. This fear weakens the strength and willpower required to lead through chaos, or accomplish anything meaningful.

The typical results of this mentality are:

- **Stagnation**: Shying away from bold projects or challenges denies opportunities for growth and improvement. Inaction becomes a perceived shield against failure, creating a self-fulfilling cycle of mediocrity.

- **Rigidity**: Fear of disorder fosters inflexibility in mind and spirit. Teams that can't tolerate disruption can't adapt to change. Instead, they lose ground to more agile and resilient competitors.

- **Short-sighted decisions**: The desire for stability leads to decisions that feel safe, now, but cost far more later. Long-term value is sacrificed for momentary comfort.

- **Eroded resilience**: Without the alignment of Forward Integration, stress builds, trust decays, and your top talent distances—or leaves entirely.

Even the most well-resourced, experienced teams can fall victim to Disorientation. Though often associated with underperformance or inexperience, history offers a striking counterexample: in 1777, Disorientation crippled a global superpower.

Britain's Blunder

1777 marked a turning point in the American Revolution. Two key events shifted the war decisively in the American's favor. First, the British suffered a catastrophic defeat at the Battle of Saratoga. Second, France entered the war as an American ally, transforming the colonial rebellion into a world war. Britain now faced the challenge of not only quelling a revolt 4,000 miles from home, but also of defending its global empire against hostile powers like France and Spain.

Saratoga, 1777, the turning point of the American Revolution.
British General John Burgoyne surrenders to American General Horatio Gates. The British campaign was plagued by Disorientation from the start. London failed to clarify strategy, coordinate roles, or align the team. The result: isolated commanders, a divided army, and a catastrophic defeat. (Photo: Courtesy of Alamy)

But, in 1777, something critical didn't happen—an event that could have been a major turning point in Western history. Britain's Hudson campaign, designed to sever New England from the rest of the colonies and split the rebel colonists, failed spectacularly. It remains one of history's great "What Ifs," a scenario that could have crippled the American Revolution politically, economically, and militarily. Though the strategy was unique, it was crippled by some of the worst planning and execution ever committed by a global power.[118]

The failure of the 1777 campaign is striking because Britain held nearly every conceivable advantage. Their military was led by competent generals, equipped with state-of-the-art tools, reinforced by proven organizational systems, and bolstered by the prestige of being the world's reigning superpower. Yet, they suffered a strategic defeat at the hands of a rebellion led by farmers, blacksmiths, tradesmen, and artisans. This is a story of Disorientation at the highest levels of leadership.

From a Rebellion to an Insurgency

The American Revolution began in 1775 when colonial militias thwarted British forces attempting to confiscate their gunpowder. This motley group of citizen-soldiers not only defeated two British forces at the Battles of Concord and Lexington, but they pursued His Majesty's troops into Boston, bottling them up in the city. The British later regrouped and launched a counterattack at Bunker Hill. While the British technically won the battle, the Americans abandoned the fight after running out of ammunition.[119]

In the summer of 1776, Britain launched one of the largest invasion forces in history against New York. They fought the Continental Army at the Battle of Long Island and nearly routed them. Luckily for the Americans, General George Washington and the Continental Army were able to flee under the cover of a surprise fog, narrowly avoiding total destruction.

The defeats kept coming for the Americans. Over the next

few months, the British pursued Washington and his evaporating army. By early December 1776, the entire Continental Army teetered on the brink of collapse, and the American cause of freedom was at its nadir.[120]

On Christmas night, 1776, however, a miracle occurred. During a blinding snowstorm, Washington led a weakened yet determined force of 2,400 men in a surprise attack on a British garrison in Trenton, New Jersey.[121] It was a stunning tactical victory with far-reaching strategic implications. The American cause for freedom was not only alive, but it was now reinvigorated. To the dismay of British political and military leaders, the conflict was far from over—it was escalating.

The British Strategy for Success

The situation in North America was serious. The kingdom was already burdened by crippling debt, and the war in the colonies was driving spending even higher.[122] Britain needed to end the conflict quickly, but there was no end in sight. The Americans refused to fight decisive battles where the British held the advantage. Worse, they refused to admit defeat even when beaten. Meanwhile, international support for the rebellion grew. France, Prussia, and Spain—Britain's historical rivals—began smuggling aid to the rebels. Intensifying the pressure for an immediate resolution was the matter of British honor and reputation. They were the world's preeminent superpower, and yet they were struggling to defeat an armed civilian uprising. Something had to be done, and fast.

The newly appointed Secretary of State for the American Department, Lord George Germain, had a solution. Responsible for overseeing all military operations in America, Germain conceived a strategy of divide and conquer. The idea was for British forces to isolate New York and New England, the financial hub of the thirteen colonies, from the rebels. This would not only cause them major economic harm, but it would also deny them access to large numbers of potential recruits. Once secured, this area would act as a giant military operating base where English armies could come and go freely, striking out as they pleased. Over time, the traitors would realize the folly of their ways and beg to return to the Crown's good graces.

Success of the entire strategy hinged on controlling the Hudson River. To do this, a British army in Canada would march south along the river while another in New York marched north. The two forces would meet halfway, lock arms, and form an impenetrable wall.

General William Howe, commander of all British forces in America, and General John Burgoyne, under Canadian command, were selected to lead both prongs. Both men submitted their respective plans to make Germain's vision of success a reality.

Burgoyne, with 8,000 soldiers—including American Indian allies—proposed to advance south along the river. A secondary force, under Colonel Barry St. Leger, would serve as a diversion by attacking eastward along the Mohawk River Valley. Both forces would converge on Albany.[123] Howe, commanding 20,000 troops, proposed to first capture the rebel capital of Philadelphia. However, he promised to leave a garrison in New York City to support Burgoyne's movements.[124]

Lord Germain approved both plans.

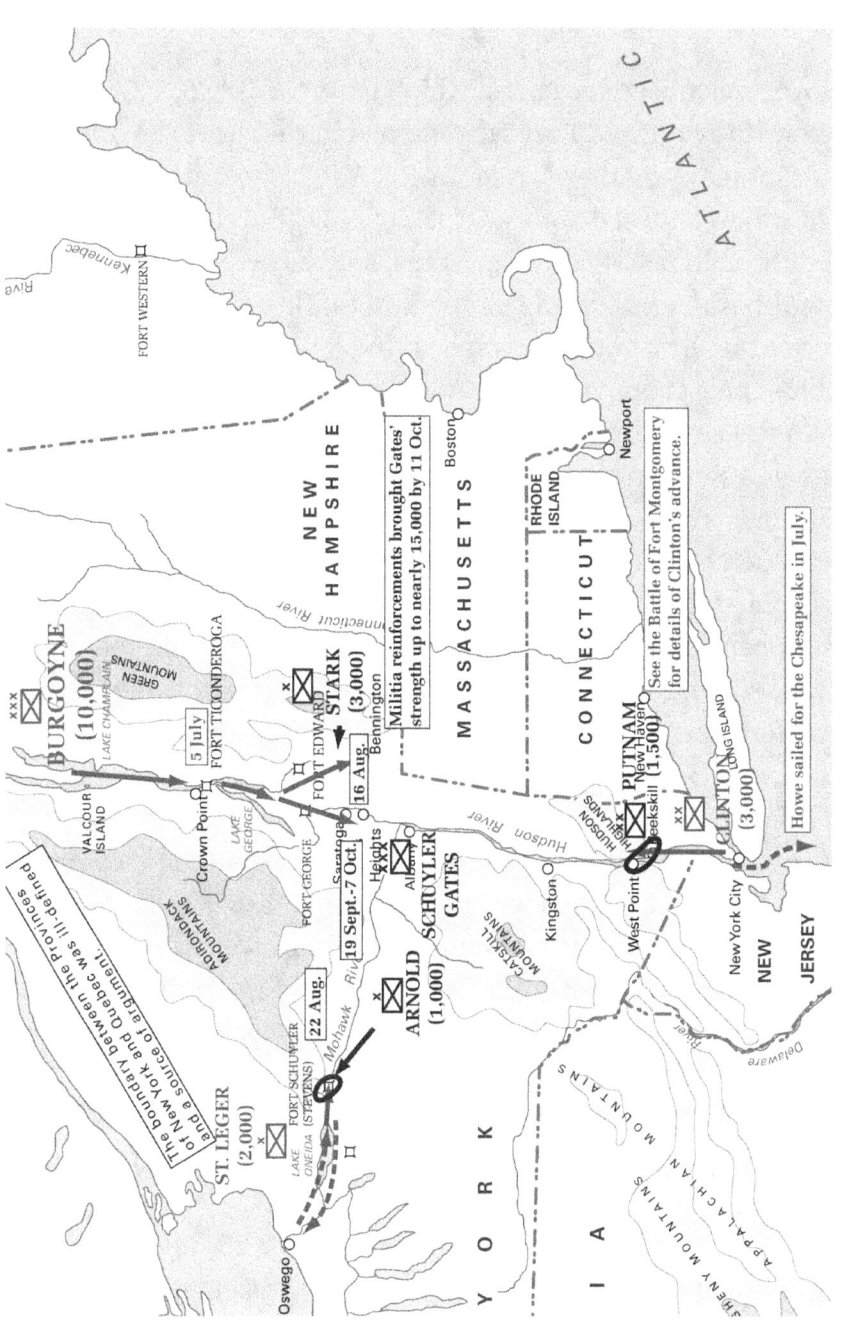

The British Strategy of 1777. Burgoyne advanced from Canada, expecting support from Howe. But Howe diverted to Philadelphia, leaving Burgoyne stranded. Surrounded near Saratoga, he was forced to surrender. (Map courtesy of the United States Military Academy Department of History)

The Illusion of Alignment

Burgoyne's campaign began on a high note. On July 6, 1777, his forces swiftly captured Fort Ticonderoga in New York, dealing a significant blow to American morale.[125] Yet, his initial successful march quickly turned into a grueling slog. Burgoyne's troops waded through marshes and swamps, all while contending with constant harassment from colonial forces. British progress had its costs: the further they advanced, the longer—and more vulnerable—their supply lines became. Local resistance grew with every mile, and so did British casualties. By early September, Burgoyne's tired and overstretched army reached the out skirts of Saratoga. There, they encamped briefly—only to face a reinforced rebel army under the command of General Horatio Gates.[126]

The First Battle of Saratoga began on September 19 and ended inconclusively. A stalemate ensued, and over the following weeks, Burgoyne, now desperate, sent repeated requests for reinforcements. His diversionary force in the west had been blocked, and Howe's garrison in New York could offer little more than belated pledges of help. It was too late anyways. The Second Battle of Saratoga began on October 7, and within the following ten days, Burgoyne surrendered his army to Gates.[127]

Where was Howe? Surely he was en route, preparing to link up, right? No. The majority of his army was in Pennsylvania, pursuing a slow and needlessly circuitous campaign to capture Philadelphia. This gave George Washington, whose army was positioned outside the city—and between both British armies—the opportunity to send critical reinforcements north to aid in the fight against Burgoyne.

Howe captured Philadelphia on September 26, unopposed. The Continental Congress had escaped, and Washington's army remained intact—and still a threat. Weeks later, while enjoying the comforts and delights of the city, Howe received devastating

news: Burgoyne had surrendered.[128] An entire British field
army was gone. Moreover,
France had officially joined the
war on the side of the rebels, followed by Spain and Holland.[129]

Lessons Learned

How could the British fail so
badly, given their overwhelming military power and tactically competent leaders? This
self-induced disaster stemmed
from two critical errors that
created Disorientation: flawed
planning and failed leadership.

Nearly every major British
planning assumption was
wrong. The idea that New
England and New York could
be cut off from the other colonies was grossly unrealistic.

Lord Germain, charged with
directing Britain's war effort in
America. Rather than assert control over his tactically brilliant
commanders, he deferred to their
judgment and left them to interpret his strategy alone. The result
was a disastrous campaign that intensified pressure on Britain militarily, economically, and politically.
(Photo: Courtesy of Alamy)

The British army and navy on the continent simply lacked the
numbers for such a giant undertaking. Even more damning was
the belief that most Americans remained loyal to the Crown and
would support a campaign against their neighbors—a notion
that proved wildly inaccurate.

The second—and most critical—reason for the British failure
was Lord Germain. Simply put, he failed to take control of his
team, ensuring unity of purpose and of effort on the parts of his
subordinates. Any governing body, "worth its salt," writes historian William B. Wilcox, "has the responsibility to see the entire

picture and plan accordingly – to determine the priorities of different theaters, allocate resources to them, and above all require from their commanders cooperation in a common effort."[130] Germain failed this essential test of leadership, one that applies equally across all levels—whether from the front, managing in the middle, or overseeing at the top.

To be clear, Germain's failures as a leader weren't just missed opportunities—they were a devastating liability to his own team. Consider that for the Americans, the Hudson River was as critical to their cause as it was to the British.[131] Arguably, even the *perception* of British control over this vital waterway—however disorganized—could have thrown the rebels into disarray, undermining morale and decision-making. That kind of psychological pressure might have fractured American leadership further. Washington's detractors, already emboldened by his defeats, could have pushed harder for his removal as Commander-in-Chief. In hindsight, that would have been catastrophic. Washington's leadership proved indispensable to the war effort. His absence might have spelled disaster for the Revolution, and for the American cause of freedom.

In the context of chaos, a leader's failure to assert control over subordinates creates a vacuum. Control-oriented individuals, if not aligned to a common effort and goal, will often seize the opportunity to act independently, pursuing their own vision of success. This is exactly what happened with Howe. In Germain's absence, he acted unilaterally, initiating his own campaign in Pennsylvania and ultimately derailing the British strategy.

The resulting Disorientation manifested in four distinct ways: strategic misalignment, counterproductive organization, inadequate systems, and a regressive cultural effect.

Strategic Misalignment

Disorientation arises from a failure to understand. Without clear alignment to the mission's *intended* objective and purpose, teams develop conflicting visions of success and pursue diverging approaches to achieve them. In the absence of that shared understanding, even the slightest difference in preference or style can shape expectations of success; those expectations then determine approaches that undermine the strategy from the outset:

- **Germain** envisioned success through a swift and violent campaign to crush the rebellion. To him, Britain would dictate terms, and the colonists would submit without reservation. Securing the Hudson River was the linchpin of his strategy, marking the first major step in a larger plan to unleash punishment on the traitors.

- **Burgoyne** pursued a hybrid strategy of intimidation and persuasion, but his vision of success never extended beyond Albany. His campaign was designed to serve as a spectacle of British dominance. By projecting strength and the inevitability of British success, he aimed to rally Loyalist support and sway neutral or undecided colonists toward the Crown.

- **Howe**, known for his sympathies to the Americans, prioritized a negotiated settlement achieved through military pressure. For him, strategic success centered on capturing Philadelphia, the rebel capital. He believed holding the colonial capital would destabilize the rebels and potentially force Washington into a decisive battle—a long-sought goal of British military and political leadership. Howe treated the Hudson campaign as a secondary concern, a distraction to be addressed only after achieving his vision of success.

Counter-Productive Organization

The problems with a misaligned strategy were magnified by an incompatible organization.

First of all, Howe and Burgoyne were the two prongs of a two-pronged strategy. Yet, both acted as independent commanders. Technically they were: British forces in Canada and America were two different command structures. They had no formal obligation to coordinate or support each other.

Another aggravating issue was the customary reliance on Hessians, or German mercenaries, in the British army structure. Their employment was seen as a profound betrayal of trust. Many colonists still viewed themselves as culturally English and bound by shared language, faith, heritage, and traditions. The rebellion was, thus, a family dispute—not a war with a foreign power. By employing German soldiers of fortune, however, the Crown sent a clear signal: the colonists were no longer part of the same national family. They were now enemies to be subjugated—indistinguishable from any foreign adversary. This decision hardened colonial resentment and destroyed any lingering sense of unity across the Atlantic.

Then there was the employment of Native Americans in Burgoyne's army. The murder and mutilation of Jane McCrea by Native auxiliaries in July 1777 outraged local populations so deeply that it accomplished the exact opposite of Burgoyne's intent: it drove colonists away from the Crown. Within weeks of the killing, enraged locals joined Colonial forces at the Second Battle of Saratoga, swelling their numbers to over 12,000—double the size of Burgoyne's dwindling army.[132]

Left: General Burgoyne. Right: General Howe. Two highly competent and respected commanders with impressive tactical records. Confident, poised, and in full control of their respective commands—but without clear strategic alignment by their superior, Lord Germain. Their individual decisions ultimately fueled the rebellion's momentum instead of breaking it. (Images: Courtesy of Alamy)

Finally, there's the issue of roles. Simply put, Howe was the wrong man for the job. A stellar tactical record does not mean one is ready for the challenges of strategic leadership, where understanding the broader picture is just as important as mastering the battlefield. Furthermore, Howe's fixation on personally delivering the decisive blow of the war sabotaged Burgoyne. (It must be noted that Burgoyne just happened to be armed with the reinforcements that Howe jealously coveted.) While Howe was not completely insubordinate, he did leave a garrison in New York as promised. It was a token gesture, a pretense of cooperation, and woefully inadequate for such a critical mission.

Inadequate Systems

Finally, the one issue that still plagues most leaders—communication—was also the central impediment among British leadership. And it was completely self-inflicted.

Major communication obstacles were ignored. Messages between London and the colonies took six to eight weeks by ship.[133] In the colonies, delays in message exchanges were compounded by the difficulty of locating armies in the field, as well as the constant threat of spies and guerrilla intercepts. Despite knowing these constraints, Germain failed to oversee the establishment of any systems or processes to manage them—or to ensure they were actually used. He assumed his generals would coordinate on their own and work together to execute his vision. They were seasoned, senior commanders. Surely they would meet this most basic expectation of teamwork, right?

Wrong.

Howe and Burgoyne operated largely in isolation, with almost no communication between them.[134] For two highly experienced professionals, responsible for executing a strategy that hinged on coordination and mutual support, this lack of contact was completely unacceptable—and predictably catastrophic.

The Cultural Effect

Not surprisingly, the 1777 strategy laid bare a "backward" mindset. Obsessed with preserving imperial glory, Germain, Burgoyne, and Howe clung to Old World tactics—strategies that had once crowned Britain a superpower but no longer fit the war they were fighting. Faced with a rebellion defined by speed, defiance, and irregular warfare, they stubbornly adhered to the slow, "Gentlemanly" doctrines of European battlefields, seeking to destroy vast armies on open ground. Their refusal to adapt turned fleeting tactical victories into lasting strategic failures—dooming their Old World campaign in the New World.

British society bore the weight of its army's failures. Financial strain mounted domestically. The war grew increasingly unpopular. And the grim procession of maimed soldiers returning from an endless conflict shattered national morale. Political factions, haunted by past defeats, splintered into bitter debate—some demanding escalation to preserve imperial glory, others calling for retreat and peace. Trapped in cycles of fear and blame, Britain began to lose the resolve and unity that had once fueled its rise as a global power.

The loss of the American colonies marked the beginning of darker days. Crippling debt, growing disunity, and widening strategic vulnerabilities left Britain dangerously exposed. The timing couldn't have been worse. Revolutionary France was rising. It, and its new leader, Napoleon, would test the nation's resilience and adaptability for decades to come.

When Leadership Prevents Recovery

The British campaign of 1777 reveals the full complexity of Disorientation, especially how it can emerge even when the odds appear very favorable. A single misalignment in one element of FINT can destabilize the rest, triggering a breakdown in direction, cohesion, and execution. Britain's defeat wasn't just a military failure; it was the result of failing to achieve clarity, alignment, and sustained progress toward a shared goal.

For modern leaders, Germain's example is a stark reminder: when alignment is missing at the outset, the mission is already at risk before it even begins. In my experience, this holds true just as much in the boardroom as on the battlefield.

Disorientation, however, doesn't always stem from missing key ingredients for direction and order. Sometimes, it stems from the leader. Their outright incompetence becomes the indisputable bottleneck to success. Teams can't recover because their leaders won't allow it. The effect becomes so destructive that Turmoil takes hold. That's where we turn next.

Chapter 14
Turmoil

Turmoil is the third level of Destructive Chaos. At its core, it stems from incompetent leadership. To be clear, the leader may be technically proficient or even respected as an expert, but their inability to both lead and manage people cripples the team's effectiveness. In Turmoil, the leader becomes *the* bottleneck to success.

Turmoil is especially damaging because it amplifies existing chaos, deepening Disunity and intensifying Disorientation. Here, the team fragments: loyalties split, and factions begin to form. Team members face a dilemma: remain loyal to a faltering leader, or act in the organization's best interest by defying them. This internal conflict breeds mistrust and resistance, ultimately transforming passive disengagement into active opposition.

In this chapter, we'll define the mechanics of Turmoil—what it is, why it matters, and how it breaks teams from the inside. You'll see the self-destructive dynamics that fuel it, and learn how to recognize and stop Turmoil before it spreads. Finally, we'll examine one of history's least-known but most revealing case studies of how Turmoil undermines strength—and opens the door to collapse.

Why Turmoil Matters

Turmoil destroys a team's ability to perform, crippling any chance of achieving its Productive Power. Consider its impacts:

- **No discretionary effort**: People stop going above and beyond. They're not just discouraged from speaking up— they're actively disincentivized, often by the threat of punishment for overstepping.

- **Reduced operational duration**: Teams are forced into reactive, day-to-day survival mode. Instead of driving big goals, they scramble to put out fires, chasing one emergency after another.

- **Dependence, not independence**: Restrictive systems create reliance on senior leaders to intervene or approve decisions that middle management should own.

- **Contribution disappears**: The focus shifts from thriving to merely avoiding failure. People stick to basic expectations, showing little interest in innovation or collaboration beyond their silos.

- **Growth denied**: Development opportunities vanish as crises consume attention. Lessons go unlearned, and future leaders remain undeveloped because no one feels they have the time.

For senior leadership, Turmoil's impact is most visible in bottom-line results. Keep in mind this does not account for the cost of missed opportunities.

- **Decreased productivity**: Assignments are delayed or missed, creating bottlenecks that ripple across the organization.

- **Wasted resources**: Teams produce poor results that burn extra time and resources fixing problems they created themselves. Worse, what high-value projects were sidelined for this failure? The long-term damage is often invisible but very real.

- **Toxic culture**: Stress and frustration breed toxicity that spreads like wildfire through the ranks. Employee engagement and satisfaction plummet, dragging down overall performance and morale. And of course, the customer feels it.

- **High turnover**: Talent departures put more strain on the remaining team, who are forced to pick up the slack, triggering greater dissatisfaction that escalates into burnout.

- **Damaged brand**: Customers bear the impact of unhappy employees. They'll make it known through negative testimonials and bad reviews. A tarnished reputation doesn't just hurt business; it makes it harder to attract talent.

The Causes of Turmoil

What is it about incompetent leaders that causes team members to stop caring about the mission altogether—or worse, to become so resentful they actively sabotage the team's success?

In my experience, five key factors drive this breakdown. Use them to categorize performance gaps, guide hiring decisions, and shape the development of future leaders:

- **Professional Knowledge:** A significant gap in understanding how to manage people or lead a team effectively.

Common signs include excessive tactical thinking, vague or contradictory communication, and a lack of defined routines.

- **Personal Awareness:** Leaders who lack a clear understanding of their own strengths, values, and worldview often misinterpret situations, make inconsistent decisions, and struggle to connect with their team. The result is poor judgment, misaligned priorities, and lost trust in their ability to lead.

- **Behavioral Awareness:** A leader's behavior sets the tone, but many don't realize how their actions shape team dynamics. The result is unnecessary conflict, alienated contributors, and hardened silos. This is how cultures of fear and apathy take over.

- **Character Fitness:** Leaders who lack the maturity, discipline, or honesty expected of their role undermine their own authority. Pettiness, unreliability, and poor self-control create a vacuum—inviting resentment and even sabotage.

- **Coachability:** Some leaders reject feedback and resist growth. They expect the environment—or reality—to bend to their wishes, and get cynical when it doesn't. This rigidity stalls their development, frustrates others, and drives disengagement.

How Do Incompetent Leaders Cause Turmoil?

Most of you reading this have a thousand opinions on the above question. Below are the four most common explanations I've witnessed in my career.

Role Incompatibility

The simplest answer is that the wrong person is in charge. Not because they're unethical, but because they're a bad fit for the role. How did they get there?

In most cases, the role itself wasn't clearly defined. Leaders are often chosen for their technical expertise, not their ability to lead a team of technical experts. The assumption? That great individual performers will naturally make great managers.

Not all leaders are built for every role. Consider that in Corporate America, leaders tend to fall into **two broad categories**:

- *Technical* leaders thrive in environments that reward precision, specialization, and control. They're often best suited to small teams, niche domains, or project-based work. Think of engineers, IT specialists, or scientists.

- *People* leaders excel at managing larger teams and navigating broader dynamics. They're typically generalists who thrive on interaction, embrace risk, and focus on big-picture outcomes. Many are extroverted and comfortable taking charge.

Each has value. But if the demands of the role don't match the natural talents of the person in it, the mismatch creates friction:

- Technical leaders may cling too tightly to perfection, isolate themselves and their teams, prefer hands-on control, and struggle to scale when speed or ambiguity increases.

- People leaders may delegate too much, challenge structure, avoid hard conversations, or relax standards in pursuit of unity or ambitious goals.

It's not that either type is wrong. The problem is miscasting: when a leader's behavioral style or functional strengths don't match the true demands of the role, regardless of what their résumé says.

Overcompensation

Team members need to feel safe to perform. They must truly believe they're in capable hands. This psychological reassurance allows them to move forward with confidence, especially when circumstances demand extraordinary effort.

Incompetent leaders, by definition, lack the ability or know-how to create that safety. To retain authority, however, they must convince others otherwise. This leads to overcompensation—a cognitive bias and defense mechanism rooted in deep feelings of inadequacy.

These leaders exaggerate their capabilities, embellish their accomplishments, or outright lie. They must know everything. They must be good at everything. If not, they fear being exposed as imposters.

So they compensate. They spin the truth, perform for the eyes that matter, and project a false sense of certainty and confidence. But overcompensation is always a façade. Teams eventually see through it.

The result? The leader signals to everyone that they are in over their head. They lose the moral authority required to inspire others to take risks on their behalf. Trust erodes. And with it, the team's ability to function as intended.

Spotting Overcompensation

Understanding why people overcompensate is less important than being able to identify the signs. Below are some common clues.

General Red-Flags

These are the least controversial and easiest to spot:

- **Blind optimism**: They paint an unrealistically rosy picture of an obviously bad situation. It's as if they believe sheer willpower or positive thoughts will override reality.

- **Selective pessimism**: They frame any deviation from *their* plan as catastrophic, using fear to shut down change.

- **Dishonesty**: They distort inconvenient or unfavorable facts to protect themselves from being held accountable or highlighting their mistakes.

Performance-Based Red Flags

These impact daily function and team performance:

- **Resistance to feedback**: They reject or diminish other people's evaluations or assessments about their performance or decisions.

- **Bias reinforcement**: They reward team members who confirm their preferences or preconceived notions. They also punish those who challenge them—often through exclusion or by blocking opportunities for advancement.

- **Overconfident decision-making**: They double down on failed strategies, forcing the team to continue down clearly ineffective and unproductive paths.

- **Inappropriate structuring**: They place people in

key roles based on personal preferences rather than qualifications.

- **Appeal to credentials**: They rely on past successes to justify present decisions. More often, they use prior achievements (real or exaggerated) to deflect criticism or shut down feedback.

Behavioral Red Flags

Incompetent leaders often go into "behavioral overdrive": the act of compensating for their lack of knowledge by exaggerating their dominant behavioral style. In other words, a lack of substance (learning) compels them to rely on style (behaviors). Common types include:

- **The Cheerleader**: Pushed by an overly excited **Relationship Trait**, they try to soothe bad news with naïve optimism and hollow reassurances like "It will all work out" or "Something great will happen." Behind the smile, there's no plan—just hope. To them, positivity is all they know in a moment of perceived powerlessness.

- **The Little Napoleon**: Dominated by a fiercely competitive **Vision Trait**, they manage through fear, punishing perceived insubordination and silencing dissent. To them, victory requires total, unchallenged obedience to their authority. Anything less is a guaranteed path to defeat.

- **The Unquestionable Expert**: Driven by a rigid **Task Trait**, they intellectually intimidate others using technical jargon, posture, and tone. Their goal is to shut down dissent by signaling that others can't grasp the real issue at hand. To them, success depends on their expertise, not others' amateur input.

- **The Deflector:** Guided by an overly cautious **Team Trait**, they hide behind consensus. Instead of owning decisions, they convene endless meetings, defer to group input, and avoid making a clear call. This isn't collaboration; it's evasion. To them, maintaining order at all costs is the key to surviving chaos—especially when their reputation is on the line.

"Behavioral drift"

This occurs when a leader's personal style becomes the default operating standard, even when it doesn't fit the mission, the moment, or the people involved.

Leaders without behavioral self-awareness tend to believe their way is not just correct but the only way. Their style becomes the yardstick for judging others. The result is a subtle but powerful form of control. People who don't match the leader's behavior get sidelined, discouraged, or pushed out, regardless of competence or value.

Imagine a hammer leading a toolbox. It expects every tool—screwdrivers, pliers, saws—to act like it. Every challenge becomes a nail. Bolts and screws are treated like nails. Wood that needs cutting is pounded until it breaks.

Behavioral drift creates friction by misaligning people's strengths with the demands of the mission. In effect, it prioritizes the leader's comfort over the team's true value.

The Case of Charlie

Meet Charlie T., a 20-year veteran in sales. He's intense, driven, and relentless—a classic hard charger who thrives on speed and results. At 45, Charlie still looks like a college football player, radiating the same raw energy that propelled him early in his career.

Charlie's team mirrors his personality: aggressive, fast-talking, and laser-focused on closing deals. His mantra? "Don't worry about the paperwork. Just get the deal." And it works—his team delivers. But there are always hiccups: missed steps, back-end fixes, and issues that eat up time and resources.

What's missing in Charlie's orbit? The quiet, detail-oriented voices who ask, "What's the long-term impact of this deal?" or "Have we really thought this through?" Planners, analysts, and methodical thinkers don't last long. They're dismissed as slow or seen as "not getting it."

But Charlie's Behavioral Drift comes at a cost. His team's impatience and constant push for quick wins sacrifice precision and foresight. Poorly negotiated contracts lock the company into bad deals—and expose just how little control senior leadership actually has.

Charlie's hard-charging style may work in high-pressure sales, but it blinds his team to the broader needs of the business. The result: a high-energy team with major blind spots—unable to adapt or innovate when the situation demands more than brute force. His Behavioral Drift doesn't just limit the team: it also erodes the company's strategic flexibility and compromises its ability to grow.

The Broader Impact

Behavioral Drift is more common than you might think. It leads to Turmoil in several ways:

- **Favoritism**: Leaders often mistake behavioral similarity for competence—rewarding those who mirror their own style. Fast-paced leaders chase speed. Detail-obsessed ones prize expertise. But this creates blind spots in performance, overlooking different strengths the team actually needs. That's how valuable contributors get sidelined, silos form, and bad hires get made.

- **Unspoken expectations**: When leaders fail to clearly communicate what they want, team members are left guessing. But there's no safe way to guess because outcomes are still judged by the leader's subjective, unspoken standard. The result is second-guessing, anxiety, and a loss of initiative. People don't act. They wait to be told what's right.

- **Arbitrary expectations**: When a leader's standards feel like the opposite of clear, professional guidelines, respect starts to erode. The mission gets sidelined by fear of overstepping. That's when teams fracture into factions of loyalty and survival.

- **Reduced discretionary effort**: People only have so much energy to give. When they're forced to spend it guessing expectations and adjusting, energy gets burned on survival, not performance. What's left isn't enough to go above and beyond. Even if it were, there's no motivation to use it.

Confrontation, or the Fighting Gene

Does the leader fight? Put differently, to what extent will they confront others to gain and retain control? Answering this question is a powerful predictor of potential turmoil.

Confrontation is a direct dispute, an emotionally charged clash between two or more parties. And it is an unavoidable aspect of leadership. Leaders must hold people accountable and deliver open, frank feedback—even when it provokes resistance or resentment.

Successful leaders master this emotional tightrope. Incompetent ones do not. Instead, they fall back on their natural impulses. Aggressive leaders often default to confrontation, quashing dissent and creating unnecessary enemies through the threat—direct or implied—of punishment for the perceived challenge to their authority. Meanwhile, less-confrontational leaders avoid hard conversations altogether, allowing problems to fester and rendering their teams powerless.

This spectrum of confrontation can be understood as two extremes: Hard Turmoil and Soft Turmoil.

Hard Turmoil

At one extreme are leaders who rely on confrontation as their primary tool for control. They have no problem upsetting others emotionally. They are typically intensely mission-oriented. They conflate honest dissent with disloyalty. Their "my way or the highway" approach creates an unsafe environment for feedback. Ironically, their approach cripples their own ability to make sound decisions.

Costs to the team:

- Constant anxiety over making even minor mistakes

- Fear of speaking up or offering ideas that might offend

- Humiliation after being called out or labeled insignificant

- Defensiveness, as energy is spent avoiding blame instead of solving problems

- Simmering anger from being disrespected or dismissed

- A need for retribution after being made to feel powerless

Some behavioral clues that Hard Turmoil is being practiced:

- **"I must be in charge"**: These leaders bulldoze others into compliance, using position of authority, experience, even physical presence to intimidate and dominate. Their communication is direct, intense, and blunt—"Get out of my way, I'll do it" or "That's a dumb idea"—leaving little room for discussion or dissent.

- **"I must be right"**: These leaders intellectually intimidate to gain control. They bury the team in data, weaponize logic, and dismiss contrary views as naïve or uninformed. Disagreement is framed as ignorance or incompetence. The result is fear-driven compliance, which is mistaken for respect.

- **Combined hard traits**: Leaders with both traits don't just intimidate—they suffocate. Meetings revolve around their opinions. Conversations become performances. And all decisions funnel through them. The result is a paralyzed team that stops thinking independently. People become executors, not contributors. Adaptation ends. So does any reason to fully support them.

Soft Turmoil

At the other end are leaders who avoid confrontation entirely. They maintain control by disempowering others—designing environments where no action occurs without their personal permission. These leaders are often exclusively people-oriented. They withdraw from tough decisions under the guise of preserving harmony. But by sidestepping tension, they allow problems to fester. Their "don't rock the boat" mentality favors comfort over progress, leaving the team disengaged and powerless.

Costs to the team:

- Frustration from being invited to give input, only to be ignored when it matters

- Demotivation from knowing their efforts won't be valued or recognized

- Devalued, as their talents are never used or seen

- Powerlessness to fix obvious problems or influence meaningful change

- Anger with the lack of seriousness, realizing their time is wasted

- Regret for not leaving sooner, even shame for having been fooled by the illusion of a "good, friendly" workplace

Some behavioral clues that Soft Turmoil is being practiced:

- **"Stay in process no matter what!"**: These leaders hide behind rules and standardized procedures to avoid making hard decisions. They stall urgency with excessive planning and drag out committee reviews—choosing safety over speed, even when inaction puts the mission at risk.

- **"I want everyone to be happy"**: These leaders prioritize positivity over performance. They want to be liked—even if it means being ineffective. To them, respect feels impersonal or cold. They reframe even glaring mistakes as harmless "learning opportunities," avoiding the discomfort of holding anyone accountable.

- **Combined soft traits**. These leaders avoid confrontation at all costs, retreating into process and positivity to sidestep tough calls. They obsess over harmony and structure, using endless meetings and gentle language to mask their unwillingness to enforce standards or confront failure. Over time, accountability erodes, urgency fades—and so does any desire to help them succeed as leaders.

The question isn't whether a leader confronts—every leader must. The question is how. Done poorly, confrontation becomes either aggression or avoidance. Both wreck teams equally. Both lead to Turmoil.

While the four causes of Turmoil often go unnoticed in modern organizations until damage is done, history offers a striking warning. One of the clearest examples comes from a little-known chapter of Western history—a moment that shows just how destructive incompetent leadership can be, even when the odds are stacked in their favor.

How Turmoil Unfolds

Few leaders in history have demonstrated the ability to overcome chaos like Hernán Cortés. Widely regarded as one of history's Great Captains, his campaign in Mexico forever altered the course of the Western Hemisphere. Even at the height of his campaign, Cortés commanded no more than 2,000 Spanish conquistadors at one time. But his strategic genius allowed him to compensate by recruiting tens of thousands of indigenous allies into his army. In doing so, Cortés achieved the unthinkable: the complete subjugation of the Aztec Empire, a vast domain spanning 125,000 square miles and ruling over several million subjects.[135]

The Spanish Conquest of Mexico is one of the most fascinating sagas in Western history. As chronicled by Bernal Díaz del Castillo in *The True History of the Conquest of New Spain*, it tells the story of a violent collision between two diametrically different civilizations. It's also a story of absolute chaos, violence, and horror. Failure didn't just mean defeat for the Spanish—it often meant a fate worse than death. The Aztecs didn't fight to kill as the Spanish did; no, they fought to capture. Spanish prisoners, along with their horses, were ritualistically sacrificed on blood-soaked altars and then beheaded. In some cases, the Aztecs cannibalized the bodies of the Spanish prisoners.

Yet not all threats to Cortés came from the Aztecs. One of his greatest challenges came from within. Another Spanish conquistador, Pánfilo de Narváez, was sent with orders to hunt him down—right in the middle of his Aztec campaign. Armed with both an army and a royal mandate, Narváez was sent to arrest Cortés. In reality, though, he was far more likely to hang the "traitor."

The Hunt for Cortés

In 1518, Diego Velázquez de Cuéllar, the Governor of Cuba, chartered Hernán Cortés to explore the New World—modern-day Mexico. His mission was simple: establish a Spanish colony in this new world, expand the empire's influence, and funnel the wealth back to Cuba.

But Cortés had far grander ambitions. Promising his men untold riches, he redefined the mission into a full-blown conquest of "New Spain." In other words, he went rogue. Over the next several months, his army pushed deeper into the mainland, seizing enormous treasure. But instead of sending the loot back to Velázquez, Cortés kept most of it and sent a portion to the King of Spain to curry favor.

Governor Velázquez felt betrayed and humiliated. He immediately revoked Cortés's charter and ordered his arrest, selecting the veteran conquistador Narváez to carry it out. Narváez was tasked with detaining Cortés and taking command of the expedition—bringing it back under Velázquez's authority.

Narváez had everything he needed and more. His force of nearly 1,600 Spanish soldiers was almost three times the size of Cortés' army. He maintained secure connections to Cuba, ensuring a steady flow of reinforcements and supplies. He also had access to native allies who could potentially add thousands of warriors to his already superior numbers.

Most critically, Narváez's army was Spanish. They had the same weapons, tactics, and discipline as Cortés' men. This wasn't a battle against indigenous Mexican warriors who, despite their extraordinary bravery, were hopelessly outmatched in training and technology. This was a clash of equals—two European armies, evenly matched in skill and culture. But Narváez had the clear advantage: more soldiers, more horses, more cannons, more gunpowder, and superior logistics.

Plus, the timing of Narváez's arrival couldn't have been better for him. Cortés was dangerously exposed. His forces were stretched thin across four regions. His largest detachment—just a few hundred men—was holed up in Tenochtitlán, the heart of the Aztec Empire. There, at the center of a city with over 250,000 inhabitants, Cortés and his men held Emperor Montezuma II hostage. He was their royal "guest." But the illusion was fading. The city's inhabitants grew increasingly suspicious, and with each passing day, hostility edged closer to open revolt.[136]

Finally, Narváez's mere presence threatened to fracture Cortés' army from within. The legal and moral authority of the expedition was now in question. If Cortés was acting outside the law, their entire campaign—and every man in it—was potentially criminal. Aggravating an already precarious situation, loyalties among Cortés' officers were split. Some were sympathetic to Narváez, others still loyal to Velázquez. These divisions planted the seeds of disunity, and many began to wonder if they should defect before it was too late.

The Battle of Tenochtitlán. Narváez came to arrest Cortés, ignoring the chaos Cortés was already wrestling with. He misjudged the man and walked into a storm of his own making. (Image: Courtesy of Alamy)

Set for Success

Narváez seemingly had everything he needed to secure victory—and more. He was poised to defeat the "traitor" Cortés, win the favor of Governor Velázquez, and cement his place in history. Except he didn't.

Despite being outnumbered, outgunned, and outmatched in almost every measurable way, Cortés decisively defeated Narváez at the Battle of Cempoala in May 1520.

How? Because Narváez lacked the one advantage that mattered most: leadership.

In military thinking, leadership is a force multiplier: it amplifies a team's effectiveness far beyond what their numbers or resources would suggest. It transforms ordinary individuals into extraordinary performers, making them resilient and adaptive under conditions that would overwhelm most.

Narváez's incompetence squandered his immense advantages, while Cortés masterfully exploited his every weakness. For Narváez, the mission failed before it even began.

The Spanish Conquest of Mexico offers a masterclass in Chaos Studies in Leadership. It's a case study in how Cortés's exceptional leadership overcame massive material, tactical, and strategic disadvantages.

Let's break it down.

The Foundation of Failure

On paper, Narváez looked like the ideal man for the job. He projected authority: he was tall, robust, and commanding, with the type of booming voice that could inspire courage and rally troops.[137] Narváez was experienced, a second-generation conquistador, approximately ten years older than Cortés.[138] His résumé included the colonization of Jamaica and he played a key role in the brutal conquest of Cuba. Politically, Narváez was well-connected. The King of Spain knew of him, and he was related to Governor Velázquez.[139]

Yet, despite his impressive background, there were red flags.

Narváez was a conventional thinker, more suited to executing orders as a warrior than devising strategies as a general. In *The Conquest of Old Mexico,* historian William H. Prescott describes him as "a man of some military capacity, though negligent and lax in his discipline."[140] This raises a critical question: Could Narváez unify his new team and ensure they did the right things when they were out of his sight?

Narváez was also "intensely emotional," with a reckless streak that often drove him to act impulsively without careful thought or consideration.[141] Bernal Díaz del Castillo, the noted chronicler of the Spanish conquest, described him as "carelessly brutal in most things; sometimes brutally careless."[142] This penchant for violence posed unnecessary risks, especially in an unknown land filled with strange peoples and customs. It raised a critical question: would his recklessness undermine discipline or derail the mission entirely?

Finally, there was Narváez's personality. By all accounts, his only concern was himself.[143] Prescott describes him deeply arrogant—a man with "an overweening confidence in his powers" and "deaf to the suggestions of others more sagacious than himself."[144] Would his self-centeredness and inflated self-belief drive the mission forward or drive it off a cliff?

In the end, Prescott offers a damning summary of Narváez. He was "together deficient in that prudence and calculating foresight demanded in a leader who was to cope with an antagonist like Cortés."[145]

This evaluation reveals a critical flaw in Narváez's leadership. His impulsive nature and lack of strategic insight left him fundamentally ill-equipped to navigate the complexities of a mission that demanded adaptability, foresight, and sound judgment—especially in an unknown land, among unknown peoples.

The Crux of Failure

Beyond his personality flaws, Narváez failed the basic tests of leadership. Success as a team begins with fully understanding the assignment. Only then can a leader effectively position and leverage the resources needed to achieve it.

Narváez fell short in three critical ways.

First, Narváez's vision of success was too narrow. He interpreted his mission as a purely military one—just as it always had been. Not surprisingly, his only tool was the sword.

Left: Pánfilo de Narváez. Right: Hernán Cortés. Two conquistadors, both extremely ambitious, but only one understood his role as a leader. Narváez projected brute strength but lacked foresight, emotional control, and the ability to read his environment. Cortés, facing impossible odds, outmaneuvered him with strategic clarity, self-control, and ruthless cunning. (Images: Courtesy of Alamy)

Cortés, by contrast, understood that different enemies required different instruments. Against his Spanish countrymen (and future reinforcements), gold was the smarter choice at the moment. So, he bribed Narváez's men with Aztec gold. "Why fight one another?" one imagines Cortés asking. "There's enough treasure here for everyone."

Second, Narváez failed to account for the significance of legitimacy. In Spanish culture, respect for law and order was a deeply ingrained value. True, Narváez represented the Governor of Cuba, but Cortés claimed to act on behalf of the King of Spain. That raised a serious question: who had the ultimate authority? Narváez's men now began to hesitate. Were *they* on the wrong side of the law? Could they be punished for attacking a fellow Spaniard acting under royal orders? These doubts eroded Narváez's moral authority, further generating Disunity and Disorientation.

Finally, Narváez failed to understand the motivations of his own people. These were conquistadors—ambitious, risk-taking *adventurers* driven by the promise of wealth and glory. While they fought as warriors, they were not *soldiers*, bound by strict oaths of loyalty.

Narváez not only ignored their aspirations—he alienated them. He hoarded what they saw as their fair share of the spoils. He also threatened punishment for anyone who took what he considered his.

Historian William Prescott confirmed not only their estrangement but also their confusion about the purpose of the mission. Cortés, through intercepted messages, learned:

The soldiers, in general, they said, far from desiring a rupture with those of Cortés, would willingly cooperate with them, were it not for their commander. They had no feelings of resentment to gratify. Their object was gold. The personal influence of Narváez was not great, and

his arrogance and penurious temper had already gone
far to alienate from him the affections of his followers.[146]

Cortés responded with precision. He promised some of
Narváez's top officers' wealth and opportunity—terms they saw
as both fair and honorable. Then, of course, he sealed the deal
with a generous bribe.

The Campaign Unravels

In April 1520, Narváez and his army landed near modern-day
Veracruz, in nearly the same location where Cortés had arrived two years earlier. Narváez quickly gathered intelligence
about Cortés' successes and location. He even established secret
contact with Montezuma II, who, as a royal hostage of Cortés,
pledged his full support to Narváez—including aiding in Cortés'
capture or assassination.[147]

Narváez initially seemed poised for success—that was until
Cortés learned of his presence and began to resist. From that
moment on, Narváez's campaign slowly unraveled. A series of
poor decisions deepened disunity among his followers and wors-
ened confusion about the team's direction.

First and foremost, Narváez confused the mission from the
beginning. His obsession with confiscating treasures for personal gain sent conflicting signals to his men. Were they truly there
to capture Cortés, or just to help Narváez enrich himself?

Narváez sabotaged his own campaign. On multiple occasions,
he seized the very gifts Cortés had given to local chiefs as good-
will gestures—an act that insulted the natives and squandered
any chance of gaining them as allies. Whether due to his "bluster-
ing conceit," disdain for the locals, or overconfidence in his own
strength, Narváez forfeited a critical source of reinforcements

and intelligence—one that might have decisively shifted the balance of power in his favor, both militarily and politically.[148]

In contrast, Cortés leveraged their full potential. By showing respect—and by vowing to help them defeat their detested neighbors, the Aztecs—he augmented his army of hundreds with tens of thousands of indigenous warriors and gained early warning about Narváez and his army.

Finally, Narváez's disregard for organization and systems only deepened his team's disunity. Instead of strengthening his decision-making with objective feedback and diverse perspectives, he surrounded himself with sycophants and careerists—people who told him what he wanted to hear in exchange for access, favor, and privilege. Indeed, his arrogance made him so gullible that he was "wax in the hands of clever flatters and diplomats."[149]

The team breaks at the point of greatest stress.

Cortés and his men attacked Narváez and his vastly superior army on the stormy night of May 27, 1520, achieving near-total surprise.[150] The victory was immediate and decisive: Narváez's forces surrendered, and Cortés suffered only two casualties.[151]

One reason for this devastating defeat was that Narváez allowed a culture of complacency to take root within his army. He openly mocked Cortés and dismissed his abilities in front of the troops—a sentiment reinforced by his sycophantic entourage. Unsurprisingly, this arrogance trickled down the ranks, eroding any incentive to remain disciplined or vigilant. During the storm, several of Narváez's guards left their outpost, seeking warmth and shelter. In doing so, they broke a cardinal rule of soldiering: they abandoned their posts. It was exactly the opportunity Cortés and his men needed.

Another reason for Narváez's downfall was his arrogance. Despite firsthand reports that Cortés and his men were on the move, he dismissed the warnings as baseless gossip, fueled by fear. Egged on by his fawning lackeys, he scoffed at the idea, declaring the weather too severe for anyone to mount an attack. "If I wouldn't strike under these conditions," he likely reasoned, "then certainly no one else would dare."

Finally, Narváez failed to protect his team from outside influence. In the weeks leading up to the battle, he and Cortés communicated through messengers. These exchanges gave Cortés the perfect opportunity to buy the loyalty of key men. Returning to camp, these newly incentivized soldiers spread tales of Cortés' successes and the riches he had amassed, igniting gossip that raced through the ranks like wildfire: imagine what treasures could be waiting for them, too, if they joined his campaign!

Narváez realized his team was broken only when it was too late. By the time Cortés attacked, approximately 150 of Narváez's men had already switched sides.[152] Others engaged in Deliberate Resistance: cannons were sabotaged so they couldn't fire properly, and horse bridles were cut, causing riders to be thrown as soon as they mounted. Many men simply

The Battle of Cempoala. Cortés decisively defeats Narváez in a battle that lasts only minutes. Overconfident and unprepared, Narváez is captured and wounded. By morning, most of his army defects to Cortés, more than doubling his strength just in time for the crisis in Tenochtitlán. (Image: Courtesy of Alamy)

stood by, letting the attack unfold and waiting to see how the chips fall.[153]

The battle ended almost as quickly as it began. Narváez and his men were caught completely off guard. During the melee, Narváez took a spear to the eye, and his demoralized forces promptly surrendered.

Narváez spent the next two years as Cortés' prisoner, while most of his men joined Cortés' expedition. They immediately marched back to Tenochtitlán to confront the new brewing crisis in the Aztec capital.

Narváez's legacy did not end with his clash against Cortés. Years later, he would make a name for himself again—once more, for all the wrong reasons. In 1527, he led a disastrous expedition to colonize Florida. Poor planning and an inability to adapt doomed the mission from the start. After losing most of their supplies and men to hostile encounters and a brutal environment, Narváez and the remnants of his force attempted to escape by sailing west along the Gulf Coast on makeshift rafts. The desperate move ended in tragedy. Most perished—including Narváez himself. True to form, his arrogance and incompetence proved fatal, sealing a legacy defined by Turmoil and failure.[154]

When Toxicity Turns Radioactive

Turmoil is the product of incompetent leadership. At its core, it stems from a leader's failure to unify the team under stress, provide clear direction, and prepare it to adapt to the unexpected. More deeply, it reflects an inability to confront reality as it is—and to guide the team toward a shared vision of success amid chaos and distraction.

Whether by alienating followers, imposing personal bias through Behavioral Drift, or silencing dissent and opposing perspectives, Turmoil erodes trust, suppresses initiative, and dismantles a team's collective capability. The cascading effects are clear: lost productivity, wasted resources, fractured cultures, and teams unable to meet even their most basic objectives.

But Turmoil is not the worst form of Destructive Chaos. Eventually, toxicity mutates into betrayal. The team no longer believes in the leader's intentions or the system's fairness. That's when Distrust takes hold. Chaos becomes truly radioactive—destroying the team's DNA and crippling the broader organization, often beyond recovery. In other words, everything needed to overcome chaos is eliminated.

Chapter 15

Distrust

L eadership in chaos is about strength—or at least, it should be.

Strong leaders embrace chaos. They see uncertainty as fuel for growth, sharpening their resilience and pushing toward success. They fight for the future, even when the odds are against them, refusing to let fear dictate their choices.

But there are those who will never be strong. They mistake *endurance* for strength. So, they don't rise to challenges—they *survive* them. They aren't building anything—they are *clinging for life*. And when their survival is threatened, they don't rise to the occasion—they embrace failure.

These are the leaders of Distrust. They fear chaos because they can't control it. They see every risk as a threat, every slipup as an indictment of their own limitations. And rather than confront those limitations, they hide behind the things that make them feel safe—bureaucracy, groupthink, and power structures that shield them from the accountability of leadership.

This chapter is about those people: leaders who mistake endurance for strength, evasion for resilience, and coercion for influence. We'll break down the four distinct types of distrustful leaders—their methods, their motivations, and the damage they leave behind. Then, we'll examine a tragic case study—how the U.S. Army turned against one of its strongest officers, Captain Roger Hill.

But first, we need to understand the core issue that makes Distrust a reality: The Survival Paradox.

The Survival Paradox

A million years ago, a lone hunter stands at the mouth of a cave, gripping a crude spear. His ribs press against his skin—he hasn't eaten in days. Inside, his people wait, weak and starving. Outside, the dark sky rumbles. Shadows shift in the forest. The cries of unseen beasts echo through the trees.

This world is not safe. But survival has never depended on safety; it demands risk. If he stays, they starve. If he leaves, he might never return. There are no good choices. He exhales, steadies his grip, and steps forward—vanishing into the unknown.

Inside the cave, the others watch in silence. One clutches his stomach, convincing himself the hunger will pass. Another mutters that the hunter is a fool, that waiting is better. To them, one thing is certain: it's safer inside, away from the chaos outside.

They're wrong.

Survival isn't about staying still or avoiding danger. On the contrary, it demands action, adaptation, and ultimately, engagement with chaos.

This fundamental truth has been largely forgotten in the modern Western world. The basic necessities of life—food, shelter, security—are no longer hard-won achievements but assumed entitlements. We have inherited massive wealth, stable institutions, and technological convenience without enduring the titanic, often life-or-death struggles that built them. Over time, comfort has been mistaken for safety, breeding complacency and the illusion that stability is the natural order of things.

This is the Survival Paradox: the gross error of equating survival with safety. It is the illusion that merely staying alive—more truthfully, avoiding discomfort—leads to real security and, eventually, happiness.

But man is the most complex of animals. His survival is not defined by mere existence, but by his ability to think, create, and build. Physical security alone is never enough. Man requires purpose: his own chosen path to self-actualization as an independent, proud, self-reliant being. Without something that gives his life meaning, survival becomes hollow, stripped down to nothing but existing, breathing, waiting.

Purpose fuels resilience and adaptability. Without it, people don't progress—they stagnate. They mistake physical comfort for personal fulfillment, and not dying for truly living.

The Root of Distrust

Distrust is the consequence of the Survival Paradox. Leaders without personal purpose cannot unify their teams around a mission because they lack the internal drive to push forward and meet the demands of chaos. Instead, they default to self-preservation in the moment, making decisions that shield themselves from risk rather than taking the difficult road to strengthen their team for the challenges ahead. They don't rise to meet chaos; they avoid it, leaving their people misaligned, unprepared, and vulnerable.

This is where Distrust takes root and festers:

- Some leaders buckle under pressure, sabotaging others to shield themselves from failure.

- Those who can't contribute exploit others who can, manipulating them for personal gain instead of driving results for the team.

- Others project moral superiority to mask their cowardice or incompetence, hijacking missions and resources for personal crusades.

- And in the most dangerous cases, entire institutions—with proud histories and hard-won reputations—are corrupted from within, repurposed to serve insiders at the expense of everyone else.

This is the real cost of Distrust: Betrayal fractures teams, corrodes institutions, and leaves lasting damage in its wake. Everyone who believed in the mission—everyone who gave their time, their trust, and their life's work—pays the price.

Four Types of Corrupt Leaders

There are all kinds of reasons for corruption. But in chaos, *why* matters less than *how.* You can't control someone's motives, but you can anticipate their behavior. Patterns are predictable, and that makes them useful: they're early warnings for what's coming your way.

Over the years, I've noticed four patterns that show up everywhere, no matter the sector, industry, or organization. Each represents a distinct type of corrupt leader—one with their own unique brand of dysfunction and damage.

Table 9. Four Types of Corrupt Leaders

Type	Defining Action	Description
Sell-outs	Buckle and betray	Side with power for safety, sacrifice others to maintain position.
Parasites	Exploit and leave	Extract resources, then abandon the host before being exposed.
Crusaders	Hijack and impose	Weaponize the organization to push their moral or ideological agenda.
Institutionalists	Capture and control	Reshape the institution to serve themselves, ensuring their survival.

Before we dive in, remember two things as you move through this chapter:

- **Like natural behaviors, these traits often overlap**—you're more likely to encounter a mix than a single, pure form of corruption.

- **Think of this section as a tool, not just a list of descriptions**. Use it to help you:

  o *See* exactly where you stand in relation to harmful leadership.

  o *Determine* what kind of fight you're in, and whether you can win it.

  o *Understand* that competence and effort won't be rewarded the way you expect.

Once you understand these types and their motivations for betrayal, you'll stop waiting for things to change. Instead, you'll finally see the game for what it is. More importantly, **you can confidently decide whether to fight, adapt, or walk away**.

Table 10. What You're Really Facing: Recovery Odds by Corrupt Leader Type

Type	Motivation	Purpose	Chance of Recovery
Sell-outs	Immediate survival	**Stay afloat** by avoiding accountability	Possible, but unlikely
Parasites	Short-term opportunism	**Prosper** by exploiting opportunities to extract maximum resources and influence	Difficult if they appear to be valuable
Crusaders	Moral validation	**Be important** by being seen as virtuous	Very difficult, need a drastic culture change
Institutionalists	Status preservation	**Stay powerful and relevant** by hijacking the institution for their own benefit	Extremely difficult, likely need a radical organizational change

Sell-outs

Sell-outs are leaders who buckle under the pressure of chaos and sell others out to save themselves. These are the executives who let disasters unfold, knowing the consequences but staying silent to protect themselves. They are the managers who manipulate results for their bosses instead of telling the hard truths that no one wants to hear. They are the employees who witness fraud and do nothing—telling themselves, "It's not my fight."

Sell-outs trade integrity for survival—not just morally, but at the cost of their own autonomy. They become passive beings, no longer pushing their own destiny but reacting to whatever keeps them safe in the moment. Those who take this path cannot adapt to a changing world—instead, they become dependents, relying on the competence and ingenuity of others to survive.

If someone can't take charge of their own life, how can they possibly lead others? And yet, in many organizations, they do. People who've never mastered themselves are put into positions of authority. And when pressure comes, they don't rise, they fold.

How Sell-outs Betray Their Teams

When faced with hard choices, Sell-outs take the easy way out—even if it costs their subordinates everything.

Take, for example, a mid-level manager in a large company. One of his direct reports—let's call her Megan—volunteers to lead a time-sensitive project. She stays late, keeps it on track, and delivers real results. But when senior leadership takes notice, the manager takes the credit. Megan's name is barely mentioned. *He* needs the win.

At first, she brushes it off. Maybe there are things behind the scenes she doesn't see. Maybe recognition will come later.

It doesn't.

When promotion season rolls around, Megan is passed over. Leadership sees her as a doer, not a thinker—reliable, but replaceable. Meanwhile, her manager gets a bonus and a bigger role.

Then something goes wrong on the next project. Again, Megan is useful—this time as a scapegoat. Her boss deflects. It's her fault. She has to work overtime again to salvage the situation.

The damage is done. Her reputation is stained. Her complaints are dismissed as emotional or disloyal. And her drive to be the best—once the reason she stepped up—is gone.

This is how Sell-outs operate:

- Make promises they never intend to keep.

- Take credit for others' success while dodging failure.

- Block strong employees from growing or advancing.

- Undermine morale by making good people question whether integrity even matters.

- Spread gossip to turn people against each other.

The Sell-out's Descent

Most don't start out corrupt; many begin with ambition and good intentions. But when pressure mounts—deadlines, expectations, or an unforgiving environment—they retreat into self-delusion and rationalization.

Once they crack, they stop leading and start reacting:

- They fake competence, prioritizing perception over performance.

- Success is no longer about achievement; it becomes about avoiding scrutiny.

- They shift blame, cover failures, and sacrifice others to protect themselves.

Sell-outs don't just fail. They pull others down with them. Instead of confronting reality, they double down on denial:

- They cut corners and lie to others—and to themselves—just to stay afloat.

- They excuse their behavior as a one-time thing, until it becomes a pattern.

- They justify their actions: "Everyone else is doing it."

- They exploit others' mistakes to shield themselves from blame.

- Over time, they don't just tolerate dysfunction—they enforce it to stay in the system.

Why Sell-outs Exist

Chaos forces people to make hard decisions—not just for their team, but for themselves. But instead of rising to the challenge, Sell-outs retreat from the responsibilities of leadership in chaos. Why? Because they lack the one thing chaos always demands: Productive Purpose.

Strong leaders define themselves by the choices they make. They know where they're going in life and work—and why. Because of that clarity, they see the world as one of untapped possibilities, not an endless landscape of traps.

Sell-outs have no real purpose. Lacking a North Star, they drift. Their decisions are driven by short-term pleasure and momentary convenience. Thus, unethical shortcuts don't feel wrong to them because there's no long-term in their lives to consider. What matters—what feels *right*—is *whatever* works *right now*.

Sell-outs are self-imposed prisoners of their own cowardice. They abandoned their obligations as productive human beings, avoiding the trials of life that build real strength: taking risks knowing that failure is an option, developing the courage to get back up and potentially lose again, and—most of all—facing reality as it is, not as they wish it were.

Sell-outs exist only to survive. Their legacy is betrayal—first of themselves, then of everyone around them.

Parasites

Parasite leaders aren't just toxic—they're radioactive. They poison organizations from within while siphoning every ounce of value before moving on. Unlike Sell-outs, who crumble under pressure, Parasites exploit it. Every challenge, crisis, or moment of instability becomes an opportunity for personal gain.

They are deliberate actors, predators who know exactly what they're doing. Many are technically competent, even talented. But their focus isn't the mission. It's themselves.

Parasites don't work to build, improve, or protect the organization. They work to extract. Access, power, resources, and credit are what they crave, and they pursue them while making themselves appear indispensable. To them, teams and institutions are temporary vessels for self-enrichment—nothing more.

Unlike Sell-outs, Parasites do have a form of Productive Purpose, but it's corrupted. They aim to get ahead at the lowest possible cost, chasing the rewards of victory without earning them.

Their sense of entitlement fuels everything. They act as though they are superior, deserving of the rewards others have worked for. Deception, in their mind, isn't unethical; it's proof of intelligence. If others were better, they'd be in charge. But they're not. So, there's no reason to play fair.

Confusion and inefficiency serve their goals. A disoriented team is easier to dominate and manipulate.

How Parasites Take Over

Parasites manufacture the illusion of offering value in order to gain influence and, ultimately, access. They form alliances only with people who serve their interests and are easy to control. Their loyalty is purely transactional. Betrayal is inevitable the moment the power dynamic shifts and they begin to lose their influence.

To Parasites, leadership is about dominance, not duty. Power is something to be seized, not earned.

They gain and maintain power by:

- Exploiting crises to justify intervention and eventual control.

- Sabotaging others through calculated obstruction.

- Cultivating false dependency: "Without me, everything falls apart."

- Rewarding sycophants instead of competent contributors.

- Purging dissent under the guise of "alignment" or "cultural fit."

- Demanding allegiance—unquestioning obedience—rather than earning loyalty.

- Centralizing decisions, making others reliant on their approval to act.

- Redirecting resources to serve their personal agenda, even at the organization's expense.

The Big Shot

Charles L. perfectly embodies the Parasite leader.

On paper, this Chief Operating Officer commanded respect—a supposed A-list executive whose pedigree and connections shielded him from scrutiny. His history with prestigious companies gave him instant credibility. His elite network and international experience made him appear indispensable. His resume, stacked with high-level roles at name-brand firms, gave him instant credibility. And he knew it.

A big man himself, Charlie carried an air of authority and expertise. Of power. Resources. Credit.

Every few years, he'd move to a new company under the understanding of helping to take it to "the next level." Within months, it became clear he wasn't there to lead any major transformation—he was there to infiltrate and extract. His pattern over the years never changed:

- **He commandeered teams.** He wrestled control of key functions from existing leaders, gutted them of talent, and restaffed them with loyalists.

- **Once in power, he did nothing.** No innovation, no improvement—just wheel-spinning and blame. Progress stalled because, he claimed, others weren't executing *his* vision.

- **He built a firewall.** He groomed a handful of ambitious executives into a loyal inner circle—a buffer that shielded him from accountability and silenced dissent.

- **He sought total control**, even trying to take the chief executive's job. His coup failed spectacularly. But before he could be fired, he cashed out—bonus, severance, and equity—and jumped ship on "pleasant" terms.

- **When exposed, he did what all Parasites do:** framed his exit as a strategic move—another "next big thing"—before the damage could stick to his name.

Charlie didn't come off as a bad or evil man. If you met him, you'd probably like him. That's what made him dangerous. His affability was disarming, his value an illusion. Charlie cared about one thing: Charlie. He used others' trust—and their hard-earned money—to advance himself at their expense.

Charlie's impact lasted long after he left:

- Shareholders lost hard-earned money to his deception.

- The company lost valuable talent, disgusted by his behavior.

- Charlie's loyalists—some well-meaning—were tainted by association.

- Certain executives saw their credibility shattered after allowing themselves to be manipulated by him.

Parasites are neither leaders nor team players. They are predators. No matter their credentials, they are liabilities—never the assets they want you to believe they are.

Crusaders

Crusaders are self-righteous activists driven by ideology rather than their oaths or contractual obligations. To them, power isn't a responsibility—it's a tool they feel entitled to. They use their position to reshape the world in service of their chosen cause or agenda. And if that means sacrificing an organization's hard-earned reputation, culture, financial stability, or even its survival, then so be it.

Crusaders are a perversion of Productive Purpose. They haven't earned real fulfillment in their own lives, so they compensate. They strive to *appear* fulfilled—even important—by championing fashionable social causes that make them seem morally superior to their peers. It's not conviction—it's camouflage. Like a comedian chasing applause instead of laughs, they're chasing validation, dressed as righteousness.

Bud Light's Crusade

In 2023, Bud Light launched a marketing campaign featuring Dylan Mulvaney, a politically divisive activist-influencer, as part of an effort to align the brand with progressive social causes. The company's leadership justified the shift not based on consumer demand, but rather on the belief that it was a necessary and socially responsible move.[155]

The result? A historic backlash, a mass boycott, and billions in lost revenue.[156] Instead of acknowledging their miscalculation and reversing course, Bud Light's executives doubled down—insisting that their customers were the ones who needed to change, not them.

The market responded. For the first time in decades, Bud Light lost its position as America's most popular beer. Two years later after the debacle, it still has not recovered its 40% market share loss.[157]

In other words, Bud Light's leadership needlessly alienated half its customer base. They were no longer selling beer; they were selling moral virtue.

Why Did This Happen?

The organization was hijacked by Crusaders. Senior executives allowed the brand to be repurposed for a political movement that had nothing to do with its product or market.

The executive in charge of the campaign even mocked the existing audience, dismissing them as "fratty and out of touch."[158] She framed the marketing shift as a necessity—not because it made business sense, but because it was supposedly the morally right thing to do.

This wasn't leadership. It was activism.

- The goal wasn't to please the customer; it was to virtue signal.

- The strategy wasn't market-driven; it was ideological.

- And when it failed, the response wasn't accountability; it was blame-shifting.

When the backlash hit, Bud Light's leadership refused to reverse course. Instead of admitting fault, they issued a statement saying, "We never intended to be part of a discussion that divides people."[159] But the market delivered the only verdict that mattered: billions lost, reputation destroyed, and a permanent shift in consumer perception.

This is the Crusader's mindset at work.

What Defines a Crusader?

Crusaders exploit people's need for purpose. But instead of connecting their work to the mission, they substitute it with a moral agenda. Performance becomes secondary to belief. Competence gives way to ideological purity. People stop seeing themselves as professionals on a mission and start seeing themselves as foot soldiers in a cause.

And causes need leaders.

Success demands total commitment—in body and especially in spirit. So Crusaders wrap their agenda in moral language. Following them isn't just right—it's righteous.

The danger isn't just that they believe they're right—it's that Crusaders believe anything is justified in service of their cause. Their "higher purpose" gives them moral license to do whatever they feel is necessary. Thus, any opposition to them is an attack on morality itself. Critics become existential threats that must be silenced. And that sense of moral superiority makes them nearly impossible to challenge.

Crusaders gain and maintain power by:

- Weaponizing guilt to enforce moral conformity and suppress independent judgment.

- Policing language by banning forbidden terms and promoting approved ones.

- Appointing ideological enforcers—bureaucratic commissars tasked with rooting out opposition.

- Purging dissenters and replacing them with loyalists, regardless of competence.

- Staging public outrage to isolate dissenters and intimidate would-be challengers.

Crusaders can ignite teams, mobilize energy, and even boost short-term performance, but never for the mission. They're not here to serve. They're here to convert—and everyone else pays the price.

Institutionalists

An Institutionalist is a leader who abuses the brand and authority of an institution for personal gain.

An institution is more than an organization. It has a distinct identity and often an irreplaceable mission. It carries legacy, credibility, and public trust. Think of the U.S. Navy, a constitutional court, or an elite research university. These aren't just functional entities. They represent enduring values built on decades, sometimes centuries, of earned legitimacy. Individuals are forgotten over time; institutions are not.

At first, Institutionalists serve a higher purpose: defending justice, advancing knowledge, or protecting national security. But over time, they stop serving and start protecting the institution itself. Not as guardians, but as bureaucrats. They aren't serving the mission; they are protecting the system that keeps them in power and relevant.

Change becomes the enemy. Reform is resisted. Innovation is smothered by red tape.

The institution, now corrupted by self-serving bureaucrats, begins to harm the very people it was meant to serve—those who still believe in its mission and depend on it to operate effectively.

How Institutionalists Betray Their People

Their security depends on maintaining the status quo. So, anyone pushing for change becomes dangerous. And when that happens, even the most loyal, well-intentioned people become enemies to these entrenched bureaucrats. Here are the ways they betray their people:

- **They Delay Progress.** Solving real problems would

expose uncomfortable truths—like how things got so bad in the first place. So they stall innovation, bury inquiry, and hide behind bureaucracy.

- **They Co-opt Projects.** They intervene and slap their name on high-visibility initiatives to inflate their importance and boost their own reputation. The project becomes a monument to their career, not a solution for the mission.

- **They Gaslight Loyalty.** They pressure people into equating loyalty to them with loyalty to the institution, creating the illusion that challenging their authority means betraying the entire establishment.

- **They Reward Loyalty Over Competence**. Talent is a threat because it can innovate, disrupt, and expose their inadequacies. So, they promote mediocrity instead—it's their survival mechanism.

- **They Use Bureaucracy as a Weapon.** They actively manipulate process to kill progress. Committees, approvals, and delays aren't mistakes: they're tools used to block change while creating the illusion of momentum.

- **They Defend the System Even When It's Corrupt.** They deceive those who trust them by insisting everything is fine when it isn't. Whistleblowers are crushed. Cover-ups become standard. Failures are buried.

- **They Leverage Your Commitment Against You.** Your time, your effort, your identity—it's all tied to your devotion to the institution. And they use that investment to keep you obedient. "Do you want to be a team player or throw it all away for nothing?" The threat is clear:

everything you've built will be lost if you don't show loyalty. What they call duty is unquestioning submission.

Why Institutionalists Are So Dangerous

Removing Institutionalists is extremely difficult. Parasites can be toppled and Crusaders removed. But with Institutionalists, you're not dealing with a single actor—you're facing a system. A network of acolytes and sycophants, all working to prevent exposure and protect their own.

Firing one of them solves nothing. By then, they've already seeded loyal disciples across the organization. This Deep State—an entrenched network of bureaucratic loyalists whose identity is fused directly with the institution—continues the work of self-preservation long after their leader is gone. In some cases, senior Institutionalists still pull strings through former protégés now embedded in leadership roles.

Expect Deliberate Resistance when a reformer shows up. The Institutionalist network pushes back—hard. The greater the change, the greater the confrontation. This isn't ordinary resistance; it's calculated obstruction. Expect a coordinated counterattack, one with ferocity: it's their reputations, status, and livelihoods on the line.

By the time you realize you're dealing with an Institutionalist, only three options remain:

1. Play along to protect yourself—but at what cost?

2. Try to fix it and risk being destroyed—or worse, corrupted.

3. Walk away—take the loss and don't lose any more time.

Institutionalists can't be reasoned with or reformed. The only real remedy is an extreme reckoning—a force that exposes the rot and holds people accountable—or a revolution from within that topples the old guard completely.

What happens when the system sees you as the threat, when just doing your job with integrity is enough to trigger its wrath?

Roger Hill and the Ultimate Betrayal

Captain Roger Hill is what we veterans would call a "stud." A West Point graduate and infantry officer, he earned the Ranger Tab, saw heavy combat in both Iraq and Afghanistan, and was awarded a Bronze Star and the highly coveted Combat Infantryman Badge (CIB).

Hill was exactly the kind of leader soldiers trusted with their lives. As the commander of Dog Company, 1st Battalion, 506th Infantry Regiment, he led from the front, training his men to be disciplined and ready for the mayhem of battle. His company carried the storied lineage of the original *Band of Brothers*, the famed World War II paratroopers of the 506th Infantry Regiment. They earned their place in that legacy. Dog Company also had the highest retention rate in the battalion, a testament to the company's leadership, and to the men's desire to take on the toughest challenges.

In Afghanistan, however, Dog Company faced more than one enemy. Their story is told in *Dog Company: A True Story of American Soldiers Abandoned by Their High Command*. As the book itself warns, it is a story the U.S. Army doesn't want you to read.

The War Within

From the moment Hill and his men arrived in Wardak Province, Afghanistan, in 2008, the situation was far worse than expected. The Army had designated Wardak a low-threat sector, but on the ground, it was anything but. Instead of a quiet deployment, Hill and his soldiers found themselves in the middle of a quickly escalating and hotly contentious fight.

Dog Company, with its 90 soldiers, was responsible for securing a region the size of Connecticut, home to half a million people. And it was teeming with Taliban insurgents. It was one of the most dangerous areas in Afghanistan. Worse, Hill's sector had been wrongly classified as peaceful by Army leadership. In reality, it was a hornet's nest. Intelligence later revealed that the area was being used as a rest and refit zone for approximately 2,000 veteran Taliban fighters.[160]

Captain Roger Hill. West Point graduate. Ranger. Decorated combat leader. Hill embodied everything the Army claims to value—discipline, courage, and mission-first leadership. His soldiers trusted him with their lives. (Photo: Courtesy of Roger Hill)

To make matters worse, Hill's battalion and brigade leadership consistently failed to fulfill requests for critical supplies, like ammo, food and water. Requests for better intelligence and logistical support were ignored. Tactically, orders were issued that contradicted the realities on the ground. Mandated patrols became needlessly risky. The lack of support and guidance left Hill's men isolated, operating without the resources and direction they needed to survive in hostile territory.

Then came the casualties. Thirty percent of Hill's men were wounded within seven months of hitting the ground.

The worst came in August 2008, when a roadside bomb-initiated ambush killed 1st Lt. Donnie Carwile and Specialist Paul Conlon critically wounding several others, and rendered Hill's 3rd platoon combat ineffective.

Just prior to third platoon's loss, Hill's men were called to support a recovery mission where U.S. soldiers from a unit passing through their sector had been overrun and captured by Taliban fighters. Their bodies were discovered—mutilated—arms severed, a heart removed from one soldier's chest. Later, U.S. intelligence reports surfaced that American soldiers' fingers were being sold as war trophies in the local bazaar.

Something was wrong: Dog Company was hit too often, too precisely. It was as if the Taliban knew their comings and goings. Then came the intelligence report from Hill's Special Forces counterpart: they absolutely did. Spies were inside the base. Local Afghan interpreters and workers—all "vetted" by Hill's higher command—were feeding intelligence to the Taliban. Including Hill's own personal interpreter.

Hill requested help from battalion. As usual, his requests were ignored.

At the same time, credible intelligence indicated the enemy was planning to overrun Hill's base. Believing he had no other choice—and that his men's lives were in immediate danger—Hill and his First Sergeant (1SG), Tommy Scott, detained a dozen confirmed spies and placed them under armed guard.

But the Rules of Engagement (ROE) were clear: without charges, detainees could only be held for 96 hours. Without formal proof of their crimes, they would be released, just as Hill's men had been forced to do a dozen times before. Only the next level of command could bring charges, but Hill's higher headquarters refused to collect the spies as required.

Hill was in an impossible position. A confession would serve as unclassified evidence, allowing Afghan authorities to take custody of the spies and stop the 96-hour countdown toward their release. But if released, they would almost certainly return to the Taliban with fresh intelligence on Dog Company's movements, positions, and readiness—and launch retaliatory attacks.

Blindfolded and separated, the detainees were subjected to psychological tactics to elicit answers about their early warning operations. 1SG Scott allegedly straddled the chest of at least one bound detainee, slapping him while demanding answers. Hill fired his pistol into the ground, 20 yards from the nearest prisoner—a scare tactic meant to break their resolve. It was a classic *ruse de guerre*, a deception allowed under the Law of War.

It worked.

Captain Roger Hill (center) at the Wardak Jirga, 2008. He met with Afghan leaders to investigate the Highway 1 Jingle Truck Massacre, where over fifty U.S. supply trucks were destroyed, Afghan drivers were beheaded, and others kidnapped for ransom. But the real weight of the moment runs deeper. Hill's posture reflects more than fatigue. It foreshadows the frustration, isolation, and betrayal still to come. (Photo: Courtesy of Roger Hill)

Their confessions corroborated the classified intelligence

collected by the counterintelligence team supporting Hill's men. The Afghan authorities could now take the spies into custody now. The 96-hour detention limit no longer applied.

Betrayed from the Top

A medical examination ordered by Hill's command confirmed that none of the detainees had been harmed. Yet Hill and 1SG Scott were formally charged under the Uniform Code of Military Justice (UCMJ) with detainee abuse and dereliction of duty—not for brutality, but for failing to report the use of tactics their command deemed improper.

The Army escalated the charges further, branding their actions as "war crimes" and psychological torture. Keep in mind: this is the same language used to prosecute Nazis for genocide in World War II.

The same superiors who had ignored Hill's repeated pleas for support now treated him as a criminal. Battalion and brigade leadership, eager to shield themselves from scrutiny, framed the interrogation as an unforgivable breach of conduct—not as the desperate act of a commander abandoned in the field.

Hill faced an Article 32 hearing, the military's equivalent of a grand jury.[161] Despite overwhelming evidence that Dog Company had been systematically neglected, the Army focused solely on Hill's actions—not the leadership failures that had forced him into an impossible position.

Witnesses testified that Hill had exhausted every proper channel, that battalion had outright refused to take custody of the detainees, and that releasing known spies would have directly endangered American lives. But none of it mattered. His command wasn't interested in context or accountability. They were interested in a scapegoat.

To make matters worse, the Army suppressed key evidence that could have exonerated Hill. The investigating officer's final report was mysteriously sealed, denied even to Hill's defense team. His attorney later stated that the report likely implicated senior commanders, exposing how they had abandoned Dog Company in the field. Rather than risk accountability, leadership buried the findings—making them inaccessible even through a Freedom of Information Act (FOIA) request.[162]

Hill had no real options. He could face a court-martial, a potential prison sentence, and the permanent label of a war criminal. Or he could take a deal. He chose the latter.

A week after accepting the deal, the Division Commander requested a meeting. In a face-to-face conversation, the Commanding General proposed an alternative: Hill could continue his Army career with a lateral transfer to another brigade in the division—if he admitted that his actions had been immoral.

Hill refused. In February 2009, he resigned from the Army with a General Discharge.

1SG Scott met a similar fate, along with three other soldiers who had simply stood guard during the interrogation. All were expelled from the military and denied honorable discharges. Their years of service and clean records were permanently stained, making it difficult to secure civilian employment. They also lost all military benefits. No access to VA services. No Post-9/11 GI Bill. Nothing.

Roger Hill, today. Veteran turned family man, author, and advocate. Hill now speaks out on behalf of service members and law enforcement officers. His fight continues for truth, accountability, and recovery. (Photo: Courtesy of Roger Hill)

Then, in 2016, an attorney who had served on the prosecution against Hill and his men during their Article 32 hearing in 2008 contacted Hill to express his regret. He admitted the case had been a *witch hunt*, driven by the command's need for a scapegoat to cover up its own failures in supporting Dog Company.[163]

Then, in February 2025, after discovering *Dog Company*, Hill was contacted by an NSA analyst who had been assigned to Hill's division during the 2008 deployment. The analyst's role was to conduct signals intelligence sweeps of U.S. bases in Afghanistan. He disclosed that within the first week of Dog Company's arrival, he had identified multiple insider threats on Hill's base. When he reported this intelligence to Division command, he was told to *stand down*—an explicit order not to alert Hill or his men. No justification was given.[164]

The Division leadership knew. They knew there were insider threats on Hill's base. And they did nothing—watching as chaos unfolded and Dog Company suffered dozens wounded and killed in action.

The Cascading Effects of Destructive Chaos

Roger Hill's case isn't just about Institutionalists—it's also a blueprint for how Destructive Chaos unfolds to its lowest level.

At the first level, Disunity was undeniable. Hill and his leadership were fundamentally misaligned, creating friction in decision-making and disruption in day-to-day operations. The disconnect extended beyond the unit itself—American forces and their Afghan partners were never truly operating on the same page. For many Afghans, the divide was understandable: within thirty years, two superpowers had invaded and occupied their country.

At the second level, Disorientation took hold due to the absence of a clear mission. Without a defined objective or vision of success, there was no coherent strategy. What did success even look like? Lacking strategic clarity, warfighters found themselves bound by a system that prioritized compliance over combat effectiveness. Instead of enabling decisive action, restrictive Rules of Engagement institutionalized hesitation—ultimately valuing enemy lives over those of American soldiers.[165]

At the third level, Turmoil set in as Hill's leadership abandoned him. They failed to provide resources, intelligence, or guidance, forcing him to assume responsibilities far beyond his rank. Instead of making decisions appropriate for a company-grade officer, he was left making calls that belonged to a battalion or brigade commander. In corporate terms, it was like holding a mid-level manager accountable for choices that should have been made by a director or VP—without giving them the tools, access, or authority to do the job.

But Hill's case plunges deeper into Destructive Chaos, culminating in its fourth and final level: Distrust. This isn't just about corrupt leadership. It's about systemic rot that enables corruption to thrive.

The Institutional Collapse Behind Hill's Betrayal

- **Congress has abdicated its responsibility to declare war.** The last time it did so was in 1941—World War II, our last decisive military victory. Since then, the executive branch has been free to wage endless interventionist wars that drain national blood and treasure while manufacturing the next crisis, ensuring perpetual conflict.

- **Perpetual war is profitable.** Flag officers, including generals and admirals, often retire into lucrative board positions with defense contractors, as long as those companies' products remain in demand. In 2021, 80 percent of America's four-star generals went to work for the very industries that profit from prolonged conflict.[166]

- **Accountability is inverted.** As Lieutenant Colonel Paul Yingling famously put it, "A private who loses a rifle faces harsher consequences than a general who loses a war."[167] Hill's mistake? Trying to fix a problem that shouldn't have existed in the first place. His leadership didn't punish him because he was wrong—they punished him because his actions exposed the system's failure.

- **The military deceives the public.** "Green-on-blue" attacks—when Afghan partners murdered their American allies—were labeled as "workplace violence" to downplay the reality of the war.[168] Meanwhile, as of 2024, the Pentagon has failed seven consecutive audits, preventing public transparency and shielding corrupt leadership from accountability.[169]

- **A self-serving bureaucracy exists to survive, not win.** Today, 40 four-star generals and admirals oversee 1.1 million troops, the same leadership that oversaw failures in Iraq and Afghanistan. By contrast, in World War II, just seven four-star generals led a 12.2-million-strong military that decisively defeated Germany and Japan, nations with comparable firepower, tactics, and lethality.[170] The fact is, the more top-heavy a system becomes, the less it tolerates disruption, especially anything that threatens a promotion. Hill rocked the boat, and the Army's response was simple: remove him.

- **Self-crippling Rules of Engagement (ROE) protect the enemy.** Today, combat units don't just deploy with rifles—they also deploy with lawyers. Every engagement requires legal justification. Every decision is second-guessed. Officers are trained to hesitate rather than act, because any misstep can end their career or land them in prison.

The enemy fights to win. The U.S. Army, as in Hill's case, operates within a system designed to sustain itself, not achieve victory. We win battles, but not wars—because winning isn't the priority.

Hill's case is the ultimate proof of the destructive power of Distrust. When I asked him what he would say to a young man or woman considering military service, his response was unflinching: "Absolutely not."[171] He wasn't condemning military service. He was condemning a system that devours its own, shields corruption, rewards vice, and values appearances over victory.

Any institution that willingly sacrifices its own—especially its strongest—cannot survive. And it doesn't deserve to.

CONCLUSION

Chapter 16
Your Turn

W e've come full circle. It's time to take everything you've learned in this book and apply it.

In this chapter, you'll find five ways to build the capabilities needed to gain strength in chaos, both within your team and across your organization. Each supports the core goals of this book: to help you pinpoint, predict, and prepare for chaos.

- A **checklist** to measure progress across the levels of Constructive Chaos.

- Guidance for **selecting the right behavioral tool** to help you pinpoint your team's current Control Outcome on the Control Scale.

- A recommended **educational framework tailored for chaos**, specifically for sharpening pattern recognition and developing critical competencies.

- An introduction to **specialized workshops** to quickly prepare teams for chaos: what they are, why they matter, how they work, and what is needed to build them.

- An **innovative approach for chaos-focused learning** that is fun, engaging, and very effective in a fast-moving world.

I've used these exact tools with clients across industries to build flexible strategies and high-performing teams—with incredible results.

Let's get started.

Chaos and You

Here's the bottom-line: Chaos is coming your way, whether you like it or not. Your ability to guide your team toward success—even in your absence—will define your effectiveness as a leader.

In this book, we've explored how chaos affects leaders and teams, both positively and negatively. It is a source of constant friction that is unavoidable, and it is one that you must come to terms with—no matter what.

Your first task is to reflect on what you've learned and apply it. Use the following questions to gauge where your team falls on the chaos scales. Better yet, ask them directly:

- Would you call this team "professional"? If not, why?

- Are we unified? Are we putting aside our differences and functioning as a cohesive unit? If not, what's getting in the way?

- Do we have clear direction and a shared sense of purpose? Or is every day just putting out fires? What needs to happen to get everyone aligned?

- Do we have standardized systems and processes that support efficient work? Are we actually using them? If not, why not?

- Can the team operate effectively without your constant oversight? If not, what do they need from you to succeed?

- Most importantly, are we reliable as a team? Where do we fall short? Where do we excel—and why?

Chances are, you'll find opportunities for improvement across the board. Your job is to identify the most critical one: the obvious bottleneck to success. Then trace it back to the core issue creating the most friction. Use the Constructive and Destructive Chaos scales to define the problem with precision. From there, map out a solution. This process shifts your focus away from symptoms and toward root causes.

Measuring Progress

As a leader in chaos, your number one job is to help the team reach its Productive Power. To do that, you must satisfy all four levels of Constructive Chaos. Use the checklist below to guide your actions and track your progress:

LEVEL 1 - UNITY	
Seamless Integration	Team members commit to mutual support and cooperation.
Social Contract	Leaders and followers uphold shared obligations.
Discipline	Systems, standards, and practices are consistently followed.
Identity	The team takes jealous pride in its work and membership.

LEVEL 2 - FORWARD INTEGRATION	
Strategy	A clear, simple direction is selected and communicated.
Organization	Roles and structure match the strategy's demands.
Systems	Workflows and standardized processes enable efficient execution.
Culture	A forward-focused mindset of optimism, growth, and resilience prevails.

LEVEL 3 - MISSION COMMAND	
Assuming a Loss of Control	The team performs effectively in your absence.
Balancing Pillars	Both people and mission are given equal weight.
Thinking in Outputs	Success is clearly defined; the team determines how to achieve it.
Sharpening Delegation Skills	Team members act with discretion, making sound decisions within defined limits and owning the outcome.
Developing/Protecting Trust	Reliability is the norm—in words and actions.

LEVEL 4 - TRUST	
Reinforcing Unity	Leaders balance mission demands with team well-being.
Improving FINT	The team proactively engages, adjusts, and contributes intelligently.
Embracing Mission Command	Leaders achieve Disciplined Initiative; teams show audacity with prudence.
Development	Relentless improvement drives the team toward industry leadership.

Finding the Right Behavioral Tool

No other leadership resource is more valuable for understanding and working with others—or for anticipating how they'll react to control and chaos.

As you know, there are thousands of so-called "personality" tools out there, and let's be honest—not all of them are worth your time. Don't confuse popularity with quality. Picking the right tool takes skill, discernment, and a clear understanding of what you actually need.

With that in mind, I want to emphasize that everything shared here reflects my personal experience and professional perspective. Nothing is aimed at any specific provider, and if any descriptions, labels, or terminology resemble those used in commercial tools, it's purely coincidental. My only goal is to equip you with the insight needed to make informed, strategic choices about behavioral tools—resources that are often misunderstood or misused.

In my experience, a select few tools that measure natural behavior are both accurate and useful. When choosing one, look for at least three essential features:

First and foremost, **the tool must be scientific.** It should be grounded in a distinct body of knowledge and tested with high confidence in its results. Scientific tools are critical for identifying individual strengths and, just as importantly, for minimizing confirmation bias.

Non-scientific tools, by contrast, offer little accuracy. But they *do* make us feel good—especially when they affirm what we already believe or want others to believe about us.

Here are some red flags to spot a non-scientific tool:

- **The tool claims to measure "personality."** As covered in Chapter 4, personality is a catch-all term. What exactly is being measured—natural behaviors, psychological traits, decision-making patterns, lived experience? Any tool that claims to assess "personality" must define its terms clearly. If it doesn't, it's not measuring anything useful.

- **They are free.** As in life, you get what you pay for. Quality tools don't have to break the bank, but they should require some investment. Free tools are free for a reason: they often lack the rigor and reliability needed for meaningful insights. Many are little more than horoscopes for professionals.

- **The tool's questions fail to guard against confirmation bias.** Agree-or-disagree statements like "I like big ideas" or "I am decisive" invite predictable, flattering responses. After all, who aspiring to be on a high-performing team would admit, "No, I'm not into big ideas"? Without checks for bias, people will answer based on how they want to be seen—not who they actually are.

- **The tool uses labels that may unintentionally divide the team.** A title like "Rock Star" can seem more desirable than "Engineer," breeding resentment among those assigned less glamorous roles. Color-coded traits also invite misinterpretation—does "Red" mean passionate or hot-tempered? Does "Blue" signal calmness or indifference? These oversimplifications reinforce stereotypes and obscure real strengths.

- **The tool's intellectual property is not protected.** A major red flag is when the tool's name is part of a business name—common among certain coaches and consulting firms. These versions are often modified with proprietary tweaks, diluting or even undermining the tool's scientific validity (assuming it had any to begin with).

Second, **the tool must detect how a person masquerades**. Scientific tools distinguish between who someone naturally is and who they're trying to be, behaviorally speaking. For example, job candidates often adjust their behavior to match what they think the company wants. This kind of "masquerading" also happens at work, as people adapt to cultural pressures or a boss's personality. Over time, suppressing natural behaviors weakens performance and eventually leads to burnout.

Third, **the tool must provide a snapshot of a person's stress levels**. This is critical for identifying the environmental factors causing burnout. I've sat down with people who seem happy or at least content, only to learn they feel like they're walking on their heads. They're so burned out that when I ask, "Are you thinking about looking for another job?" their eyes widen, like I just read their mind. Other times, the stress is temporary, caused by a short-term change in their environment. In those cases, simply explaining that what they're feeling is normal and will pass often gives them a visible boost. Instead of worrying, they leave reassured and ready to reengage as contributing members of the team.

As an added value, the best tools reveal how a person's energy is distributed across the project lifecycle. This insight helps assign tasks more effectively, ensuring each person's workload is manageable and aligned with their strengths.

Finally, make sure you enlist the help of an **expert**, not simply a **vendor**.

Many coaches and consultants use "personality" tools as the foundation of their services. In effect, they're vendors, because their expertise largely begins and ends with the tool. While they can explain its features and how it applies to human relationships, they often lack the depth to connect the results to broader aspects of leadership and management—like strategy, organization, systems, or decision-making.

Experts, on the other hand, use precision tools to complement their wider knowledge. They interpret behavioral surveys in the context of navigating chaos and create actionable plans—packed with verbs—that move individuals and teams toward Productive Power. Without expert guidance, you risk losing the critical link between behavioral science and its real-world application.

When the tool is used without expert support, it often gets dismissed. That's why many managers and executives, in my experience, see "personality" tools as, at worst, a waste of time, and at best, an interesting but ultimately forgettable exercise. Either outcome is completely unacceptable if you're serious about gaining strength in chaos.

An Education Fit for Chaos

Leadership *training* can be useful—but in chaos, its true value comes from *education*. James P. Carse said it best: "To be prepared against surprise is to be trained. To be prepared for surprise is to be educated."[172]

Education, in this context, isn't solely about gathering facts or checking skill boxes. It's equally about developing the ability to see what others miss—to spot patterns hidden in the world and to be able to reasonably anticipate what comes next. That's not a skill set. That's a mindset. And it only comes from mastering essential leadership competencies like critical thinking, cross-functional communication, flexible planning, and focused execution.

Leaders who build that mindset don't just respond to chaos—they shape it.

If that's your goal, continuous education must be a top priority. Focus on:

- **Honing conceptual thinking** to recognize patterns and solve root problems.

- **Sharpening analytical skills** to isolate what matters most.

- **Enhancing systems thinking** to understand how everything connects.

- **Improving communication** by mastering the Control Factor in leadership.

- **Boosting influence** by speaking the language of decision-makers and customers.

Relying on a Broad Range of Subjects

Leadership education can't rely solely on leadership theory. Every theory reflects someone's interpretation of the world—their assumptions, their worldview, their religion, their philosophy. Why not build your own?

To do that, you'll need a broader foundation. The best leaders master their profession by studying multiple disciplines, each offering a different perspective on how the world works. Spotting recurring patterns in human behavior—across seemingly different fields, functions, and time periods—sharpens pattern recognition and reveals the core dynamics of how people and systems respond under pressure.

Here are four fields I've found essential to mastering chaos. They'll strengthen your thinking about people and decision-making, revealing the deeper forces shaping leadership performance.

History

History is the science that explains the past. Stripped of ideological spin, it becomes exciting, relevant, and invaluable. It also provides comfort, reminding you that the challenges you face today aren't new. Others have likely faced them too, but likely often under greater stress. Most importantly, history reveals key lessons from others' decisions, shaped by the unique pressures of their time.

History can also inspire. Take billionaire and business tycoon Ted Turner. His admiration for the classics profoundly shaped his worldview and decision-making. As he explained in a 2001 interview with Ken Auletta in *The New Yorker*:

> *"They laughed at me when I started CNN. They laughed at me when I bought the Braves. They laughed at me when I bought M-G-M,"* Turner recalled. *"I spent a lot of time thinking, and I did not fear because of my classical background. When Alexander the Great took control when his dad died, he was twenty years old. He took the Macedonian Army, which was the best army in the world at the time, and conquered Greece, got the Greeks to all join with him, and then marched across the Hellespont and invaded Asia...He kept marching. He hardly ever stopped."*[173]

Philosophy

Ideas matter—and competition is the ultimate testing ground.

Philosophy is the science of understanding the nature of reality and our place in it. A person's interpretation of the world shapes everything about their decisions, from how they solve problems to how they treat the people around them. It's often the clearest window into how a leader responds under pressure.

Philosophy helps you understand how someone reasons. No matter how unusual or irrational a worldview may seem, it operates within its own internal logic. The conquistadors learned this the hard way: the Aztecs didn't fight to kill their enemies, as the Spanish and other Western armies were trained to do. They fought to capture prisoners for ritual sacrifice. Their heavenly ideals often cost them dearly in battle, but they pursued them anyway.

A smart leader recognizes the underlying logic behind decisions and strategic calculus—even when it seems irrational—and learns to capitalize on it. A mediocre one dismisses it as "crazy" and misses the opportunity inside.

Philosophy also gives you a framework to anticipate behavior and decision-making. You don't have to agree with someone's beliefs, but you must recognize their logic, no matter how flawed. This is the starting point for real persuasion and lasting influence.

Economics

Leadership in chaos demands management, which requires foresight and the ability to balance finite resources effectively to achieve goals. This means leaders must understand the true cost of decisions, in terms of how limited energy and resources are distributed. Enter the discipline of economics.

In my experience, there's no better resource on the subject than Henry Hazlitt's masterpiece, *Economics in One Lesson*. His examination of the "broken window" fallacy sharpens critical thinking by exposing the often-overlooked concept of opportunity costs. His explanation of inflation—how it occurs and flows—is a masterclass in systematic thinking, showing how a single action can ripple through an organization and produce distinct effects.

Economics in One Lesson is an education in reality-focused thinking. It strengthens your defense against charismatic but misguided or manipulative leaders. For example, Hazlitt trains you to recognize language designed to mask reality. When you translate the phrase "investing in the future" into its real meaning, "spending money and resources," the entire discussion shifts.

Finally, economics teaches leaders a fundamental truth that Thomas Sowell captured perfectly: "There are no solutions, but only trade-offs."[174] Perfection in decision-making is a myth. Every leadership decision carries a cost—some visible, others hidden. The ability to anticipate those trade-offs and weigh them intelligently is what separates effective leaders from the rest.

Military history

No other discipline integrates all the elements of leadership and management like military history. It's a specialized science that examines the ultimate test of strategy and human resilience: war. Yet today, it's a dying discipline in the United States.

Consider the gem *Fighting Power* by Martin Van Creveld. This book explores the performance differences between the US Army and the German Army during World War II. How could the Germans be tactically superior to the Allies *in nearly every circumstance*, yet still lose the war? Van Creveld's analysis ranges from macro-level issues like culture to micro-level factors such as systems of rewards and punishments, uncovering the deeper organizational forces at play.

These lessons are organizational gold for any leader serious about performance. For instance, why did the Americans prioritize **intellect** while the Germans emphasized **character**? Why were the most capable German officers sent to the front lines, while the brightest Americans stayed in the rear? These differences weren't random; they were rooted in national logic, history, and geography.

Similar forces shape your team and your decision-making. Military history provides a lens to better understand the systems, behaviors, and cultural factors influencing how your organization operates and competes. By studying these dynamics, you gain actionable insights that can transform your approach to leadership.

"Controlled Chaos" Learning Opportunities

Two major obstacles stand in the way of meaningful development for leaders and teams.

The first is limited time. There's never enough of it to learn what we need, when we need it. How often have you heard—or even said—"I wish I had known that years ago?"

The second obstacle is the quality of education. Most learning today is deductive: people sit in conference rooms and passively receive information through presentations or facilitated sessions. You try to process all the material, connect it to real situations in your mind, and then use what you've learned in the real world. That works—until the next expert shows up with their take on a new method or process, forcing you to scrap everything and start over.

With all our technological advantages, shouldn't leadership education be faster, more engaging and, frankly, more fun? Shouldn't we be able to collapse years of learning into weeks or months?

We can. The key is combining behavioral science with technology—specifically, through computer wargaming.

Controlled Chaos Workshops

For years, I've run workshops that immerse teams—whether on the frontlines or in the C-Suite—in trials of controlled chaos. Over two to three days, executives, middle managers, or a mix of both engage in real-time strategy (RTS) simulations.

Participants must work together as a military staff to create nations, develop economies, and build armies. Their opponent—typically artificial intelligence (AI)—does the same. Both sides pursue goals that are unknown to each other. As the conflict unfolds, the question becomes: can the team accomplish its mission before the chaos intensifies and engulfs them?

These workshops are loosely based on my experiences as a staff officer in the US Army. For five years, I participated in extensive exercises where commanders and staff from different units came together for days of nonstop, real-time computer-simulated war scenarios. While inspired by my military experience, my workshops are adapted to reflect the realities of corporate challenges.

The difference between military simulations and typical corporate workshops? Mine aren't just fun, they are also intense and extraordinarily immersive. There is 100% engagement; no one can hide in the back of the room and not participate.

The experience is also *very* revealing. Everyone's strengths under pressure—and their weaknesses—are laid bare for all to see. Most importantly, how participants behave in the simulations, whether in communication, planning, or decision-making, mirrors exactly how they operate in the office. The lessons learned in the computer lab carry straight back to their real-world roles.

Controlled Chaos workshops are extremely powerful because participants discover essential lessons of leadership in chaos through inductive learning. In effect, they learn by doing—personally verifying critical insights through "aha" moments. The lessons stick because they're grounded in emotion and direct experience, not passive instruction or academic models with no real-world relevance.

These workshops also expand each participant's understanding of their own role—and their boss's role—when leading through chaos. They confront challenges they've never been formally trained to handle, and they do it under real-time pressure. Most importantly, they feel the impact of their decisions. They see, almost immediately, how their actions affect the team and the mission.

It's no exaggeration: the insights gained in these sessions would normally take years—if not decades—to acquire.

How do the workshops work?

A single team of six to ten people is given a mission that—unbeknownst to them—mirrors the real-world conditions their company is currently facing. As the simulation unfolds, an AI-controlled force executes a competing mission.

Each role in the workshop reflects a critical function found in any organization:

- **Operations** control the computers, representing frontline personnel. They direct military forces on land, sea, and air, as well as civilians gathering resources and building infrastructure.

- **Intelligence** collects and analyzes data on competitors, and then converts it into actionable insights to support the team's strategy.

- **Planning** develops and refines the team's strategy. They coordinate across all roles to deliver clear direction and guide execution on the ground.

- **Commander** is a single person responsible for the team's success or failure. They oversee the entire operation, including team structure, strategic direction, intelligence prioritization, and overall performance.

Additional Organizational Benefits

Clients who participate in Controlled Chaos workshops take what they learn in the simulation and immediately apply it at work. They turn simulation templates into strategic blueprints, and lessons of leadership in chaos into operational doctrine. One client, for example, used the strategy template while scaling to a billion dollars in sales. That same company later executed a successful initial public offering (IPO).

The shared experience of the workshop provides a lasting benefit: a central reference point that reinforces the importance of mutual understanding across all levels of the organization. Participants develop a shared language that transcends rank or title.

Most teams learn the hard way. In the simulation, they experience firsthand what happens when leadership's intent isn't clear or followed. Those failures become unforgettable lessons—real experiences, not gaming scenarios—that carry straight back to the office.

These lessons stick. They're practical, personally validated, and earned—not abstract theories that vanish once the slides go dark. Participants refer to them in real business situations, using the language and metaphors forged in the heat of the simulation.

One senior executive explained the company's acquisition of a vendor to the leadership board by referencing how, in the simulation, his army cut off the enemy's gold supply, denying the competition access to vital resources. In a different vein, a fast-moving frontline manager was frequently reminded by colleagues, "Don't forget to draw the map." The phrase came from the simulation where, in her impatience, she began assigning tasks immediately after receiving the mission—without first establishing a frame of reference for the landscape and conditions. As a result, her team scrambled to align her instructions with the frontline environment.

Controlled Chaos workshops also deliver immediate organizational value by validating structural decisions. Most participants don't realize that senior leadership is quietly observing during the simulations—linking what they see directly to real-world performance.

In one case, a senior director was promoted to vice president shortly after excelling as a commander. Her performance confirmed both leadership ability and managerial strength. In another, a senior VP of sales was let go after the workshop exposed why his team's poor results persisted. His behavior revealed the root cause, giving leadership the clarity and confidence to make a long-overdue decision.

How to Build Your Own Controlled Chaos Workshop

If you don't have the resources to bring in expert help, you can still create a similar workshop on your own. Below are six non-negotiables to ensure an effective education in controlled chaos:

1. **Incorporate behaviors.** Every participant completes a behavioral survey and shares the results with the team.

By confirming their natural tendencies—including their current stress levels—they create transparency and take ownership of how their behavior impacts team performance. It also sends a clear signal: *this person is serious about contributing to the team's success.*

2. **Test the mind, not the body.** Computer simulations are ideal because they engage everyone—regardless of age, physical ability, or technical skill. But watch out: some "gamers" may try to dominate the exercise by controlling the computer. Don't let them turn the workshop into a solo mission. The real value lies in the collective team experience. Everyone should stay actively involved, supporting the leader by preparing maps, developing plans, drafting orders, and contributing to intelligent, coordinated action as a team.

3. **Connect simulation conditions to work performance.** The simulation should mirror the core competencies required in leadership: critical thinking, cross-functional communication, resource allocation, strategic and operational planning, and managing personalities under stress. Assign roles that match participants' actual responsibilities—for example, placing a finance leader in charge of resources. Alternatively, assign them to a different role entirely so they can experience—and feel—the pressures their teammates face.

4. **Rotate everyone into the Commander role.** Every participant should step into *the* senior leadership role and feel the pressure of juggling competing demands. While a simulation can't fully replicate executive responsibilities, it does create realistic stressors: time constraints, limited resources, competing priorities, and team dynamics.

Participants quickly discover what it takes to lead under pressure, and what happens when they don't.

5. **Make it a safe place to fail.** Participants need to experience the consequences of their decisions—good and bad—in a controlled, supportive environment. Mistakes should be expected, even encouraged, as long as they drive learning. Better to fail here, where the cost is nothing, than in the real world, where failure could jeopardize the team, the mission, or the company.

6. **A strong facilitator.** The effectiveness of any Controlled Chaos workshop depends on the facilitator's ability to draw out lessons and link them directly to on-the-job performance. They must manage personalities, keep the team focused, and confront poor performance without hesitation. That means pushing back on rationalizations and addressing misalignment the moment it appears—directly and constructively, in front of the group.

   But this kind of candor only works with full buy-in from the very top. Controlled Chaos workshops aren't feel-good training sessions. Real emotions surface, and people finally voice hard truths that have gone unspoken. And in some cases, the workshop reveals that certain people aren't a fit for the roles they're in.

   The facilitator must handle all of it—without flinching. In the end, the workshop must deliver what matters: clarity, alignment, and a team capable of delivering under pressure.

The long-term value of Controlled Chaos workshops depends on what happens afterward. Treat the workshop as a one-off event, and the breakthroughs disappear. Nothing changes.

To prevent that, reinforce the lessons and embed them into

daily routines. Reference takeaways in meetings. Build habits around them. Turn key language from the simulations into a shared lexicon. Let the lessons from controlled chaos become your strength in real chaos.

Reimagining Learning for Chaos

Books can never be replaced. But today's digital age offers powerful complements—options that fit our busy lives. Podcasts, video lectures, online archives, and even unconventional resources like movies and documentaries can deepen your understanding. Used wisely, they help refine what you've learned about leadership, behavior, and decision-making through both reading and experience.

That said, modern methods have limits. Most are built to entertain, not to educate. They can support your learning, but should never replace the written word, where sources and context are preserved.

The danger lies in their convenience and persuasiveness. Dramatized portrayals—especially of historical figures—are often simplified, exaggerated, or distorted for narrative impact. But if you can engage with these characters as written, without mistaking them for real historical accounts, you unlock a powerful new resource for expansive learning.

Done right, modern tools offer immense value. Take Jodi M., a senior manager at a Fortune 150 company. Prior to COVID, she introduced an innovative professional development program for her team using popular streaming services. She divided her 20-person team into smaller learning groups based on behavioral profiles and assigned a ten-part series to watch and analyze. Over six weeks, they met weekly for one-hour discussions facilitated by Jodi, focusing on characters, team dynamics, strategy, decision-making, and behaviors. The engagement level was extraordinary. "Some employees saw their mindsets and behaviors play out on the big screen," Jodi said. One of her employees reflected, "I never realized that's how I came across."[175]

This unconventional approach yielded tangible business results: a 15% increase in inclusion, an 18% boost in teamwork, and a remarkable 40% increase in innovation.[176] New ideas flowed from employees who had previously been quiet in traditional settings. By making the experience fun and emotionally engaging, employees internalized the lessons, driving meaningful change and measurable impact.

When COVID struck and her employees were stuck at home, Jodi continued the program. Now, though, employees invited loved ones to join in, turning professional development into a shared family experience. Some even thanked her for continuing the process, citing the insights and connections it fostered during a challenging time.

Modern learning tools, when used thoughtfully, are not just a supplement to traditional methods—they are a powerful way to reinforce adaptability and innovation in the face of chaos.

Now It's Your Turn

You've explored the complex terrain of chaos. You can now identify its patterns, measure its effects, and guide your team through the storm. The challenge now is to transform that knowledge into a competitive advantage that benefits your team, your organization, and yourself.

Let this book be your ultimate resource for chaos. Leaders and teams who embrace these ideas and lessons will thrive where others sink into self-destruction.

The five tools from this chapter—the Constructive Chaos

checklist, selecting the right behavioral tool, a chaos-tailored education track, Controlled Chaos workshops, and a modern approach to chaos-focused learning—form the foundation for mastering the uncontrollable.

Never forget: chaos is inevitable. Don't let fear of it drive you into futile attempts to control or avoid it. Instead, embrace it. Meet it head-on with certainty, competence, and confidence. In doing so, you'll uncover your true potential—not just by building a strong team but by creating a legacy of leadership defined by resilience and adaptability.

This is just the beginning of your journey to gain strength in chaos.

The world needs strong leaders now more than ever.

Be that strong leader.

Endnotes

Chapter 1: Strength in Chaos

1 Kevin Black, "Why Behaviors Are a Critical Yet Largely Untapped Resource for Leaders," Forbes, August 22, 2019, https://www.forbes.com/councils/forbescoachescouncil/2019/08/22/why-behaviors-are-a-critical-yet-largely-untapped-resource-for-leaders/

Chapter 3: The Metaphysics of Chaos

2 Will Durant, *The Life of Greece: The Story of Civilization, Volume II* (New York: Simon and Schuster, 1939), 99.
3 W.T. Jones, *A History of Western Philosophy I: The Classical Mind* (New York: Harcourt, Brace & World, Inc., 1969), 14–15.
4 W. T. Jones, *A History of Western Philosophy: Kant and the Nineteenth Century*, Vol. IV (New York: Harcourt, Brace & World, 1969), 258.
5 Edward N. Lorenz, *The Essence of Chaos* (Seattle: University of Washington Press, 1995), 5–9.
6 Gleick, James. *Chaos: Making a New Science.* New York: Viking, 1987, 8.
7 Fiedler, Klaus, Johannes Prager, and Linda McCaughey. "Metacognitive Myopia: A Major Obstacle on the Way to Rationality." *Current Directions in Psychological Science* 32, no. 1 (2023): 49-56.
8 Ayn Rand, *Introduction to Objectivist Epistemology*, (New York: New American Library, 1979), 91.
9 Carl von Clausewitz, *On War*, ed. and trans. Michael Howard and Peter Paret (Oxford: Oxford University Press, 2006), 88-89.

Chapter 4: The Driver of Chaos

10 James Gleick, *Chaos: Making a New Science* (New York: Viking, 1987), 8.

11   Kevin Black, "Why Behaviors Are a Critical Yet Largely Untapped Resource for Leaders," *Forbes*, Forbes Coaches Council, August 22, 2019, https://www.forbes.com/councils/forbescoachescouncil/2019/08/22/why-behaviors-are-a-critical-yet-largely-untapped-resource-for-leaders/.

Chapter 5: Leadership in Chaos

12   Ed Cray, *General of the Army: George C. Marshall, Soldier and Statesman* (New York: W. W. Norton & Company, 1990), 591.
13   Friedrich Nietzsche, *Twilight of the Idols, or, How to Philosophize with the Hammer*, trans. Richard Polt (Indianapolis: Hackett Publishing Company, 1997), 6.

Chapter 6: How Chaos Unfolds in a Team

14   *New York Times*, "May 11, 1973: Charges Dropped Against Pentagon Papers Leakers," *The Learning Network*, May 11, 2012, https://archive.nytimes.com/learning.blogs.nytimes.com/2012/05/11/may-11-1973-charges-dropped-against-pentagon-papers-leakers/index.html.

Chapter 7: What Success in Chaos Looks Like

15   Plutarch. *Plutarch's Lives*, trans. Bernadotte Perrin (Cambridge, MA: Harvard University Press; London: William Heinemann Ltd., 1920), vol. 21, part 9.
16   Livy, *The History of Rome*, book 30, chap. 31, trans. Frank Gardner Moore, *Perseus Digital Library*, Tufts University, https://www.perseus.tufts.edu/hopper/text?doc=Perseus%3Atext%3A1999.02.0159%3A-book%3D30%3Achapter%3D31.
17   B. H. Liddell Hart, *Scipio Africanus: Greater Than Napoleon* (Cambridge, MA: Da Capo Press, 2004), 152.
18   David Eggenberger, *An Encyclopedia of Battles: Accounts of Over 1,560 Battles from 1479 B.C. to the Present* (Mineola, NY: Dover Publications, 1985), 452.
19   Cornelius Nepos, *Life of Hannibal*, scientific ed. Bret Mulligan (Cambridge: Open Book Publishers, 2015), sec. 28, https://doi.org/10.11647/OBP.0075.
20   Livy, *The History of Rome*, trans. Frank Gardner Moore (Cambridge, MA: Harvard University Press; London: William Heinemann Ltd., 1949), book 22, chap. 49.

21 Will Durant, *Caesar and Christ: The Story of Civilization, Volume III* (New York: Simon & Schuster, 2011), 52.

22 Hart, 62.

23 Klima, Kenneth T., Peter Mazzella, and Patrick B. McLaughlin. "Scipio Africanus and the Second Punic War: Joint Lessons for Center of Gravity Analysis." *Joint Force Quarterly* 88 (January 2018).

24 Hart, 63–64.

25 Ibid., 90.

26 Ibid., 94.

27 Ibid., 119.

28 Ibid.

29 J. F. Lazenby, *Hannibal's War* (Norman: University of Oklahoma Press, 1998), 203.

30 Ibid., 205.

31 Ibid., 208.

32 Ibid., 209.

33 Eggenberger, 487.

34 Polybius, *The Rise of the Roman Empire*, trans. Ian Scott-Kilvert (Harmondsworth, NY: Penguin, 1979), 477.

35 Livy, *The History of Rome*, book 30, trans. Frank Gardner Moore, *Perseus Digital Library*, Tufts University, https://www.perseus.tufts.edu/hopper/text?doc=Perseus%3Atext%3A1999.02.0159%3Abook%3D30s.

36 Hart, 63.

37 Livy, *A History of Rome: Selections*, trans. Moses Hadas and Joe Park Poe (New York: Modern Library, 1962), 344.

38 Edward Luttwak, *The Grand Strategy of the Roman Empire from the First Century A.D. to the Third* (Baltimore: Johns Hopkins University Press, 1976), 141.

Chapter 8: Unity

39 Jon R. Katzenbach and Douglas K. Smith, "The Discipline of Teams," *Harvard Business Review*, March 1993.

40 Ibid.

41 Peter F. Drucker, *The Practice of Management* (New York: Harper & Row, 1954), 159.

42 Victor Davis Hanson, *Carnage and Culture* (New York: Anchor Books, 2002), 64.

43 Encyclopaedia Iranica Foundation, "ARMY i. Pre-Islamic Iran," *Encyclopaedia Iranica*, Link: https://www.iranicaonline.org/articles/army-i.

44 Hanson, *Carnage and Culture*, 64.

45 Xenophon, *Anabasis*, trans. Carleton L. Brownson (Cambridge, MA: Harvard University Press, 1922), Book 1, Chapter 8, Sections 26–29, p. 321.

46 Hanson, *Carnage and Culture*, 64.

47 Xenophon, Book 2, Chapter 5, Section 39; Chapter 6, Section 3, p. 401.

48 Ibid., Book 3, Chapter 4, Sections 4-6.

49 Ibid., Book 4, Chapter 3, Section 2.

50 Ibid., Book 4, Chapter 7, Section 24.

51 Ibid., Book 4, Chapter 8, Sections 9-18.

52 Robert J. Bonner, "The Organization of the Ten Thousand," *The Classical Journal* 7, no. 9 (June 1912): 358.

53 Shane Brennan, "On the Enduring Appeal of Xenophon's *Anabasis*," *Literary Hub*, December 17, 2021. https://lithub.com/on-the-enduring-appeal-of-xenophons-anabasis/.

54 Ibid.

55 Xenophon, Book 3, Chapter 1, 36–41, p. 433.

56 Ibid., Book 4, Chapter 5, 8–14, p. 41.

57 Bonner, "The Organization of the Ten Thousand," 354–55.

Chapter 9: Forward Integration

58 Andrew S. Grove, *Intel Keynote* (presentation, Academy of Management Annual Meeting, San Diego, CA, August 9, 1998), https://www.intel.com/pressroom/archive/speeches/ag080998.htm.

59 Robert A. Burgelman et al., "Fading Memories: A Process Theory of Strategic Business Exit in Dynamic Environments," *Administrative Science Quarterly* 39, no. 1 (1994): 24–56.

60 Andrew S. Grove, *Only the Paranoid Survive: How to Exploit the Crisis Points That Challenge Every Company and Career* (New York: Currency Doubleday, 1996), 34.

61 BBC News. "Former Intel Chief Andrew Grove Dies Aged 79." *BBC News*. March 21, 2016, https://www.bbc.com/news/business-35866274.

62 Oliver Staley, "Silicon Valley's Confrontational Management Style Started with Andy Grove," *Quartz*, April 8, 2016, https://qz.com/656708/silicon-valleys-confrontational-management-style-started-with-andy-grove.

63 Ibid.

64 Grove, *Intel Keynote*.

65 Grove, *Only the Paranoid Survive,* 140.

66 Grove, *Intel Keynote*.

67 Grove, *Only the Paranoid Survive,* 96.
68 Grove, *Only the Paranoid Survive,* 97.
69 Grove, *Only the Paranoid Survive,* 153.
70 Grove, *Intel Keynote.*

Chapter 10: Mission Command

71 Arthur Herman, *To Rule the Waves: How the British Navy Shaped the Modern World* (New York: Harper Perennial, 2005), 359.
72 David Eggenberger, *An Encyclopedia of Battles: Accounts of Over 1,560 Battles from 1479 B.C. to the Present* (Mineola, NY: Dover Publications, 1985), 305–6.
73 Herman, *Waves,* 353.
74 Michael A. Palmer, *Command at Sea: Naval Command and Control Since the Sixteenth Century* (Cambridge, MA: Harvard University Press, 2007), 5.
75 Palmer, *Command,* 13.
76 Herman, *Waves,* 359.
77 Ibid., 357.
78 Palmer, *Command,* 11.
79 Roger Knight, *The Pursuit of Victory: The Life and Achievement of Horatio Nelson* (London: Penguin Books, 2006), 297.
80 Herman, *Waves,* 360.
81 Ibid.
82 Knight, *Victory,* 286.
83 Palmer, *Command,* 13.
84 Herman, *Waves,* 357.
85 Knight, *Victory,* 139.
86 Herman, *Waves,* 296.
87 Ibid., 286.
88 Donald E. Vandergriff, *Adopting Mission Command: Developing Leaders for a Superior Command Culture* (Annapolis, MD: Naval Institute Press, 2019), 27–28.
89 Kevin Black, "Ep. 33 – 'Mission Command: A Leadership Philosophy of Initiative, Empowerment, and Flexibility – Part 1 of 2,'" *Black Market Leadership* (podcast), March 15, 2023.

Chapter 11: Trust

90 Ed Cray, *General of the Army: George C. Marshall, Soldier and Statesman* (New York: Cooper Square Press, 2000), 658.

91 Ibid., xii.

92 Ibid., xi.

93 Tunku Varadarajan, "For FedEx Founder Fred Smith, the Sky Is Still the Limit," *Wall Street Journal*, April 15, 2022.

94 Thomas E. Ricks, *The Generals: American Military Command from World War II to Today* (New York: Penguin Books, 2013), 35.

95 Cray, *General of the Army*, 168-171.

96 David Eggenberger, *An Encyclopedia of Battles: Accounts of Over 1,560 Battles from 1479 B.C. to the Present* (New York: Dover, 1985), 153–54.

97 Cray, *General of the Army*, 177.

98 Ibid., 177.

99 Ricks, *The Generals*, 33.

100 George C. Marshall, *George C. Marshall: Interviews and Reminiscences for Forrest C. Pogue*, ed. Larry I. Bland (Lexington, VA: George C. Marshall Research Foundation, 1991), 534.

101 Ricks, *The Generals*, 35.

102 George C. Marshall to General John S. Mallory, November 5, 1920, George C. Marshall Papers, George C. Marshall Research Foundation, Lexington, VA.

103 Thomas E. Ricks, "Why Our Generals Were More Successful in World War II than in Korea, Vietnam, or Iraq/Afghanistan," *UC Berkeley Events, The Fleet Admiral Chester W. Nimitz Memorial Lecture*, March 22, 2011, YouTube video, 1:26:47, https://youtu.be/AxZWxxZ2JGE?si=NvBHm20vaYnlIG8V.

104 Ibid.

105 George C. Marshall, *The Papers of George Catlett Marshall*, ed. Larry I. Bland and Sharon Ritenour Stevens, vol. 2 (Baltimore: Johns Hopkins University Press, 1981), 622.

106 Richard Demartino, Jack Clarcq, and Michael Palanski, "George C. Marshall: An Enduring Model of Leadership Effectiveness," *Journal of Character & Leadership Integration* 2, no. 1 (Fall 2011): 21, https://www.usafa.edu/app/uploads/JCLI-Fall-2011.pdf.

107 Ibid., 22.

108 Ricks, *The Generals*, 37.

109 Samuel J. Cox, "H-008-5: Admiral Ernest J. King—Chief of Naval Operations, 1942," *Naval History and Heritage Command*, July 2017, https://www.history.navy.mil/about-us/leadership/director/directors-corner/h-grams/h-gram-008/h-008-5.html.

110 Cray, *General of the Army*, 9.

111   Mark A. Stoler, *George C. Marshall: Soldier-Statesman of the American Century* (Boston: Twayne Publishers, 1989), 108.

112   Cray, *General of the Army*, 436.

113   Ibid., 178.

114   *The Civil War*, directed by Ken Burns, Episode 3, "Stonewall," PBS, originally aired September 24 1990, approx. 75 min.

Chapter 12: Disunity

115   Fleming, Michael. "The Agent." *The New Yorker*, July 10, 2006. https://www.newyorker.com/magazine/2006/07/10/the-agent.

116   United States Congress, House, Committee on Foreign Affairs, Subcommittee on International Organizations, Human Rights, and Oversight, and Subcommittee on Europe. *Extraordinary Rendition in U.S. Counterterrorism Policy: The Impact on Transatlantic Relations.* Joint Hearing, 110th Congress, 1st session, April 17, 2007. Washington, D.C.: U.S. Government Printing Office, 2007.

117   Lawrence Wright, "Missed Opportunities," *The New Yorker*, July 10, 2006, https://www.newyorker.com/magazine/2006/07/10/missed-opportunities

Chapter 13: Disorientation

118   William B. Willcox, "Too Many Cooks: British Planning Before Saratoga," *Journal of British Studies* 2, no. 1 (1962): 56.

119   David Eggenberger, *An Encyclopedia of Battles: Accounts of Over 1,560 Battles from 1479 B.C. to the Present* (New York: Dover, 1985), 66.

120   W. H. Moomaw, "The Denouement of General Howe's Campaign of 1777," *The English Historical Review* 79, no. 312 (July 1964): 498.

121   Eggenberger, *Encyclopedia*, 444.

122   Richard M. Ketchum, *Saratoga: Turning Point of America's Revolutionary War* (New York: Henry Holt, 1997), 67.

123   Ketchum, *Saratoga*, 84.

124   Willcox, *Cooks*, 61.

125   Ketchum, *Saratoga*, 116.

126   John Luzader, *Decision on the Hudson: The Saratoga Campaign of 1777* (Clemson, SC: Americana Collection, 1975), 40.

127   Eggenberger, *Encyclopedia*, 386.

128   Robert Middlekauff, *The Glorious Cause: The American Revolution, 1763-1789* (New York: Oxford University Press, 2005), 402.

129   Middlekauff, *The Glorious Cause*, 386.

130 Willcox, "Too Many Cooks," 65.
131 Thomas S. Wermuth and James M. Johnson, "The American Revolution in the Hudson River Valley: An Overview," *Hudson River Valley Review* 20, no. 1 (2003), 9.
132 Ketchum, *Saratoga*, 395.
133 Willcox, "Too Many Cooks," 65.
134 Ibid.

Chapter 14: Turmoil

135 Miguel León-Portilla, *The Broken Spears: The Aztec Account of the Conquest of Mexico* (Boston: Beacon Press, 1962), xxiii.
136 León-Portilla, *The Broken Spears*, xix.
137 Frank Goodwyn, "Pánfilo de Narváez: A Character Study of the First Spanish Leader to Land an Expedition to Texas," *Hispanic American Historical Review* 29, no. 1 (February 1949): 150.
138 Hugh Thomas, *Conquest: Montezuma, Cortés, and the Fall of Old Mexico* (New York: Simon & Schuster, 1993), 354.
139 Goodwyn, "Character Study," 152.
140 William Hickling Prescott, *The Works of William H. Prescott* (Philadelphia and London: J. B. Lippincott Company, 1904), 30.
141 Goodwyn, "Character Study," 153.
142 Thomas, *Conquest*, 354.
143 Goodwyn, "Character Study," 154.
144 Prescott, *Works*, 30.
145 Ibid., 30.
146 William H. Prescott, *History of the Conquest of Mexico* (United Kingdom: Random House Publishing Group, 2010), 504.
147 Thomas, *Conquest*, 364.
148 Goodwyn, "Character Study," 154.
149 Ibid., 155.
150 Joaquín Telesforo de Trueba y Cosío, *Life of Hernan Cortes* (United Kingdom: Constable and Company, 1829), 216.
151 Hernán Cortés, *Cartas y relaciones de Hernán Cortés al emperador Carlos V*, second letter, 140–43, in *The Conquest of Mexico*, ed. and trans. Nancy Fitch (2004).
152 Thomas, *Conquest*, 375.
153 Ibid., 379-380.
154 Douglas Preston, "Brutal Journey," *Sarasota Magazine*, December 2006.

Chapter 15: Distrust

155   Mike Rowe, host. *The Way I Heard It with Mike Rowe*, "424: Anson Frericks – Last Call for Bud Light," podcast audio, February 5, 2025, Apple Podcasts, https://podcasts.apple.com/us/podcast/424-anson-frericks-last-call-for-bud-light/id1087110764?i=1000688865792.

156   Gavin Newsham, "How the Decline of Budweiser Was Decades in the Making," *New York Post*, January 25, 2025, https://nypost.com/2025/01/25/lifestyle/how-the-decline-of-budweiser-was-decades-in-the-making/.

157   Rowe, *The Way I Heard It*, "424: Anson Frericks – Last Call for Bud Light."

158   Sonia Thompson, "3 Inclusive Marketing Lessons from Bud Light's Fumbled Dylan Mulvaney Controversy," *Forbes*, April 21, 2023, https://www.forbes.com/sites/soniathompson/2023/04/21/3-inclusive-marketing-lessons-from-bud-lights-fumbled-dylan-mulvaney-controversy/.

159   The Enquirer, "Anheuser-Busch CEO Brendan Whitworth Releases Statement Amid Dylan Mulvaney Bud Light Backlash," *Cincinnati Enquirer*, April 14, 2023, https://www.cincinnati.com/story/news/2023/04/14/anheuser-busch-ceo-brendan-whitworth-releases-statement-amid-dylan-mulvaney-bud-light-backlash/70116412007/.

160   *Roger Hill, interview by Kevin Black, Black Market Leadership*, Episode 57, "Dog Company: The Pentagon's Betrayal of American Heroes in Afghanistan, Part 1 of 2," Apple Podcasts, December 20, 2022, https://podcasts.apple.com/us/podcast/ep-57-dog-company-the-pentagons-betrayal-of/id1523238553?i=1000590418381.

161   "Article 32 Investigation Ends," *DVIDS*, March 5, 2008, https://www.dvidshub.net/news/27178/article-32-investigation-ends.

162   Roger Hill, interview by Kevin Black, *Black Market Leadership*, Episode 58, "Dog Company: The Pentagon's Betrayal of American Heroes in Afghanistan, Part 2 of 2," Apple Podcasts, December 22, 2022, https://podcasts.apple.com/us/podcast/ep-58-dog-company-the-pentagons-betrayal-of/id1523238553?i=1000592182730.

163   Roger Hill, email message to author, March 17, 2025.

164   Ibid.

165   Roger Hill, "American Military Culture Values Enemies Above U.S. Troops," *Washington Times*, April 12, 2017,

https://www.washingtontimes.com/news/2017/apr/12/american-military-culture-values-enemies-above-us-/.

166   William D. Hartung, *March of the Four Stars: The Role of Retired Generals and Admirals in the Arms Industry*, Quincy Institute for Responsible Statecraft, October 4, 2023, https://quincyinst.org/research/march-of-the-four-stars-the-role-of-retired-generals-and-admirals-in-the-arms-industry/.

167   Paul Yingling, "A Failure in Generalship," *Armed Forces Journal*, May 1, 2007, https://armedforcesjournal.com/a-failure-in-generalship/.

168   Hill, interview by Black, *Black Market Leadership*, Episode 58.

169   Dress, Brad. "Pentagon Fails 7th Audit in a Row but Says Progress Made." *The Hill*, November 15, 2024. https://thehill.com/policy/defense/4992913-pentagon-fails-7th-audit-in-a-row-but-says-progress-made/.

170   Douglas Macgregor and Joshua Whitehouse, "America's Four-Star Problem," *The American Conservative*, September 29, 2022, https://www.theamericanconservative.com/americas-four-star-problem/.

171   Hill, interview by Black, *Black Market Leadership*, Episode 57.

Chapter 16: Your Turn

172   Carse, James P. *Finite and Infinite Games: A Vision of Life as Play and Possibility*. New York: Ballantine Books, 1986, 18.

173   Ken Auletta, "The Lost Tycoon: Now He Has No Wife, No Job, and No Empire, but Ted Turner May Just Save the World," *The New Yorker*, April 23, 2001.

174   Thomas Sowell, *The Vision of the Anointed: Self-Congratulation as a Basis for Social Policy* (New York: Basic Books, 1995), 224.

175   Black, Kevin. "Leveraging Streaming Services for Leader Development." *Forbes*, September 15, 2020.

176   Ibid.

Bibliography

1. Aristotle. *On the Soul*. Translated by J. A. Smith. In *The Complete Works of Aristotle*, edited by Jonathan Barnes, Vol. 1, Book III, chap. 2. Princeton: Princeton University Press, 1984.
2. Auletta, Ken. "The Lost Tycoon: Now He Has No Wife, No Job, and No Empire, but Ted Turner May Just Save the World." *The New Yorker*, April 23, 2001.
3. B. H. Liddell Hart. *Scipio Africanus: Greater Than Napoleon*. Cambridge, MA: Da Capo Press, 2004.
4. BBC News. *"Former Intel Chief Andrew Grove Dies Aged 79."* BBC News. March 21, 2016. https://www.bbc.com/news/business-35866274.
5. Black, Kevin. "Ep. 33 – 'Mission Command: A Leadership Philosophy of Initiative, Empowerment, and Flexibility – Part 1 of 2.'" *Black Market Leadership* (podcast), March 15, 2023. https://podcasts.apple.com/us/podcast/ep-33-mission-command-a-leadership-philosophy/id1523238553?i=1000538375852.
6. Black, Kevin. *"Leveraging Streaming Services for Leader Development."* Forbes, September 15, 2020. https://www.forbes.com/councils/forbescoachescouncil/2020/09/15/leveraging-streaming-services-for-leader-development/.
7. Black, Kevin. *"Why Behaviors Are a Critical Yet Largely Untapped Resource for Leaders."* Forbes. August 22, 2019.

https://www.forbes.com/councils/forbescoachescouncil/2019/08/22/why-behaviors-are-a-critical-yet-largely-untapped-resource-for-leaders/.

8. Bonner, Robert J. "The Organization of the Ten Thousand." *The Classical Journal* 7, no. 9 (June 1912): 354–55, 358. https://www.jstor.org/stable/3287577

9. Brennan, Shane. "On the Enduring Appeal of Xenophon's Anabasis." *Literary Hub*, December 17, 2021. https://lithub.com/on-the-enduring-appeal-of-xenophons-anabasis/.

10. Burgelman, Robert A., Liisa Välikangas, and Steven R. Osborn. "Fading Memories: A Process Theory of Strategic Business Exit in Dynamic Environments." *Administrative Science Quarterly* 39, no. 1 (1994): 24–56.

11. Burns, Ken, dir. *The Civil War*. Episode 3, "Stonewall." PBS, originally aired September 24, 1990. Approx. 75 min.

12. Carse, James P. *Finite and Infinite Games: A Vision of Life as Play and Possibility.* New York: Ballantine Books, 1986.

13. Chandler, Alfred Dupont. *Strategy and Structure: Chapters in the History of the American Industrial Enterprise.* United Kingdom: Doubleday, 1990.

14. Clausewitz, Carl von. *On War.* Edited and translated by Michael Howard and Peter Paret. Oxford: Oxford University Press, 2006.

15. Combined Joint Task Force, 101 Public Affairs Office. "Article 32 Investigation Ends." *DVIDS*, March 5, 2008. https://www.dvidshub.net/news/27178/article-32-investigation-ends.

16. Cornelius Nepos. *Life of Hannibal.* Translated and edited by Bret Mulligan. Cambridge: Open Book Publishers, 2015. Section 28. https://doi.org/10.11647/OBP.0075.

17. Cortés, Hernán. *Cartas y relaciones de Hernán Cortés al emperador Carlos V.* Second letter, 140–43. In *The Conquest of Mexico*, edited and translated by Nancy Fitch, 2004.

18. Cox, Samuel J. "H-008-5: Admiral Ernest J. King—Chief of Naval Operations, 1942." *Naval History and Heritage Command,*

July 2017. https://www.history.navy.mil/about-us/leadership/director/directors-corner/h-grams/h-gram-008/h-008-5.html.

19. Cray, Ed. *General of the Army: George C. Marshall, Soldier and Statesman.* New York: W. W. Norton & Company, 1990.

20. Demartino, Richard, Jack Clarcq, and Michael Palanski. "George C. Marshall: An Enduring Model of Leadership Effectiveness." *Journal of Character & Leadership Integration* 2, no. 1 (Fall 2011): 21–22. https://www.usafa.edu/app/uploads/JCLI-Fall-2011.pdf.

21. Diaz del Castillo, Bernal. *The Conquest of New Spain.* United Kingdom: Penguin Books Limited, 2003.

22. Dress, Brad. "Pentagon Fails 7th Audit in a Row but Says Progress Made." *The Hill*, November 15, 2024. https://the-hill.com/policy/defense/4992913-pentagon-fails-7th-audit-in-a-row-but-says-progress-made/.

23. Drucker, Peter F. *The Practice of Management.* New York: Harper & Row, 1954.

24. Durant, Will. *The Life of Greece: The Story of Civilization, Volume II.* New York: Simon and Schuster, 1939.

25. Edward Luttwak. *The Grand Strategy of the Roman Empire from the First Century A.D. to the Third.* Baltimore: Johns Hopkins University Press, 1976.

26. Eggenberger, David. *An Encyclopedia of Battles: Accounts of Over 1,560 Battles from 1479 B.C. to the Present.* Mineola, NY: Dover Publications, 1985.

27. Encyclopaedia Iranica Foundation. "ARMY i. Pre-Islamic Iran." *Encyclopaedia Iranica.* https://www.iranicaonline.org/articles/army-i.

28. Fiedler, Klaus, Johannes Prager, and Linda McCaughey. "Metacognitive Myopia: A Major Obstacle on the Way to Rationality." *Current Directions in Psychological Science* 32, no. 1 (2023): 49–56.

29. Fleming, Michael. "The Agent." *The New Yorker*, July 10, 2000. https://www.newyorker.com/magazine/2000/07/10/

the-agent.

30. *Game of Thrones*. Season 3, episode 6, "The Climb." Directed by Alik Sakharov. Written by David Benioff and D. B. Weiss. Aired May 5, 2013, on HBO.

31. Gleick, James. *Chaos: Making a New Science*. New York: Viking, 1987.

32. Goodwyn, Frank. "Pánfilo de Narváez: A Character Study of the First Spanish Leader to Land an Expedition to Texas." *Hispanic American Historical Review* 29, no. 1 (February 1949): 150–55.

33. Grove, Andrew S. *Intel Keynote*. Presentation at the Academy of Management Annual Meeting, San Diego, CA, August 9, 1998. https://www.intel.com/pressroom/archive/speeches/ag080998.htm.

34. ———. *Only the Paranoid Survive: How to Exploit the Crisis Points That Challenge Every Company and Career*. New York: Currency Doubleday, 1996.

35. Hamilton, Edith. *The Roman Way*. United States: W. W. Norton, 2017.

36. Hanson, Victor Davis. *Carnage and Culture*. New York: Anchor Books, 2002.

37. Hartung, William D. *March of the Four Stars: The Role of Retired Generals and Admirals in the Arms Industry*. Quincy Institute for Responsible Statecraft, October 4, 2023. https://quincyinst.org/research/march-of-the-four-stars-the-role-of-retired-generals-and-admirals-in-the-arms-industry/.

38. Hazlitt, Henry. *Economics in One Lesson: The Shortest and Surest Way to Understand Basic Economics*. United States: Crown, 2010.

39. Herman, Arthur. *To Rule the Waves: How the British Navy Shaped the Modern World*. New York: Harper Perennial, 2005.

40. Hill, Roger. Interview by Kevin Black. *Black Market Leader-*

ship. Episode 57, "Dog Company: The Pentagon's Betrayal of American Heroes in Afghanistan, Part 1 of 2." Apple Podcasts, December 20, 2022. https://podcasts.apple.com/us/podcast/ep-57-dog-company-the-pentagons-betrayal-of/id1523238553?i=1000590418381.

41. ———. Interview by Kevin Black. *Black Market Leadership.* Episode 58, "Dog Company: The Pentagon's Betrayal of American Heroes in Afghanistan, Part 2 of 2." Apple Podcasts, December 22, 2022. https://podcasts.apple.com/us/podcast/ep-58-dog-company-the-pentagons-betrayal-of/id1523238553?i=1000592182730.

42. ———. "American Military Culture Values Enemies Above U.S. Troops." *Washington Times*, April 12, 2017. https://www.washingtontimes.com/news/2017/apr/12/american-military-culture-values-enemies-above-us-/.

43. ———. Email message to author, March 17, 2025.

44. J. F. Lazenby. *Hannibal's War.* Norman: University of Oklahoma Press, 1998.

45. Jones, W. T. *A History of Western Philosophy I: The Classical Mind.* New York: Harcourt, Brace & World, 1969.

46. ———. *A History of Western Philosophy: Kant and the Nineteenth Century, Vol. IV.* New York: Harcourt, Brace & World, 1969.

47. Katzenbach, Jon R., and Douglas K. Smith. "The Discipline of Teams." *Harvard Business Review*, March 1993.

48. Kenneth T. Klima, Peter Mazzella, and Patrick B. McLaughlin. "Scipio Africanus and the Second Punic War: Joint Lessons for Center of Gravity Analysis." Joint Force Quarterly 88 (January 2018). https://ndupress.ndu.edu/Portals/68/Documents/jfq/jfq-88/jfq-88_102-111_Klima-Mazzella-McLaughlin.pdf?ver=2018-01-09-102343-833.

49. Ketchum, Richard M. *Saratoga: Turning Point of America's Revolutionary War.* New York: Henry Holt, 1997.

50. Knight, Roger. *The Pursuit of Victory: The Life and Achievement of Horatio Nelson.* London: Penguin Books, 2006.

51. León-Portilla, Miguel. *The Broken Spears: The Aztec Account of the Conquest of Mexico.* Boston: Beacon Press, 1962.

52. Livy. *A History of Rome: Selections.* Translated by Moses Hadas and Joe Park Poe. New York: Modern Library, 1962.

53. Livy. *The History of Rome.* Book 30. Translated by Frank Gardner Moore. Perseus Digital Library, Tufts University. https://www.perseus.tufts.edu/hopper/text?doc=Perseus%3Atext%3A1999.02.0159%3Abook%3D30s.

54. ———. *The History of Rome.* Book 30, Chapter 31. Translated by Frank Gardner Moore. Perseus Digital Library, Tufts University. https://www.perseus.tufts.edu/hopper/text?doc=Perseus%3Atext%3A1999.02.0159%3Abook%3D30%3Achapter%3D31. Livy. *The History of Rome.* Book 22, Chapter 49. Translated by Frank Gardner Moore. Cambridge, MA: Harvard University Press; London: William Heinemann Ltd., 1949.

55. Lorenz, Edward N. *The Essence of Chaos.* Seattle: University of Washington Press, 1995.

56. Luzader, John. *Decision on the Hudson: The Saratoga Campaign of 1777.* Clemson, SC: Americana Collection, 1975.

57. Macgregor, Douglas, and Joshua Whitehouse. "America's Four-Star Problem." *The American Conservative,* September 29, 2022. https://www.theamericanconservative.com/americas-four-star-problem/.

58. Marshall, George C. *George C. Marshall: Interviews and Reminiscences for Forrest C. Pogue.* Edited by Larry I. Bland. Lexington, VA: George C. Marshall Research Foundation, 1991.

59. ———. *The Papers of George Catlett Marshall.* Vol. 2. Edited

by Larry I. Bland and Sharon Ritenour Stevens. Baltimore: Johns Hopkins University Press, 1981.

60. ———. Letter to General John S. Mallory, November 5, 1920. *George C. Marshall Papers*. George C. Marshall Research Foundation, Lexington, VA.

61. Middlekauff, Robert. *The Glorious Cause: The American Revolution, 1763–1789*. New York: Oxford University Press, 2005.

62. Moomaw, W. H. "The Denouement of General Howe's Campaign of 1777." *The English Historical Review* 79, no. 312 (July 1964): 491–504.

63. New York Times. "May 11, 1973: Charges Dropped Against Pentagon Papers Leakers." The Learning Network. May 11, 2012. https://learning.blogs.nytimes.com/2012/05/11/may-11-1973-charges-dropped-against-pentagon-papers-leakers/.

64. Newsham, Gavin. "How the Decline of Budweiser Was Decades in the Making." *New York Post*, January 25, 2025. https://nypost.com/2025/01/25/lifestyle/how-the-decline-of-budweiser-was-decades-in-the-making/.

65. Nietzsche, Friedrich. *Twilight of the Idols, or, How to Philosophize with the Hammer*. Translated by Richard Polt. Indianapolis: Hackett Publishing Company, 1997.

66. Palmer, Michael A. *Command at Sea: Naval Command and Control Since the Sixteenth Century*. Cambridge, MA: Harvard University Press, 2007.

67. Plutarch. *Plutarch's Lives*. Translated by Bernadotte Perrin. Cambridge, MA: Harvard University Press; London: William Heinemann Ltd., 1920. Vol. 21, part 9.

68. Polybius. *The Rise of the Roman Empire*. Translated by Ian Scott-Kilvert. Harmondsworth, NY: Penguin, 1979.

69. Prescott, William H. *History of the Conquest of Mexico*. United Kingdom: Random House Publishing Group, 2010.

70. ———. *The Works of William H. Prescott*. Philadelphia and London: J. B. Lippincott Company, 1904.

71. Preston, Douglas. "Brutal Journey." *Sarasota Magazine*, December 2006. https://www.sarasotamagazine.com/news-and-profiles/2006/12/brutal-journey.

72. Rand, Ayn. *Introduction to Objectivist Epistemology*. New York: New American Library, 1979.

73. Ricks, Thomas E. *The Generals: American Military Command from World War II to Today*. New York: Penguin Books, 2013.

74. ———. "Why Our Generals Were More Successful in World War II than in Korea, Vietnam, or Iraq/Afghanistan." UC Berkeley Events, The Fleet Admiral Chester W. Nimitz Memorial Lecture, March 22, 2011. YouTube video, 1:26:47. https://youtu.be/AxZWxxZ2JGE?si=NvBHm20vaYnlIG8V.

75. Rowe, Mike, host. *The Way I Heard It with Mike Rowe*. "424: Anson Frericks – Last Call for Bud Light." Podcast audio, February 5, 2025. Apple Podcasts. https://podcasts.apple.com/us/podcast/424-anson-frericks-last-call-for-bud-light/id1087110764?i=1000688865792.

76. Sowell, Thomas. *The Vision of the Anointed: Self-Congratulation as a Basis for Social Policy*. New York: Basic Books, 1995.

77. Staley, Oliver. "Silicon Valley's Confrontational Management Style Started with Andy Grove." *Quartz*, April 8, 2016. https://qz.com/656708/silicon-valleys-confrontational-management-style-started-with-andy-grove.

78. Stoler, Mark A. *George C. Marshall: Soldier-Statesman of the American Century*. Boston: Twayne Publishers, 1989.

79. The Enquirer. "Anheuser-Busch CEO Brendan Whitworth Releases Statement Amid Dylan Mulvaney Bud Light Backlash." *Cincinnati Enquirer*, April 14, 2023. https://www.cincinnati.com/story/news/2023/04/14/

anheuser-busch-ceo-brendan-whitworth-releas-es-statement-amid-dylan-mulvaney-bud-light-back-lash/70116412007/.

80. Thomas, Hugh. *Conquest: Montezuma, Cortés, and the Fall of Old Mexico*. New York: Simon & Schuster, 1993.

81. Thompson, Sonia. "3 Inclusive Marketing Lessons from Bud Light's Fumbled Dylan Mulvaney Controversy." *Forbes*, April 21, 2023. https://www.forbes.com/sites/soniathompson/2023/04/21/3-inclusive-mar-keting-lessons-from-bud-lights-fumbled-dylan-mul-vaney-controversy/.

82. Trueba y Cosío, Joaquín Telesforo de. *Life of Hernan Cortes*. United Kingdom: Constable and Company, 1829.

83. United States Congress. House. Committee on Foreign Affairs. Subcommittee on International Organizations, Human Rights, and Oversight, and Subcommittee on Europe. *Extraordinary Rendition in U.S. Counterterrorism Policy: The Impact on Transatlantic Relations*. Joint Hearing, 110th Congress, 1st session, April 17, 2007. Washington, D.C.: U.S. Government Printing Office, 2007.

84. van Creveld, Martin. *Fighting power: German and US Army performance, 1939-1945*. United Kingdom: Bloomsbury Academic, 1982.

85. Vandergriff, Donald E. *Adopting Mission Command: Developing Leaders for a Superior Command Culture*. Annapolis, MD: Naval Institute Press, 2019.

86. Varadarajan, Tunku. "For FedEx Founder Fred Smith, the Sky Is Still the Limit." *Wall Street Journal*, April 15, 2022.

87. Vincent, Lynn., Hill, Roger. *Dog Company: A True Story of American Soldiers Abandoned by Their High Command*. United Kingdom: Center Street, 2017.

88. Welles, Orson. Interview by Dick Cavett. *The Dick Cavett Show*. Aired July 27, 1970, on ABC.

89. Wermuth, Thomas S., and James M. Johnson. "The American Revolution in the Hudson River Valley: An Overview." *Hudson River Valley Review* 20, no. 1 (2003): 1–15.

90. Will Durant. *Caesar and Christ: The Story of Civilization, Volume III.* New York: Simon & Schuster, 2011.

91. Willcox, William B. "Too Many Cooks: British Planning Before Saratoga." *Journal of British Studies* 2, no. 1 (1962): 54–67.

92. Wright, Lawrence. "Missed Opportunities." *The New Yorker*, July 10, 2006. https://www.newyorker.com/magazine/2006/07/10/missed-opportunities.

93. Xenophon. *Anabasis.* Translated by Carleton L. Brownson. Cambridge, MA: Harvard University Press, 1922.

94. ———. Book 1, Chapter 8, Sections 26–29, p. 321.

95. ———. Book 2, Chapter 5, Section 39; Chapter 6, Section 3, p. 401.

96. ———. Book 3, Chapter 1, Sections 36–41, p. 433; Chapter 4, Sections 4–6.

97. ———. Book 4, Chapter 3, Section 2; Chapter 5, Sections 8–14, p. 441; Chapter 7, Section 24; Chapter 8, Sections 9–18.

98. Yingling, Paul. "A Failure in Generalship." *Armed Forces Journal*, May 1, 2007. https://armedforcesjournal.com/a-failure-in-generalship/.